Advance Praise For

ANOREXIA'S FALLEN ANGEL

"*Anorexia's Fallen Angel* is a cautionary tale, and Barbara McLintock, who has written about the controversial clinic from the beginning, is uniquely qualified to tell it. The award-winning journalist for Vancouver's *The Province* has delivered a fascinating, level-headed account of the rise and fall of [the] clinic in the form of case histories, anecdotes, and courtroom drama. In the background are the near-delusional 70-pound adolescent girls—whose tragedy is no less heartbreaking for being by now well documented..."—*Quill & Quire*

BARBARA MCLINTOCK

Anorexia's Fallen Angel

THE UNTOLD STORY
OF PEGGY CLAUDE-PIERRE
AND THE CONTROVERSIAL MONTREUX CLINIC

HarperCollins*PublishersLtd*

Anorexia's Fallen Angel: The Untold Story of Peggy Claude-Pierre and the Controversial Montreux Clinic
Copyright © 2002 by Barbara McLintock.
All rights reserved. No part of this book may be used or reproduced in any manner whatsoever without prior written permission except in the case of brief quotations embodied in reviews. For information address HarperCollins Publishers Ltd.,
55 Avenue Road, Suite 2900,
Toronto, Ontario, Canada M5R 3L2

www.harpercanada.com

HarperCollins books may be purchased for educational, business, or sales promotional use. For information please write: Special Markets Department, HarperCollins Canada,
55 Avenue Road, Suite 2900,
Toronto, Ontario, Canada M5R 3L2

First edition

Canadian Cataloguing in Publication Data

McLintock, Barbara
Anorexia's Fallen Angel : the untold story of Peggy Claude-Pierre and the controversial Montreux Clinic.

Includes bibliographical references
ISBN 0-00-200092-X

1. Claude-Pierre, Peggy.
2. Montreux Clinic.
3. Eating disorders – Treatment.
I. Title.

RC552.E18M42 2002   362.1'9685262'0092   C2002-900560-4

WEB 9 8 7 6 5 4 3 2 1

Printed and bound in Canada
Set in Monotype Janson

This book is dedicated to
Sally
Samantha
Lena
Donna
and
Rebecca

May they find now the peace
that so long eluded them on Earth.

Contents

Author's Note ix
Cast of Characters xi

1 The Stuff of Legends 1
2 The Coming of Samantha 22
3 The Miracle Show 43
4 Taking Anorexia to the Cradle 64
5 Gathering Storm Clouds 89
6 Down from the Pinnacle 115
7 The Hearing 139
8 What Montreux Said 156
9 Judgment Day 172
10 Struggling for Survival 197
11 The Walls Come Tumbling Down 219
12 The End 243

Epilogue 273
Chronology 277
Notes 280
Bibliography 283
Acknowledgments 287

Author's Note

All the stories told in this book are true. All the patients mentioned are real people, battling to overcome an illness that sometimes seems to have complete control over their lives. All the parents are real mothers and real fathers, too often living lives of desperation and mental agony that we would not even want to imagine. All the staff members are real as well, many of them people who gathered up their courage to be the ones to say, "the emperor has no clothes." The only thing that is not real is, in many cases, the names. Names were changed in order to protect the privacy of patients and staff members as they struggle to move on with their lives. I met and talked to dozens of patients and family members in the three years I covered the story of Montreux for *The Province* newspaper. All talked to me willingly, and many talked to other journalists as well. Despite that, I remain unconvinced in many cases that they could truly give informed consent for their names to be used. I would not want them to realize years from now that a book is still being read that contains their names and stories from the worst moments of their lives, especially when, as is to be hoped, they have been able to recover and find a new life free of their eating disorder. Rather than make individual decisions on which names should appear and which should not, I have chosen to use pseudonyms, even for those patients whose names have previously appeared in public. This applies to patients who have been previously quoted in the media as well as those who testified at the licensing hearing before Dr. Stanwick or whose identity was given in the 1,200-plus court documents from which much of the material in this book is taken. In the cases in which names are changed, they are noted with an asterisk the first time they appear.

Cast of Characters

THE MANAGEMENT

Peggy Claude-Pierre, founder and Program Director of Montreux Counselling Centres. Author of *The Secret Language of Eating Disorders*.

David Harris, husband of Claude-Pierre and Executive Director of Montreux Counselling Centres Ltd.

Noah Dobson, Personnel Manager 1993–95; manager of the residential program 1995–1999.

Margaret Dobson, Associate Program Director, 1993–1999.

Nicole Claude-Pierre, Peggy's daughter. Associate Program Director.

Bob Enoch, Consultant to Montreux, 1999.

THE DOCTORS

Dr. Richard Stanwick, Medical Health Officer, Capital Health Region. Writer of the decision requiring Montreux to close.

Dr. Allan Kaplan, head of the Eating Disorders Program at Toronto General Hospital. Writer of reports on Montreux operations, 2000.

Dr. Laird Birmingham, head of the Eating Disorders Program, St. Paul's Hospital, Vancouver, B.C. Reviewed the files of six Montreux patients as part of the Licensing Investigation, 1998.

Dr. David Clinton-Baker, general practitioner in Victoria. Consultant doctor for Montreux.

Dr. Mauro Bertoia, general practitioner in Victoria. Consultant doctor for Montreux.

Dr. Charles Medhurst, general practitioner in Victoria. Consultant doctor for Montreux.
Dr. Susan Sherkow, child psychoanalyst from New York who assessed Dustin after his discharge from Montreux.
Dr. Geoffrey Ainsworth, child psychiatrist from Vancouver who provided expert testimony for licensing about Dustin's treatment.
Dr. Paul Termansen, Vancouver psychiatrist and suicide expert, hired by Montreux to help reduce suicide risk at the clinic.

THE LAWYERS

Maureen Boyd, Vancouver lawyer who provided services to Montreux during the 1998 investigation.
Dennis Murray, Montreux's senior lawyer during 1999 hearings.
Fiona McQueen, Murray's junior associate during the hearings.
Chris Considine, lawyer for Montreux during the year 2000.
Guy McDannold, lawyer for Licensing branch, Capital Health Region.
Paul Pearlman, lawyer for Dr. Stanwick during 1999 licensing hearing.

THE WHISTLE-BLOWERS

Gay Pankhurst, careworker who launched first complaint to licensing investigators in 1999.
Andrew* and Randi,* careworkers who joined Gay in complaining during first investigation.
Gavin,* one of primary careworkers for three-year-old Dustin, became key witness at hearing for licensing; approached by private investigator hired by Montreux.
Heidi* and Mark,* other careworkers who testified on behalf of licensing.
Marg Eastman, nurse who became interim Montreux manager in 2000.
Pam Brambell, nurse who worked for the clinic in 2000.
Susan Trefz, dietitian who joined Brambell and Eastman in talking to licensing after quitting Montreux in the summer of 2000.

THE INVESTIGATORS

Steven Eng, head of the licensing branch for the Capital Health Region.
Lori Frame, head of licensing for adult residential facilities until moving away from Victoria in 1999.
Kim Macdonald, licensing nutritionist who took over from Frame as head of licensing for adult residential facilities.
Gerry Stearns, psychologist and former RCMP officer seconded to the Montreux investigation team by the B.C. attorney general's ministry.
Dr. Linda Poffenroth, deputy medical health officer for Capital Health Region; seconded to Montreux investigation team to provide medical expertise.
Greg Dunphy, licensing officer who provided original liaison between health authorities and Montreux.

OTHER MONTREUX STAFF MEMBERS

Kirsten Claude-Pierre, Peggy's eldest daughter, who went on to become a counsellor at the clinic.
Tessa,* a bank teller and former outpatient of Peggy's who went on to become one of her most trusted associates and head of the outpatient counselling program.
Janice, senior careworker who became one of primary workers for Dustin.
Tricia,* senior careworker for many of the most difficult clients.
Justin Williams, husband of Nicole Claude-Pierre.
Karim Nasser, manager of staff scheduling.
Kelly,* "medical liaison officer," the link between the patients and the clinic's doctors.
Jacob,* driver and careworker who at least twice became romantically involved with clinic patients.
Judy,* long-term careworker who later was put in charge of recreational programs.

THE PATIENTS

Chloe,* Victoria woman, held against her will in her own home and in Safe House in 1993.
Gemma and Amanda Lawson,* twin girls from Victoria, clients in 1992–93; Gemma committed suicide in September 1992.
Janet,* early outpatient; later part-time staff member.
Marisa,* outpatient successfully treated in earliest Montreux days; later often provided testimonials for clinic.
Susannah,* early outpatient who later provided testimonials.
Caroline,* one of earliest critically ill patients, from Chilliwack, B.C., admitted February 1993; still attached to the clinic seven years later.
Samantha Kendall, high-profile British patient admitted in May 1994; discharged herself in summer, 1995; died of anorexia October 1997.
Donna Brooks, high-profile British patient admitted in September 1994 while being filmed by *20/20*; died shortly after returning home in 1999.
Lynda,* daughter of Catherine* who introduced Montreux to *20/20*. Admitted to Montreux in summer of 1994.
Jeannie,* young woman from Scotland who arrived critically ill, recovered rapidly, and went on to become a careworker and then a member of clinic management.
Shannon,* young woman from Cleveland, Ohio, who arrived critically ill in September, 1994 after being admitted during *20/20* filming.
Kristina,* young woman who provided testimonials to media in her home state of Ohio after being admitted shortly after first *20/20* broadcast.
Robbie,* 11-year-old boy from New Mexico, admitted on *20/20* follow-up, spring 1995.
Dustin,* three-year-old boy from New York City; his treatment became one of the cornerstones of the licensing hearing.
Louise,* young woman from Britain; while still acute patient, became primary careworker for Dustin.
Marie,* young woman from New York; Moira became her team leader.
Lena Zavaroni, former child singing sensation whose treatment at Montreux sparked first complaints to licensing. Died after a brain operation, October 1999.

Carmen,* young woman from Mississippi; appeared on both *Oprah* shows.

Anna,* British teenager; long-term patient whose files were reviewed by Dr. Birmingham.

Vivian,* young woman from Israel, long-term patient whose files were reviewed by Dr. Birmingham.

Joshua,* 14-year-old boy from Louisiana; admission files reviewed by Dr. Birmingham.

Angela,* Wilma,* and Sharleen,* three other patients whose files were reviewed by Dr. Birmingham.

Sheila,* young woman who arrived from Rhode Island not only anorexic but also an elective mute; her father became a passionate spokesman for the clinic.

Brenda,* a highly acute patient from Australia; her mother became an outspoken advocate for the clinic.

Kerry,* a girl from California who was only 12 when admitted to Montreux.

Shelley,* a young woman from Nevada who had also lost a sister to anorexia before coming to Montreux.

Stacey,* a young American woman who became the last patient allowed to stay legally in the Rockland mansion after the closure was ordered.

Carrie,* a girl from Chicago who came to Montreux at the age of 13 in 1997.

Sylvia,* a professional woman from the eastern U.S.; discharged from Montreux because of her violence towards staff.

Serena,* a patient from California who went on to become the clinic's spokeswoman and its de facto manager in early 2000.

Denise,* a girl from Victoria who became a residential patient at the age of 15 and went on to become a careworker.

Becca, a teenager from Florida who became a long-term Montreux patient; died in February 2001, a few months after returning home.

Marcie,* a long-term patient from Wisconsin, who left Montreux's care to pursue a romantic relationship with one of the clinic's staff members.

Etta,* a teenager from Sweden, one of the clinic's last-admitted patients.

Esther,* a young woman from the U.S. who returned to Victoria after being discharged and seriously relapsed.

Natalie,* an early outpatient who went on to become one of the first residential careworkers.

Emma,* a nurse from Australia whom Montreux wanted to hire as "director of clinical care" shortly after her treatment ended.

Melanie,* a medical doctor from Switzerland who came to Montreux as a residential patient even after the decision ordering it to shut down.

Jessica,* a young woman from Austria; one of the last patients admitted to Montreux.

Naomi,* a young woman from Japan, one of Montreux's last-admitted patients.

FAMILY MEMBERS

Bernice Lawson,* mother of twins Gemma and Amanda; later member of clinic's "monitoring committee."

Suzy Kendall, mother of twins Michaela, who died in 1994, and Samantha, who died in 1997 after a stay at Montreux.

Thomas,* husband of Chloe, who appeared on TV alongside Claude-Pierre.

Catherine,* New York actress who introduced Montreux to *20/20* producer Alan Goldberg.

Moira,* mother of three-year-old Dustin; became Montreux team leader.

Ken, father of an early patient, managed apartment buildings and provided the clinic with suites where patients and family members could stay.

Dee,* mother of an early Montreux outpatient, later took over the non-profit society.

I

The Stuff of Legends

Chloe* was desperate. She was caught in a Kafkaesque maze, a prisoner in her own home, watched every minute of the day, searching frantically for an avenue of escape. She was no criminal. She was an ordinary suburban housewife, mother, and nurse's aide who happened to suffer from acute anorexia and bulimia. Discharged from hospital, she had been struggling to cope at home with her husband and three small children. No one had been more surprised than she when she'd answered the door of their home to find lay counsellor Peggy Claude-Pierre, Claude-Pierre's husband David Harris, and two other women whom she didn't know on the doorstep. Chloe had met Claude-Pierre only once, at the urging of her husband. He had read an article in a local women's magazine which had touted her as someone who worked miracles helping sufferers recover from their eating disorders. After that first meeting, neither Chloe nor Claude-Pierre had talked of any further counselling.

The visitors came into her living room. Claude-Pierre said she had been talking to Chloe's husband. They had decided that Chloe was so ill that the only way she could be saved was to receive round-the-clock care from Claude-Pierre's hand-picked staff. They had come to provide that 24-hour care in Chloe's own home, beginning immediately. She would not be allowed to leave the house. She would not be allowed to use the phone. She would not even be allowed to go to the washroom unobserved. Claude-Pierre herself would come to the house half a dozen times a day to feed her "nutritional drinks" from a sports bottle.

Chloe was flabbergasted. She was 24 years old. She had not been legally declared so mentally ill as to be unable to care for herself. She knew full well she should have the right to decide on her own course of treatment—and that course wouldn't include Claude-Pierre or her staff. But the workers were there, keeping her away from the phone, putting themselves between her and the door. When her husband was home, he gave them his full support.

She spent two weeks "under house arrest," as she thought of it. Although Claude-Pierre was supposed to come to feed her six to eight times a day, on many days she only managed to come once or twice. She often didn't allow the other workers to try to feed Chloe. Chloe began losing the weight she'd struggled so hard to put on while in the hospital. When she protested against the feeding, the bottle would be jammed into her mouth, once with such force her lip was cut and bleeding.

Every day she became more desperate to escape. Once, while her careworker for the day was distracted for a few minutes, she saw her opportunity. Who to call? She picked up the phone and called her regular family doctor whom she trusted implicitly. In a few seconds, she managed to whisper to him that she was being held against her will and needed help. Her last sentences were overheard by the returning careworker, who took the phone out of her hands.

The doctor was so shocked by what Chloe had told him that he immediately phoned the police department in the Victoria suburb of Saanich, where the family lived. They sent an officer over to check on her welfare. But the officer arrived too late. Chloe had already gone. The careworker had phoned Claude-Pierre and Harris, and they'd arrived several minutes before the police cruiser. Chloe remembers physically clinging to the banisters, winding her skinny arms and legs around them. But she was a small woman, and weak from her eating disorder. Claude-Pierre and Harris bundled her quickly into their own car and took her to a careworker's home, over the municipal boundary into the city of Victoria proper. After dark, they moved her again, this time to Claude-Pierre and Harris's own home. The police department were convinced it had been a domestic dispute and elected not to pursue the issue.

For the next few weeks, Chloe felt as if she had no control over her own life. Each morning, she was taken to a day program Claude-Pierre was running for a group of eating-disorder sufferers; each night she had to go back to Claude-Pierre and Harris's house. She had to sleep in a sleeping bag on the floor of the guest room with a careworker watching her to ensure she didn't escape. At one point, when Claude-Pierre's daughter, Nicole, and Nicole's new husband moved back into the family home, Chloe and the careworkers were required to share a room with Harris's young son.

While in Claude-Pierre's presence, she sometimes doubted herself, thinking maybe she really did need this kind of treatment and they were all doing what was best for her. She wrote Claude-Pierre long, apologetic letters, promising to co-operate. Sometimes she told herself that if she wrote enough letters, Claude-Pierre would relax her guard and she'd be allowed to escape. As soon as she was left alone long enough to think things out for herself, she realized that she wasn't getting any better, and that nobody had the right to hold her against her will. She again started making plans to escape.

Twice she managed to get away. Once Montreux staff members quickly found her. The other time she hid for hours, watching the searchlights of the police cars go by. She'd heard often enough from Claude-Pierre that the police were Claude-Pierre's friends, and she believed she couldn't trust them. Two police officers had even been part of the group when Claude-Pierre had taken her on an "outing" to watch a fireworks display. But soon Chloe realized she had nowhere else to go. Claude-Pierre and Harris would be waiting for her at her own home. Chloe's own husband had been convinced by Claude-Pierre that she needed such drastic treatment to keep her from dying. So had members of her own family, who were paying thousands of dollars for her "treatment." Unaware of her own doctor's previous efforts to rescue her, she didn't see calling him as a fruitful possibility this time. Reluctant and defeated, she returned to Claude-Pierre's home. It was several weeks later that she managed to stay logical and calm and talk her way to freedom. She was able to convince Claude-Pierre that she was safe now to return to her own home and be treated as an outpatient. She heard later that her parents had sought help from the Victoria police, but had been told that if their daughter was suffering from anorexia, "she couldn't be in a better place."

Chloe's treatment was to prove a prototype for the treatment Claude-Pierre would soon provide through Montreux Counselling, a residential program that attracted dozens of wealthy clients from around the world—although most patients accepted the restrictions on their freedom with far less rebellion than Chloe. Claude-Pierre called it "one-on-one care" and insisted it would save the lives of eating-disorder sufferers that no other program had been able to help. Health authorities would later call it "imposed therapy," unlawful in British Columbia unless a patient has been legally committed as mentally incompetent by two physicians—not family members, police officers, or lay counsellors. Eating-disorder experts would explain there was no evidence to back up claims of any out-of-the-ordinary success rate.

Claude-Pierre had no medical training and had not even completed her bachelor's degree in psychology. Her theories about anorexia came entirely from her own experience, the experience of a mother whose two daughters both developed eating disorders. The residential Montreux program was the culmination of events that started for Claude-Pierre in the mid-1980s, as she worked with first one daughter and then the other.

At that time, eating disorders were just beginning to come to the forefront of public attention. It was only in the few months before Peggy's daughters became ill that magazines, radio and television began to feature eating disorders as an issue of interest. Bookstores stocked only a few volumes on how to overcome an eating disorder or help your child to do so. Stories of a girl deliberately starving herself, sometimes to the point of death, were considered so rare as to be a freakish event. The idea of a girl making herself throw up everything she'd eaten was barely talked about in the popular press.

It was only in the year before Peggy Claude-Pierre's elder daughter, Kirsten, developed her eating disorder, that the first high-profile celebrity death from anorexia moved the issue to the front pages. Karen Carpenter, the pop singing sensation of the 1970s, was 32 when she died on February 4, 1983, of heart failure as the result of years of severe anorexia. She'd been battling the condition on and off for more than 15 years. It had been a relentless force in her life for the previous eight years. She had restricted her eating to almost nothing, and had been taking large numbers of laxatives and thyroid pills and forcing herself to regurgitate the little she did eat. Her death spawned an upsurge in interest in eating disorders. The public became aware that those with anorexia were suffering from a potentially fatal condition.

Those first articles gave readers the basic definitions of eating disorders. They explained that those with anorexia nervosa and bulimia nervosa suffer from an extreme and unrealistic fear of gaining weight or becoming fat. Their sense of their own body image is so distorted that they're convinced they're fat even when they've lost so much weight that others see them as gaunt and skeletal. Many become so underweight that their physical health is severely compromised. Girls and women (who make up about 90 per cent of those who suffer from eating disorders) stop menstruating. In the "restricting" type of anorexia, sufferers often begin by cutting out "unhealthy" food from their diets, then gradually restrict more and more until they're eating almost nothing at all. Many also exercise to extremes for hours a day to work off any calories they may have allowed themselves to take in. In bulimia and the "purging" type of anorexia, sufferers eat, sometimes even excessive amounts of food, but then go to any lengths to remove it from their body. Most common is forcing oneself to vomit, but other sufferers take huge amounts of laxatives or diuretics or force themselves to drink syrup of ipecac—a substance normally used to treat poisoning cases because it's almost certain to induce vomiting.

The increased interest of the early 1980s, however, had not yet spawned any large number of treatment options for those who developed anorexia or bulimia. Although numerous studies were underway to try to discover the cause of eating disorders, no conclusion had been reached. Even today, 20 years later, experts believe there is no single cause. Most experts believe the development of an eating disorder is the result of a complex interplay of biological or genetic factors and environmental factors, ranging from family dysfunction to a history of sexual abuse to the intense social and cultural pressures on women in our society.

In the 1980s, specialized eating-disorder programs were few and far between. Most whose illness was so advanced that they required residential treatment were hospitalized either on general medical wards or in psychiatric hospitals alongside patients suffering from schizophrenia, hallucinations, and psychoses. The most common method of treatment involved a strict behaviourist approach: patients were punished for refusing to eat by the withdrawal of privileges, including family visits or phone calls; they regained the privileges only by eating "normal" meals, often of high caloric value to increase their weight rapidly.

Not every patient was subject to such an approach. In 1979, pediatrician and researcher Dr. Hilde Bruch wrote *The Golden Cage*, in which she characterized anorexia as a disease suffered by those with extreme deficits in their self-esteem and sense of self. She argued that simply refeeding the patient, or insisting that she eat, would not prove successful until those deficits were addressed.

At the time Dr. Bruch was winning acclaim for her thoughts about anorexia, Peggy Claude-Pierre was a college psychology student in Kamloops, a small city surrounded by desert hills in the interior of British Columbia. She was raising two daughters and struggling with a failing marriage. Only the broadest outlines of Claude-Pierre's early life are known. She has always been reluctant to answer questions about her childhood or her life before she separated from her husband, moved to Victoria on the southern tip of Vancouver Island, and became involved with eating disorders.

She was born in 1949 in Kamloops, one of three children in the Cordinier family. Her father, John, was involved in the retail and hotel business. She married young, to a successful builder and contractor named Jurgen. They had two girls in quick succession, Kirsten in 1968 and Nicole two years later. The family remained in Kamloops, and the girls remember a household where their friends were always welcome and where they were always surrounded by pets. As the girls grew older, Claude-Pierre started attending the community college in Kamloops. As part of her courses, she began studying programs to help young offenders and, she says, undertook volunteer work with related organizations like the Elizabeth Fry Society.

However, she and Jurgen were becoming increasingly estranged, and in 1982 they agreed to separate. Claude-Pierre decided to move to Victoria and continue her studies in psychology at the University of Victoria. Nicole, then 13, came with her. Kirsten wanted to stay and finish the school term in Kamloops, and she moved in with Claude-Pierre's parents.

This is where Claude-Pierre's public history begins. According to the stories she tells about her life after that, her mother phoned several months later and said she was worried about the amount of weight Kirsten had lost. When Kirsten arrived in Victoria, she was, according to Claude-Pierre, dangerously thin, carrying less than 100 pounds on her five-foot nine-inch frame. Although little independent evidence exists to corroborate the family history, Claude-Pierre says the doctors were gloomy about Kirsten's prognosis. She checked out what specialized eating-disorder clinics she could find, but even when Kirsten was down to 84 pounds, she rejected them all because, she says, they all proposed a behaviourist approach. She was convinced such treatment wouldn't help Kirsten because, she contends, Kirsten was already obviously punishing herself so much that a reward-and-punishment scheme would only make her feel worse about herself.

Instead, she became her daughter's own therapist, talking constantly to her about her thoughts and feelings, and trying to persuade her to substitute logic for her irrational fear of eating. In all her reported conversations with Kirsten, she never mentions Kirsten talking about being afraid of gaining weight or becoming fat. Instead, Kirsten talked to her mother about feeling that she didn't "deserve" food, and said that strong internal voices were always telling her not to eat. It was the first time Peggy began a virtual 24-hour-a-day watch on a patient, because she was afraid to leave her daughter alone. She later wrote in her own book, "It was a successful day if I just kept her alive."[1] She talked her through every meal, she says, and within a few months Kirsten began to improve. Kirsten's comments had given her mother the first inklings of what were to become her theories about the cause of, and cure for, anorexia.

Nicole was highly supportive of her sister during Kirsten's bout with anorexia, but only three months after Kirsten showed signs of recovery, Nicole started showing symptoms of an eating disorder herself. According to Peggy, Nicole's anorexia was much worse than Kirsten's. She describes her younger daughter as becoming intensely suicidal and depressed, outwardly defiant of Peggy's efforts to help her, and manipulative and evasive about what she was or wasn't eating. Her behaviour grew increasingly bizarre and sometimes violent. One of the most often repeated stories has Nicole sneaking downstairs to eat dog food out of a dog dish—although the family had no dog, and her mother watched her 24 hours a day.

According to Peggy, Nicole's weight dropped significantly below Kirsten's lowest, at one point falling as low as 68 pounds.[2] Nicole, however, remembers her lowest weight ever as being 80 or 81 pounds.[3]

Peggy tells of finding notes all over the house, notes that Nicole had written in the third person, talking about how she was "a fat pig" and a bad person. Again, however, the notes apparently turned up weeks after Peggy says she put Nicole under 24-hour observation. She says she allowed herself only 90 minutes sleep a night for fear something would happen to her daughter otherwise, although doctors say so little sleep would soon seriously jeopardize a person's own health.

She tells of two occasions when Nicole collapsed on the street and she carried her home, not sure whether her daughter would actually be dead by the time they got there. Never has there been any discussion as to whether she called an ambulance or had Nicole treated for the obviously severe physical problems the anorexia was causing. No matter how exasperated they might be with the psychiatric interpretation of anorexia, most parents could be expected to call 911 in a panic if they thought their child was potentially within minutes of death.

Peggy Claude-Pierre tells of taking Nicole to several doctors but finding all of them unsatisfactory. She has never specified publicly who these doctors were, or whether any of them were eating-disorder specialists. One said Nicole was beginning to develop schizophrenia. One insisted that family dysfunction was at least part of the problem and warned Peggy that if he undertook individual psychotherapy with Nicole, he wouldn't be able to tell her about what went on in sessions. One wanted to prescribe psychiatric medications, but Nicole resisted and Peggy backed up her refusal. Ever since, although Peggy has always said publicly that it's important to have a doctor as part of an anorexic's treatment team, she has most often portrayed the medical profession as insensitive, unsympathetic, and unwilling to understand. The stories she tells of medical and hospital treatments, both of her daughters and of her later patients, would be enough to keep any sufferer and her family from seeking out conventional therapy.

When she had rejected all the doctors, Claude-Pierre took the entire burden of curing Nicole onto herself. She continued, she says, her round-the-clock supervision, while trying to give Nicole the illusion she wasn't being monitored. She tricked her into eating small amounts of her favourite foods. She worked to overcome the enormous self-hatred Nicole was feeling, trying to replace every negative thought in her mind with a positive one. Eventually Nicole, too, started to improve.

The seeds of Montreux Counselling came from Peggy Claude-Pierre's experiences with her two daughters, especially Nicole. As she struggled to come to terms with Nicole's disease, she developed the theory of what she would later call Confirmed Negativity Condition (CNC). She had always had a good relationship with both daughters, she has said, and she couldn't believe anything in her relationship with them had caused either of them to develop anorexia. There was no history of abuse that she was aware of, nor did they see her separation and divorce from their father as a particularly traumatic event. She concluded instead that the roots of the disorder came from something deep within both her daughters' personalities, something that engendered in them the deep self-loathing she had seen, almost a complete lack of an independent self. She remembered Nicole telling her one time when she looked in a mirror that this had nothing to do with efforts to be thin in order to be beautiful. "I'm not vain," she quotes her daughter as saying. "I'm looking for me. I can't find me." Since she had always previously found both Kirsten and Nicole to be unusually kind, sensitive, and helpful children, Claude-Pierre began to conclude that those personality characteristics were intertwined with the characteristics of negativity she'd seen in her daughters. She developed a theory in which the anorexia could be cured if and only if the negativity and self-blame could be removed from the patient.

According to Claude-Pierre's own book, the seeds of Montreux as a clinic for eating-disordered patients were planted during the worst of Nicole's illness. Peggy remembers one day, during one of Nicole's worst periods, when she asked Nicole what her happiest memory was. Nicole remembered a holiday trip back to the family's roots in Switzerland, especially walking on the boardwalk at Montreux, a flower-filled promenade along the shore of Lake Geneva. It was a time, she told her mother, when she'd felt filled with peace and contentment.

When Nicole remembered that, her mother told her that she would ensure Nicole recovered. After that, she told Nicole, she would develop a practice in which other children suffering eating disorders and their families could also be helped. The idea of opening a clinic, she said, gave Nicole concrete hope and "something to live for."[4] Eventually, she promised, she would open clinics all over the world so neither children nor their parents would be blamed for eating disorders. "Everyone would understand" the true causes of eating disorders then, she said. She predicted it would take about 10 years.

In the meantime, as part of Nicole's recovery, Claude-Pierre started working with other troubled young people, in part, she said, to show Nicole that she was not alone in her struggles. Some of the others had eating problems; others had difficulties with substance abuse or more general troubles at home or at school. Some of her clients were adults, including a handful of local police officers who were struggling with the stress of their jobs. One detective, at that point working in a specialized unit to combat organized crime, wrote her a general reference letter in which he talked of consulting her about "the psychological aspects of certain criminal activities" he was investigating.

Claude-Pierre had given up her university courses when Nicole became her 24-hour-a-day job. Kirsten had been willing to come along and listen to university lectures while her mother was supervising her, but Nicole never was. At various points during Peggy's media appearances, there was talk that she was working on her doctorate at that time. Talk-show host Maury Povich at one point even addressed her as "Dr. Claude-Pierre." In fact, however, she was then—and still is—a number of credits short of a bachelor's degree. After Nicole began to recover, Peggy did, for a brief period, enroll in a post-graduate program at the Adler School of Professional Psychology in Vancouver, a program that does not always insist on completion of a bachelor's degree before starting post-graduate work. Claude-Pierre says that in the psychology courses she did take, she was always particularly impressed with the work of Alfred Adler, with its emphasis on the unity between mind and body, the interconnectedness of people and their need to belong to a group. However, she never came close to completing her courses at the Adler Institute either. Long before she could do so, she says, word of her work with her own daughters got around, and she was approached by the parents of other children and teens who were suffering from anorexia and not doing well with conventional treatment.

The options in Victoria for treatment were not plentiful at that time. No doctors in the city were specialists in eating disorders. One general practitioner had developed an interest in the area and was trying to provide help for those referred to him. Children or adolescents whose disorders became so severe as to require hospitalization were usually sent to the pediatric unit at Victoria General Hospital or to B.C. Children's Hospital, and adults to the psychiatric wards at the Eric Martin Pavilion.

One of the early patients referred to Claude-Pierre turned out to be a family member of a local GP, Dr. David Clinton-Baker, a fairly recent arrival from New Zealand. The girl was only nine years old and was described as being seriously anorexic. Claude-Pierre decided to give up her studies yet again, so she could work intensively with the child. Her intervention was apparently successful, and Dr. Clinton-Baker was so impressed with her work that he became involved in providing medical backup for her patients, despite his own previous lack of expertise in eating disorders. He has been one of the regular doctors for patients at Montreux ever since.

Patient followed upon patient in quick order. Some had relatively severe eating disorders and had previously spent time in hospital. Others were adolescents struggling with a variety of issues, ranging from bulimia to alcohol abuse. Claude-Pierre did not think it much mattered what their symptoms were. Although she concentrated on eating-disorder victims, she believed that Confirmed Negativity Condition could show itself in all sorts of other behaviours as well. The same treatment would be effective for them, she believed.

Some of the patients came for a while and moved on. Others came, became enchanted by Claude-Pierre and her methods, and stayed. One of these was Tessa,* a bank teller deep in the throes of bulimia. On bad days, she would binge on virtually any item of food she could find, and then regurgitate it all. As Claude-Pierre helped Tessa overcome her problem behaviours, Tessa also became a sounding board for Claude-Pierre's theories. On many days, they would sit for hours, developing the theory of Confirmed Negativity Condition. Claude-Pierre concluded that CNC was a condition children were born with, one that would often manifest itself initially in extreme emotional sensitivity and an unusual concern for the welfare of others. Such children, she argued, developed eating disorders when they found it wasn't possible for them to make everyone around them, or indeed the whole world, happy, and then became convinced they had already failed at life.

Claude-Pierre soon saw in Tessa someone whom she wanted to join the practice, and she began teaching Tessa to be a counsellor as well, usually by having her sit in on sessions. Tessa never took any formal training, but would later move on to head the outpatient counselling program after Claude-Pierre herself chose to spend her time developing a residential clinic. In 1988, with as many patients as she could handle, Claude-Pierre, as she had promised Nicole, officially opened Montreux Counselling, at that point solely an outpatient counselling practice with an office in downtown Victoria. As she worked with her eating-disorder clients, however, she decided that some needed more intensive help than she could provide in an hour or two a day in an office setting. Some needed help eating virtually every meal. Some were too physically weak to make the trek downtown for office appointments. She began making house calls, going into the patients' own homes to feed them and talk to them. Some patients, she found, required four or five visits a day. When the home setting wasn't as supportive as she'd like, she began to bring patients into her own home, requiring them to live there for weeks or months while she tried to provide the counselling they needed.

Some parents also contacted her when their children had become so ill with eating disorders that they'd been admitted to the pediatric ward of the general hospital. She'd often be found on the ward, sitting with the most recalcitrant anorexics, persuading them to eat. Some of the nurses approved of her presence, if for no other reason than that she seemed able to afford the time needed to cajole the patients into eating, time that was always in short supply for the nurses on the floor. But other staff, including senior hospital administrators, worried when they heard she was also using her time on the wards to recruit patients and families into her practice and away from other available treatment options.

Before the counselling practice became a full-time business, Claude-Pierre had been making ends meet by working as a waitress in a restaurant. Pagliacci's, located in the heart of Victoria's downtown, was owned by a local character, Howie Siegel. Siegel had also owned a movie theatre, been a movie reviewer on TV, and even briefly had his own radio talk-show, until the station decided it was a little too provocative for the city. Pag's, as the restaurant has always been known, was a popular venue for live music, and one of the most popular bands that played there was called Balkan Jam. The fiddle player for Balkan Jam was a violinist with a degree in music, David Harris. He and Claude-Pierre met, fell in love, and were married not long afterwards.

Many of Claude-Pierre's clients from those first days remember their time with her fondly. They say she enhanced their self-esteem, gave them an ear to talk through the problems of adolescence, and helped them through a difficult time in their lives. Janet* still has the notebooks Claude-Pierre made her keep when she was 12: stenographers' notebooks with all the negative, self-blaming thoughts on the left-hand side, each countered by a more logical statement on the right. She's still pleased to show how, gradually, over the course of her treatment, the number of negative thoughts grew smaller and smaller, while the number of positive ones increased. The idea is very similar to what is known in many eating-disorder programs today as "cognitive therapy," although Claude-Pierre never gave it that name or linked it to what other practitioners were doing. When Claude-Pierre needed to increase her staff after opening the residential clinic, Janet and several of her other early patients returned to become careworkers on a part-time basis while going to college.

But not everyone's experience at Montreux was so positive. A case in point is the story of the Lawson* twins, Gemma* and Amanda.* They were identical twins who had both developed serious eating disorders during their high school years. Gemma, in particular, developed many emotional problems. She was severely depressed and had made several serious suicide attempts. Her family grew increasingly frustrated with the lack of results from her treatment in the mainstream medical system. The family put both girls into outpatient counselling with Claude-Pierre, and Gemma was one of the patients who stayed at

Claude-Pierre's own home for a time. However, their parents also recognized that Gemma's physical and psychiatric problems probably needed more treatment than the supportive lay-counselling that Claude-Pierre could provide. They again sought conventional medical and psychiatric treatment for Gemma. Gemma seemed somewhat less depressed, and in early September 1992, the twins' parents left them alone for a few days to help their elder daughter get settled into university out of town. During their absence, Gemma took a massive overdose of prescription drugs. This time her suicide attempt was successful.

The entire family was devastated, but especially Amanda. Overcome by both grief and guilt, her eating disorder soared out of control. The climax came at the end of March 1993. Amanda had been in hospital, but had begged to be taken home, and her mother, Bernice,* had agreed, hoping she might be more willing to eat in a setting where she was happier. She had home-care workers to help her look after Amanda, and she was trying Claude-Pierre's technique of offering tiny bites and vast amounts of reassurance.

But on Monday evening, March 29, Bernice reported to police in their suburb of Oak Bay that Amanda, then 21, had run out of the home and that she feared for her daughter's health and safety because she was so weakened by the anorexia. It had been, Bernice said, one of the few moments when she was not watching her daughter herself, and Amanda had apparently been able to slip by the home-care worker and out the front door, carrying a pillow and a dressing gown with her. The Lawsons lived less than a block from a large park which has been allowed to stay in its wild state, and the family suspected Amanda had headed there, where she'd often camped out before.

A search that night found no trace of her. For the next two days, trained search-and-rescue personnel, police, and firefighters combed the park as well as surrounding yards and a nearby golf course. Nothing. Helicopters and tracking dogs were brought in. Nothing. Fearfully, searchers checked the nearby bays and shoreline. Nothing.

Although no one could ever hold Claude-Pierre responsible for Amanda's peculiar disappearance, it did allow her to make her first appearance in the mainstream media. On the Friday three days after Amanda disappeared, Victoria's daily newspaper, the *Times-Colonist*, ran a lengthy interview with Bernice, detailing the horrors of living with two daughters suffering so acutely from eating disorders. As a sidebar, the newspaper ran an interview with Claude-Pierre.

Until then, word of Claude-Pierre's business had spread almost entirely through word of mouth. Her first-ever media appearance had been two months earlier in a local magazine, *Focus on Women*. The article, in which testimonials from satisfied patients were mixed with her explanation of her theories, was the one that had convinced Chloe's husband to give Claude-Pierre a free hand to try to cure his wife. However, *Focus on Women* was a small magazine, distributed for free around the Greater Victoria area, but never read outside the city.

When she was invited to comment on Amanda's case in the *Times-Colonist*, Claude-Pierre's field of influence automatically expanded. In the article, Claude-Pierre described her theories of negativity and the need to treat sufferers with unconditional love and kindness, combined with round-the-clock vigilance. Reporter Richard Watts described her as "a woman who has had remarkable success in treating the condition."[5] As would be the case for years to come, no objective evidence was offered to back up that statement.

The police and search personnel looking for Amanda were becoming increasingly concerned. They feared that her health was so fragile that if she didn't eat for several days, she could be at risk of a heart attack. They asked for volunteers to come out on Saturday to join in a massive search. The police had hoped about 300 people would turn out to cover all 21 hectares of the park thoroughly. About 450 arrived.

However, they were never required to complete the search. The story ended with the most bizarre twist of all. According to Bernice, that afternoon, Amanda simply reappeared among the family. She had never left the house at all. Instead, she had apparently spent the time hiding out in a tiny attic which she could reach only through an opening in the ceiling of her clothes closet. The rest of the family said they'd never realized it was there, and the police and search experts had apparently missed it in their checks of the house as well.

The house where the Lawsons were living was one of the best known, not just in Victoria, but in all of B.C. It is the oldest house still standing in western Canada, and it has also acquired a reputation among ghost-hunters as one of the most spectacular examples of a haunted house in the country. A porcelain cookie jar suspended on a hook was reported to swing back and forth for as long as 30 minutes at a time, and the cellar door would open itself even if it was securely latched or jammed shut with a chair. It is still visited on Hallowe'en ghost tours of Victoria each year. It is known as a house that keeps its secrets well—and it managed to hide Amanda until she chose to reappear. Although her reason for resurfacing was never made public, it would have seemed churlish to ask detailed questions about it in the midst of the happiness at her return. The volunteers gave a huge cheer as they were told their help was no longer needed because Amanda had been found alive. "There's joy as daughter comes from attic," read the headline in the next day's *Times-Colonist*.[6]

Amanda was admitted to hospital for a few days to ensure that her medical condition was stable, and then her mother turned her over to Claude-Pierre's care. Amanda stayed in her own home while receiving care from Claude-Pierre. Sometimes Chloe was brought over to Amanda's home, and the two were cared for together. Chloe felt desperately sorry for Amanda, who would often wake up in the night and call out Gemma's name, confusing Chloe with her dead sister.

That spring Claude-Pierre decided that the system of treating the more seriously ill clients in their homes was not working. She and staff members spent unnecessary time driving from place to place, and sometimes, she suspected, family members would undermine the work she was trying to do. Patients like Chloe whom she saw as needing more intensive "supervision" were particularly problematic in their own homes.

She was ready to open a residential program. There, she and her staff could provide round-the-clock supervision for their clients, ensuring that every moment of a client's day went according to their regimen.

They decided first to try out the concept in a rented house they called simply "the Safe House," located in a very ordinary residential neighbourhood not far from Victoria's downtown. Chloe would be one of the first patients, along with Amanda. Several former patients had been hired to provide the 24-hour care. Some admitted later that they were still bulimic when they started working there. Claude-Pierre used the promise of being able to join the staff to motivate others to give up the worst of their eating-disordered behaviour. Even with the four patients they started with, Claude-Pierre and Harris should have applied for a licence under the provincial Community Care Facilities Licensing Act. The legislation requires approval for any facility that provides overnight care for more than two vulnerable patients. It is doubtful, however, whether Claude-Pierre and Harris even thought of checking into such requirements. Even as the clients were moving into the Safe House, Claude-Pierre and Harris were looking for a larger and more permanent site for their operation.

With the new residential program came a willingness to take their program beyond the bounds of Victoria. About two weeks after Amanda had reappeared from her attic hideaway, reporter Wendy McLellan visited Victoria to spend time with Claude-Pierre and with many of her patients and their parents. McLellan was the health reporter for *The Province*, one of B.C.'s two major dailies, headquartered in Vancouver, across the Strait of Georgia from Victoria. Amanda's story would provide the news hook to describe the new program that was seemingly turning eating-disorder treatment on its ear in Victoria.

The illustrated two-page spread that McLellan produced made it appear that Claude-Pierre had not only revolutionized eating-disorder treatment but was curing huge numbers of people who would otherwise be dead. The 24-hour care in their own homes, it was said, was provided "for those near death."[7]

"I've got a doorful of dying kids and I have nowhere to put them except my house," she told McLellan, explaining the need for the Safe House, set to open just a week later. She said she'd been treating patients for eight years, had had 461 patients, and claimed a 90 per cent success rate. How she defined success was never explained, nor was the success rate, and the number of patients was never backed up with any documentation or follow-up studies.

McLellan watched her hand-feed Chloe, whom she later quoted criticizing the treatment she'd received in hospital, though not specifically endorsing Claude-Pierre's brand of therapy. More enthusiastic support came from Marisa,* doing well after two years of outpatient counselling with Claude-Pierre, and from Susannah,* whose story was so horrific it seemed remarkable she was still alive. Susannah said that before beginning counselling with Claude-Pierre, she was swallowing 200 laxative pills a day and drinking large amounts of over-the-counter drugs to induce vomiting. After a stay in Eric Martin Pavilion, she claimed she was discharged weighing 15 pounds less than when she was admitted, and addicted to cocaine that she'd begun to buy from another patient. After less than two years of counselling with Claude-Pierre, Susannah was one of the ex-patients who was helping work with the more acute patients admitted to the Safe House.

But the most remarkable story was that of Bernice, the mother of the twins, Gemma and Amanda. Bernice spent some time explaining to McLellan that Claude-Pierre would be the one she'd trust to get Amanda better. It would be, she said, the very opposite of what the family had done with Gemma.

"I trusted the medical model all along—and that's the last thing that works," she said. "Peggy's treatment works. None of her patients have died." Nowhere in the entire article did it mention that Gemma had also received counselling from Claude-Pierre, let alone that Gemma had lived at her house for treatment.

The Safe House opened a week later. It was filled to capacity on opening day, and a waiting list was created.

Just weeks after the Safe House's opening, their realtor showed Claude-Pierre and Harris a mansion on Rockland Avenue, in the heart of the toniest residential neighbourhood in the city of Victoria. Government House, home of B.C.'s lieutenant-governor, was just a couple of blocks down the road. The mansion was of a handsome Tudor design, brown and white, surrounded by gardens and greenery. Inside, the rooms spread over four floors, easily big enough to accommodate 8 to 10 patients, plus offices for staff. It was exactly what they wanted.

As they began moving patients in during the summer, Claude-Pierre was establishing the ground rules for the clinic, some of which became the hallmarks of Montreux treatment. Patients would always be weighed facing backwards on the scales so they would never know how much weight they might have gained. Because the patients were seen as being ultra-sensitive to negativity, nothing that could be seen as negative would be allowed around them: no TV news, no depressing or violent books or videos, no discussion among the staff of their own personal problems within patients' hearing. Because many of the clients came from difficult relationships within their families, direct family contact might also often be a negative to be avoided, at least in the first few months of treatment. Acute-care patients were never to be left alone for even a minute. It would be the job of the workers not only to counteract any negativity the patients verbalized, but also to ensure they took in everything on their daily meal plan as worked out by Claude-Pierre. Patients were not to leave the building without permission because that would, she decreed, be dangerous to them.

Staff were to be chosen not for their academic background or professional training but for their kindness, patience, and empathy. Current staff members brought their friends and siblings to try out for jobs, and many were immediately hired. About the time the Rockland mansion opened, Claude-Pierre found the couple with whom she decided she wanted to share management of the clinic. Margaret and Noah Dobson were both working in retail clothing sales at the time, although Margaret had had a year of practical nurse training in her native Scotland. They had come to visit Claude-Pierre and her husband because they were concerned about one of their staff members, who they believed was suffering from anorexia. The two couples clicked, and in less than a month, the Dobsons had quit their retail sales jobs and were employed by Montreux. Noah was appointed personnel director and Margaret "associate program director," which meant she was Claude-Pierre's most trusted assistant. Also moving to high positions in the residential program were daughters Kirsten and Nicole. Nicole led the team of careworkers that worked with the most critically ill patients; Kirsten provided counselling to those who were more advanced in their treatment. Dr. Clinton-Baker had agreed to be the clinic's medical consultant and deal with prescriptions and the patients' physical ailments.

Money was not easy to come by in the first days of the residential program. Although the waiting list was long, few British Columbians could afford the fees to cover a 24-hour-a-day residential program, at that point about $500 a day. They expected medical care in Canada to be paid for by the government, but the government had shown no interest in supporting what it saw as an experimental and unproven program—and a very expensive one at that. To finance the mortgage payments and the staff salaries, several supporters of the clinic, as well as Claude-Pierre and Harris themselves, took out second mortgages on their own homes. Loans came from well-off parents of a handful of past patients, all of whom had been satisfied with the outpatient counselling their daughters had received.

Montreux had operated as a for-profit company since it was first incorporated for the outpatient practice in 1988. At the end of 1993, Claude-Pierre and Harris decided to set up a non-profit society as well. Through the non-profit society they would be able to attract public donations and issue receipts for tax purposes. It would be a source of income that might help them offset the costs of caring for some of their acute-care patients who could never afford the full fee.

The tax laws wouldn't allow Claude-Pierre and Harris to manage the non-profit society themselves, so they enlisted the help of three enthusiastic supporters to form the first board of directors. One was Sgt. Bill Naughton, a police officer who'd sought Claude-Pierre's guidance on some of his cases; the second was Sam Travers, a newly retired civil servant from the Department of Human Resources; the third was Lori Winstanley, a consultant who'd formerly worked for the New Democratic Party government that held power in B.C. at the time. The society officially came into being on January 31, 1994.

At almost the same time, Claude-Pierre was approached to see if she would consider taking on the case of Caroline.* Caroline exemplified Claude-Pierre's belief that most of those who suffer from CNC are society's "best and brightest." She had graduated at the head of her high-school class in the Fraser Valley on B.C.'s Lower Mainland. Simon Fraser University in Burnaby was so impressed with her academic talents it awarded her a $10,000 scholarship. But Caroline had never been able to take proper advantage of it. Soon after she had finished high school, her eating disorder had soared out of control. She'd spent much of the intervening two and a half years in hospitals, and even there she wasn't getting better. When they'd tried giving her nutrition through a nasogastric tube, she'd reacted by pulling the tube out.

Her parents heard about Montreux and decided it was the only place that might save their daughter. Caroline's physician, Dr. Laird Birmingham, who headed the eating-disorder program at St. Paul's Hospital in Vancouver, was not prepared to endorse Montreux, but did admit she was not improving with the treatment she was receiving at St. Paul's Hospital. Claude-Pierre agreed to accept Caroline, despite her fragile medical condition, and despite the fact that her parents couldn't possibly pay the regular fees.

Claude-Pierre, Harris, and their supporters figured there couldn't be a better case with which to launch a campaign to lobby the provincial government for funding—one in which treatment was clearly needed, but the traditional medical system had admitted it had run out of options. Caroline's parents, friends, and family joined with Montreux to begin an intensive lobbying campaign to get the government to pony up the $500 a day for Caroline, and for other needy B.C. patients.

"Imagine your child drowning before your very eyes as you stand on shore, sealed off by a wire fence," wrote the parents in a letter to then–health minister Paul Ramsey. "There is a life preserver on the beach but you are unable to reach it to throw it to your child, so you stand there in panic, helpless."

The family's support network also co-ordinated fundraising in the community to help pay for Caroline's treatment. In six months, the town raised almost $25,000. Caroline was looking and feeling better, though she was still on 24-hour care. She was even talking about resuming her university studies.

Though the family couldn't get a promise of funding from the government, the health minister did agree to have a committee of experts conduct a thorough study of Montreux to decide whether its treatment could be considered "proven" and "effective." If so, he said, some funding would be provided to ease the burden on families like Caroline's.

2

The Coming of Samantha

At the same time that Caroline was moving into Montreux, a second set of anorexic twins was making headlines, this time in Birmingham, England. Suzy Kendall was growing increasingly desperate about ever finding the help her daughters Michaela and Samantha needed. In the winter of 1993–94, Michaela was near death. Her identical twin Samantha was not in much better shape. Both had been severely anorexic for more than a decade, and no doctor or hospital they had found had helped for long. Despairing, Suzy wrote to *Chat*, a British women's magazine that paid its readers for their true stories. Suzy hoped that someone who read the story might be able to link up the family with a program that would allow the twins to recover.

The response to her emotional plea was instantaneous. The story was picked up by Britain's national tabloids and by its more mainstream newspapers and magazines. Television shows invited Suzy and her daughters to make their plea to viewers. In a matter of weeks, the Kendall twins were Britain's best-known anorexics. For the next six years, every nuance of their lives would be dissected in the public press.

The twins didn't fit the stereotypical picture of sufferers of anorexia. The family wasn't rich. Neither of the girls appeared to be overachievers, driven to excel in school or in sports. Research showing that if one twin develops anorexia, the chances are higher than average that the second twin will as well had not yet been published. The chances are higher if the twins are identical (formed from a single egg) rather than fraternal (formed when two eggs develop at the same time in the uterus). One study showed that the chance of both identical twins developing anorexia is 14 times higher for identical twins than for fraternal.

Michaela and Samantha's natural father was in jail for burglary when the twins were born. Suzy had married him when she was only 19, against her family's wishes, and the marriage had been troubled from the beginning. The girls' father occasionally beat Suzy and spent much more time in the bar with his friends than at home with his new wife. He rarely held down a regular job. Suzy was overwhelmed when she gave birth to twins. She had not planned to get pregnant in the first place, and she had not known she was carrying two babies until the day she arrived at hospital to deliver them. Life became even worse when the girls' father walked out on the family when the twins were not yet three. Suzy had no idea how she was going to support, as well as look after, two preschoolers. It was her mother, Dorothy, who came to the rescue. She said she'd take the twins to live with her so that Suzy could get a full-time job. Suzy wasn't sure she approved of the plan, but she couldn't see any other option. It wasn't uncommon in their working-class Birmingham neighbourhood for children to be raised by their grandparents to help their mothers cope.

Looking back on it later, Samantha sometimes thought that was the beginning of all their problems. Although Suzy lived just round the corner and stayed in regular touch with her daughters, the girls felt abandoned by both their parents. When she reflected back on that time, Sam, in the throes of anorexia, would wonder if it hadn't been their fault that their parents had parted, possibly even because they were too fat. At the same time, the twins were each other's support and comfort. They always said that they were even closer and more inseparable than identical twins usually are.

The twins' grandmother, Dorothy, had spent years working as a cook in the kitchen of a company cafeteria. Food was her instinctive way of nurturing. If the girls were unhappy or lonely, she offered them a treat. If they were suffering the usual childhood ailments, she wanted to make sure they got a good meal to keep up their strength. They began to be known as "the trifle twins" because of their liking for sweet desserts after every meal. From being chunky, they soon became definitely overweight.

Other family members commented on it—with a complete lack of tact or empathy as to how the girls might feel. "Mom, they're bloody enormous," blurted one of the girls' aunts when she first saw them after a gap of several years.

Still the twins coped with their weight until they reached adolescence. They still had the confidence to get up and sing with their mother at a social club near their home. But when they reached secondary school age, the escalating taunts and bullying became too much for them. The other children started calling them "the fatties" and "the blobs." Never outstanding students, they came to hate going to school every day. Too often they turned back to the only comfort they knew—food. By the time they were 14, each weighed more than 190 pounds.

That was the summer they decided they couldn't stand it any more. They made a pact with each other to lose as much weight as they could before school started again in September. The diet they made up for themselves was extreme. Each day, they restricted themselves to one diet meal-replacement bar apiece, one apple, a little yogurt, maybe a few potato chips. Both the twins' mother and grandmother knew there was something unhealthy about the regime, but they didn't know what to do about it. It was the summer of 1981, and the issue of eating disorders was not yet well understood by the general public.

By the end of summer, Samantha and Michaela had lost more than 60 pounds apiece. At their height of five feet eight inches, they had reached a healthy weight for their age. Friends and neighbours complimented them on their appearance. They should have gone back to school feeling terrific about themselves and determined to maintain their weight with a healthy, balanced diet.

It didn't happen. Samantha would say later that they had somehow convinced themselves that if they were more accepted by their classmates at 125 pounds than at 185 pounds, they'd be even more accepted if they became even thinner.

By that fall, Suzy realized the girls had moved far beyond dieting, even extreme dieting, to the point of starving themselves. She tried to talk to them about it, and, intellectually, they seemed to understand. They'd tell her they knew they'd gone overboard with the diet, and that they'd return to normal eating the next day. "Tomorrow we'll have a proper meal," they'd tell her. But they never did.

Suzy took the twins to the family doctor and explained about the great difficulty they were having eating. The doctor talked to them as well, but didn't know what other steps might be taken to persuade them to return to a normal eating pattern.

It never really got better after that summer. For more than a decade, the twins saw a procession of doctors, psychiatrists, and professors. They were in and out of a number of hospitals, but nothing seemed to break through the anorexic mindset. As so many anorexics do, they became expert at lying convincingly about their eating habits, expert at finding ways to trick doctors and nurses about their weight and food intake. Suzy remembered hearing Samantha earnestly tell a therapist who was also a learned professor that she had started eating now and was well on the way to recovery. The professor was reassured. Suzy knew it was all nonsense.

Sometimes, for a while, they stabilized enough that Suzy would think they might yet be able to live some semblance of a normal life. They finished high school and got jobs. For a while, each had a steady boyfriend, and that seemed to lend stability to their lives.

But by that point they were having trouble holding down jobs. Their jobs most often had been working in holiday camps, but that summer, the manager apologetically said he had no choice but to let them go. Although they were well liked and competent, their appearance had become so grotesque that the guests at the camps didn't like having them around. They had begun to wear weird makeup that they thought emphasized the bones of their faces—and their thinness—even more.

In 1992, after a five-year relationship, Michaela's boyfriend gave her an ultimatum: "Is it going to be the anorexia or is it going to be me?" Michaela hesitated only briefly before telling him that, sadly, she would have to choose the anorexia because she knew she could never give it up.

When she told Samantha the story, Samantha hesitated only briefly herself. She too broke up with her boyfriend and moved back in with Michaela at their grandmother's. It was the worst thing she could have done. The twins, still strongly supportive of each other, also became supportive of each other's disordered eating, competing to see who could eat the least, sometimes even who could drink the least. According to Samantha, their daily diet in early 1993 consisted of two extra-strong mints for lunch, two potato chips mid-afternoon, and a supper of one-quarter slice of bread and a slice of black pudding (a British concoction consisting of blood and liver mixed with oatmeal and breadcrumbs, herbs and spices). Sometimes Samantha would feel she couldn't even drink a cup of tea if Michaela said they could go without.

Samantha said later she would often realize how gaunt Michaela was becoming as she lost more and more weight, but Samantha could never relate it to what she was doing herself. If she mentioned it to Michaela, the competition factor would be out in the open.

Once she urged Michaela to eat more, saying, "You look like a skeleton," but Michaela retorted, "You're only jealous."

They began using even more drastic means to lose weight. They deliberately vomited what little they ate. They took laxatives to empty their bodies of every calorie they'd taken in, sometimes as many as 100 pills a day. The effects were sometimes so extreme that they couldn't control their bowels, as if they had a bad case of intestinal flu.

The twins' health began to deteriorate drastically. Michaela, always slightly smaller and frailer than Samantha, was in the worse shape. Their mental state was no better. Michaela in particular grew so depressed that she was frequently suicidal. Suzy remembers Samantha calling her in desperation one night because Michaela had cut her wrists and then locked herself in the bathroom. When Suzy arrived and threatened to break the door down, Michaela burst out of the room and ran away screaming, the blood dripping behind her.

Throughout the years the twins had been admitted to various hospitals, mostly on general psychiatric wards rather than in specialized eating-disorder units. Various psychiatric treatments had been tried, including electroshock. Nothing brought about any lasting improvement.

As Michaela's condition deteriorated, the family and doctors agreed she must again be hospitalized. This time Michaela was adamantly opposed to the idea. The doctors took the drastic step of "sectioning" her—the British term for having her declared mentally incompetent because of a mental illness. It meant she could be hospitalized and treated against her will. She was moved to a psychiatric ward at Queen

Elizabeth's Hospital in Birmingham, where she received nutrition through a nasogastric tube. She fought every inch of the way, frequently ripping the tubes out when she was left alone. The doctors wouldn't allow Samantha to visit her because they believed that the competition between the two sisters to be the thinner was too intense. Even if they no longer had a formal "pact" not to eat, the result was still the same.

It was while Michaela was in hospital that Suzy wrote her first desperate letter to *Chat*. After her story was picked up by British tabloids and morning television, it found its way to U.S. chat-show host Maury Povich. A veteran TV news anchor and talk-show host, Povich had started his own nationally syndicated afternoon talk show three years earlier. He and his staff said the aim of the show was to put a human face on the news stories of the day. He had taken up such causes as sexual harassment in the work place and the need for more education about AIDS. His interest in issues affecting teenagers and their families was so great that he changed the entire focus of his show to adolescent problems.

In November, Suzy and Samantha were flown to New York to appear on the program. Samantha looked skeletal, and admitted she weighed about 58 pounds. Povich explained that Michaela "can't leave the hospital" to appear on the program, but viewers got to see footage of her, at 54 pounds, looking even frailer and more like a concentration-camp victim than Samantha.[8]

Both Samantha and Suzy complained about the treatments offered in Britain. The emphasis was entirely on getting the body weight up without ever trying to solve the emotional problems behind the self-starvation, they said. They complained that Samantha had never had a chance at good psychological counselling, despite all her stays in hospital. And Samantha was insistent that being placed in a general psychiatric ward, often with patients who were psychotic, hallucinating, and schizophrenic, only made her more upset and stressed and less likely to eat.

Originally she told Povich she was afraid to eat because of all the teasing and bullying she'd endured at school before losing weight. Somehow, she said, she was afraid that if she started to eat even a little, she'd regain all the weight she'd lost. Although she knew intellectually that she was seriously underweight, when she looked in a mirror she saw someone who was "normal," she said. As Povich probed gently, however, she also admitted that she had a deep reservoir of anger inside her, and that she believed the "turmoil" in which she'd grown up had contributed somehow to the disorder. She admitted to being frightened by her own condition, and told Povich, "Deep down, I want to get back to a healthy weight, yes. I don't want to die."

At the end of the show, Povich vowed to try to find suitable counselling for both Samantha and Michaela. "Now you and your sister feel like part of our family," Povich told Samantha. "We want to see how you're doing, and we don't want you to die."

Only a few weeks later, staff for the Povich show, combing local news stories for interesting tips, came across the stories that were being aired in Canada about Peggy Claude-Pierre and Montreux. His interest was immediately aroused. He got staff members to phone Victoria to ask more questions, obtain more details, and eventually to ask Claude-Pierre if she would be interested in appearing on the show, perhaps with some former patients who would provide testimonials to her work. For Claude-Pierre, it must have been exactly the break she was looking for. She'd be catapulted from being a small-scale player in a small Canadian city to a potential international star. The clinic, struggling to survive financially, could attract patients able to pay the high fees necessary for round-the-clock care.

She readily agreed to do the show. She would be flown to New York and would take with her Bernice, mother of the twins Amanda and Gemma, and Thomas,* husband of Chloe. Video footage would be shown of her sitting at Chloe's bedside, persuading her to take a little nutrition. By the time the show was ready to air in February, Caroline, whose parents were begging for government funding for the clinic, had also become a patient, and it was agreed she would be a part of it as well. There would be a video and phone link-up so viewers could see the girl, still incredibly fragile, and Povich could talk to her briefly on the phone.

Povich brought other acute anorexics onto the show as well, trying to combine all their stories to provide a picture of the mental turmoil that a victim experiences, as well as the distorted thought process that goes on in her head. One woman, who still weighed only 63 pounds, talked about how much better she felt at that weight than at her lowest of 56 pounds. "When you're 56 pounds, you feel like you're not really alive and that God just forgot to stop your heart," she said. Another talked about the fear she felt that eating a single radish would make her fat.[9]

Claude-Pierre explained for the first time to an international audience her theory that eating-disorder sufferers are exceptionally sensitive, brilliant, and kind people, "the cream of the crop" of society, who have built up a "mental negative construct" in which they are entirely unworthy of eating or living.

Emotional video footage showed Caroline at the clinic, saying that she still felt "fat and heavy and disgusting and ugly. And I just want to keep losing more weight." She explained that although she knew her condition was grave, her head was still full of "voices" that told her not to eat and that she'd be a better person if she didn't have to eat or drink at all. "The voices are always there and they never go away," she said. "They just fill up my whole head."

On the phone, Caroline said only a few words. When Povich asked her how she was feeling, she replied with a single word: "Tired." Later she added that she felt tired "all the time. And dizzy all the time."

Claude-Pierre emphasized how critical Caroline's condition had been when she came to the clinic—and how serious it still was. She described her as being "very fragile and very, very ill," and added she was "very close to death" the night she came to Montreux. She told of taking her after Caroline's mother had called and told her, "I'm not sure my daughter will make it through the night."

Bernice told the story of losing Gemma to suicide after years of anorexia and bulimia, and then of Amanda's illness, including the weeklong search for her. She told of her belief that "the medical model just does not service the needs of this condition," but again did not mention that Gemma had also been counselled by Claude-Pierre. On camera, she also did not directly link Amanda with Claude-Pierre's treatment, mentioning only that Amanda was now doing much better and was living with her older sister in Toronto to continue her recovery.

Povich was pleased to bring the viewers one piece of good news about the Kendall twins. The support the family had received after their appearance on the show had stimulated Samantha enough to re-trigger her will to live, at least briefly. In the intervening three months, she'd gained more than 20 pounds. Povich showed viewers a new snapshot of Samantha, looking significantly healthier than she had during her trip to New York. Michaela, however, had not responded as well, Povich admitted. She remained in hospital in Birmingham, still too unwell to go home or live on her own, let alone make the trip to New York for a TV appearance.

Around the time of that *Povich* show, Michaela was deciding she'd had enough. Even after close to six months in hospital, the doctors were continuing to insist she was too ill to be allowed to live on her own. But psychiatric patients in Britain, as in Canada, have a right of appeal, and Michaela took advantage of it. She was desperate not only to be on her own again, but especially to be with Samantha, whom she missed terribly. In February an appeal board ruled she was not so out of touch with reality that she could be held against her will any longer. She returned to Dorothy's house, where Samantha was living—and immediately gave up eating altogether. The months of imposed treatment had done Michaela no good at all.

Michaela's health began failing further. She was depressed and suicidal, and too weak even to leave the house. The careworker who came to the home to try to help the twins through the day worried about her increasing preoccupation with death. She was upset as well about the effect Michaela's return home was having on Samantha. Their mutual support for disordered eating and their competition to be thinner had kicked in practically the day she returned home, and she knew Samantha was quickly losing the weight she'd so painfully gained since the Povich show. At one point Michaela told the worker that if she died, perhaps "it would free Samantha to carry on and live."

Michaela and Samantha shared a double bed, and on the morning of April 20, Samantha awoke to find Michaela beside her, motionless, white, and not breathing. She had died in the night, less than two months after discharging herself from hospital. An inquest found she had taken an overdose of sleeping pills. Her own doctor had refused to prescribe her any sedatives because her health was so frail, but she'd been able to persuade her grandmother Dorothy to give her some, arguing she desperately needed to sleep and couldn't do so without medication. The overdose, said coroner Richard Whittington, had combined with a viral heart infection and her overall weakened and emaciated state to bring on a fatal heart attack. She weighed only about 60 pounds when she died.

Suzy, Samantha, and Dorothy were all devastated by Michaela's death. For Samantha, it was enough to send her over the edge into a state where she once more refused to eat at all. She'd already felt panicked and anxious with her weight at 90 pounds and had been trying to keep eating only to show Michaela it was possible. After Michaela died, she could hardly bring herself to swallow. She was attempting to survive on a handful of potato chips and soft drinks daily. Within days, she was so weak she couldn't even get out of bed. Doctors were warning Suzy that Samantha was at grave risk of dying from anorexia as well. Suzy, even more desperate than before, again appealed through the media for someone to help Samantha.

Samantha herself went public to ask for help, trying to explain how much she was grieving for Michaela but still wanted deep down to live. "It is like having to live with half of me missing, because we were so close," she said. She admitted that part of her wanted to be left alone to die in peace, but another part of her mind desperately wanted to live and to beat the eating disorder. She gave another hint of her twisted thinking when she told a reporter: "I enjoy the control I have over my body. It is the only thing I feel I have achieved."[10]

Among the other calls she made, Suzy phoned the friends she'd made at the *Povich* show to tell them the sad news about Michaela and to beg again for treatment that might be successful for Samantha.

This time Povich had an idea. He'd been fascinated with Claude-Pierre's theories at the time of the February show and especially with the story of Gemma and Amanda, a story of twins that sounded so much like the Kendalls'. He knew that Bernice gave credit to Claude-Pierre for ensuring that her second daughter did not succumb as well. Perhaps what Claude-Pierre had done for one surviving twin she could do for another. He told Suzy that he knew of a clinic in Canada that might be able to provide the sort of help Samantha appeared to need.

Suzy was ecstatic. Claude-Pierre agreed the case sounded like one the clinic might be prepared to take on. The *Povich* show agreed to pay for Claude-Pierre to fly to Britain, meet and "assess" Samantha, and decide if she could successfully be treated at Montreux. It was all decided within days. Samantha would be admitted to Montreux in mid-May, only about a month after her sister's death.

Montreux was not the only place that offered to help Samantha. Several British experts were openly doubtful about the family's decision to fly all the way to North America, rather than try some of the top programs being offered in Britain by that time. One of the most critical was Dr. Dee Dawson, who runs Rhodes Farm, a world-recognized program for adolescent anorexics on the outskirts of London. Dr. Dawson is also known throughout Britain for her vociferous speeches warning parents and schools of the need for prevention and early intervention in cases of incipient eating disorders. In an effort to avoid a "hospital" or "institutional" atmosphere, Rhodes Farm is housed in a mansion that looks remarkably similar to Montreux's mansion on Rockland. Its program combines individual psychotherapy, family work, school and extracurricular programs, and a great deal of support around eating. Dr. Dawson had much sympathy for the family over Michaela's death. Releasing Michaela from hospital when she was so ill was "a crass decision ... criminal," she said, effectively an unnecessary death sentence. At the same time, though, she said, "there is no magic cure in Canada."[11]

Similar warnings came from Dr. Janet Treasure, who headed the eating-disorders clinic at Maudsley Hospital, and from Professor Gerald Russell, who headed the program at Hayes Grove Priory Hospital, both in London. Both programs had worldwide reputations and were considered among the best in Britain. Dr. Treasure said she couldn't figure out why Samantha hadn't been referred long ago to a top eating-disorder centre rather than just admitted to regular psychiatric wards. Russell bluntly described the move to Canada for treatment as "ridiculous."[12]

However, another British therapist, Dr. Susie Orbach, thought Montreux might offer more hope than British centres. Dr. Orbach, a feminist therapist whose books include *Fat is a Feminist Issue* and who was one of Princess Diana's confidantes, said some centres in Canada provided more humane and progressive treatment than many British programs that were still adopting a strict behaviourist approach.[13]

Neither Suzy nor Samantha wanted to be dragged into debates among experts. They had become convinced that Montreux was the only place on earth that could save Samantha. They were going there, no matter what anyone else said.

It wasn't quite that simple. There was, first of all, the matter of money. Claude-Pierre had made clear that, much as she wanted Samantha as a patient, she could not afford to treat her entirely for free. Suzy and her new husband, Bob, had nothing close to the resources normally needed to pay for a Montreux stay. Eventually, several of the British media outlets agreed to co-ordinate a campaign of public donations to help defray the costs of Samantha's treatment. Donations were to be made to the non-profit society that had been set up in Victoria to aid the clinic. Over the next several months, the donations would total more than £66,000 ($135,000).

With that hurdle cleared, Samantha next needed a doctor's note, saying her health was satisfactory for air travel. Instead, the doctor who examined her immediately sent her to hospital. She had a chest infection, he said, and that, combined with her emaciated state, was enough to make air travel dangerous. Samantha stayed in hospital for three days and then discharged herself against doctors' advice. She had taken antibiotics, she said, and was feeling better.

There was one more stop for Samantha before she arrived at Montreux. That was New York, where she and Suzy met Claude-Pierre and participated together in another full-length episode of *The Maury Povich Show*.

Claude-Pierre made no secret of how serious Samantha's condition was. "I know she had an erratic pulse this morning," she told viewers. "To keep her alive for the first two weeks will be very difficult. If we do that, then there's a chance."[14] Povich did not ask on camera why someone who was so ill as to have an erratic heartbeat was doing an hour-long TV show under hot studio lights, rather than getting medical attention, or even just resting. Samantha readily admitted that the night before she'd gone out for supper with the show's producers and eaten two bowls of soup, then promptly gone to the restaurant washroom and vomited them back up.

As ill as Samantha was, her sense of humour would still come to the fore. When Povich wondered aloud how anyone could eat just two potato chips out of a bag and then throw the rest away, Samantha quipped, "Self-control," with a twinkle in her eye.

Claude-Pierre talked about her plans to provide Samantha with one-on-one or even two-on-one care, "to tell her at all times what she's worth," and how she would then begin teaching Samantha to be more objective and better able to understand her role in the world.

Samantha talked about the great relief she'd felt when she'd first met Claude-Pierre and Claude-Pierre had talked to her about how worthless she must be feeling. It had made her feel more understood and less alone than she had for a long time. "I know she can help me," she said with heartfelt enthusiasm. She felt equally relieved when, during the show itself, Kirsten Claude-Pierre started talking about the voices she'd heard in her head, condemning her and telling her not to eat. She heard voices like that too, Samantha said.

Kirsten and Nicole Claude-Pierre provided testimonials to their mother's success, telling how they had managed to get over their eating disorder once they had finally learned to trust their mother. Nicole, who was then team leader for Caroline, also updated viewers on the "incredible" progress she'd made since the show in February, moving from "shakes" to solid food eaten with a fork. It was still hard for her to eat, though, Nicole admitted.

Claude-Pierre declined to say how long Samantha might have to stay at the clinic until she was cured. But she asked Povich if she could bring Samantha back on the show in eight months, by which time "she won't be totally better, but she will be so far along that you'll notice the difference."

After Suzy asked for donations for the Save Samantha Appeal, Claude-Pierre made one last emotional appeal herself. "Could I ask the audience, please," she said, "to keep your fingers crossed and please pray. We need all the help we can get."

Even apart from Samantha's irregular heartbeat, it was a hellish few days in New York for those involved. Samantha was still taking huge numbers of laxatives, which left her with little bowel control. Her self-destructiveness was so severe that when she and her mother went shopping for souvenirs in a jewellery store, she got caught trying to shoplift several items of costume jewellery—items she neither needed nor wanted, and had the money to pay for in any case. Everyone was glad when the group finally arrived at Montreux and Samantha could begin to settle in at the mansion.

The Canadian media had also become aware of Samantha's case and the fact that she was coming to Montreux. It gave the clinic national publicity for the first time, as well as publicity in the U.S. and Britain. Newspapers across Canada ran stories repeating Suzy's claims that Samantha had exhausted every treatment available in Britain and was coming to Montreux as a last resort. No one in Canada ever learned that Samantha had not been treated in specialized eating-disorder units in Britain, or that two of those top units had offered her immediate treatment as an alternative to Montreux. Nor did they hear of her chest infection or her irregular heartbeat while in New York. The one note of caution came in a short article in the *Vancouver Sun*, in which two eating-disorder experts expressed concern over both the unproven success rates at Montreux and the level of medical supervision there for a patient as ill as Samantha.[15]

At the time Samantha arrived at Montreux, I was working as the Bureau Chief for *The Province*. *The Province* is a newspaper based in Vancouver, but my job was to cover, for a province-wide readership, news from Victoria, the provincial capital, and the southern part of Vancouver Island. Although Wendy McLellan had written the major spread on Claude-Pierre a year earlier and the newspaper had since printed several stories about Caroline's move to Montreux, I hadn't had any personal contact with the clinic.

But only a few days after Samantha's arrival at Montreux, one of our editors phoned from Vancouver to tell me my afternoon assignment was to go to the Rockland mansion, where Samantha would be holding her first news conference. Reporters from across the country had been calling Montreux to see how she was doing, and clinic management had decided she should make at least a brief public appearance. That afternoon, reporters from Britain and from across Canada jammed into the living room at the mansion. For most of the reporters, including myself, it was our first chance to see the residential program in operation. The setting was undeniably impressive. A circular driveway led from the street through gardens and greenery up to the Tudor-style house. Caroline was among the patients playing badminton on the front lawn as the TV crews arrived—a subtle testimony to success. The front door opened onto a baronial entrance hall, panelled in dark wood, with a sweeping staircase curving down. The living room seemed light, airy, and comfortable.

It was Nicole Claude-Pierre who helped Samantha, still appallingly frail, down the stairs and to the couch waiting for her in the living room. Hope and optimism radiated from every pore of her. "I know it'll work," she said with determination in her voice. "They've got it right here ... they're here to make me live."

Samantha said she liked the fact that staff members seemed to know the many tricks anorexics learn, such as hoarding laxatives. She thought the food so far was "beautiful" and found the atmosphere pleasant and relaxing. It was, she said, a huge difference from the psychiatric wards where she'd been hospitalized in Britain previously. She took advantage of the British TV crew's presence to wave hello to her family back in Birmingham. "I do love you and thanks for everything," she told them.

Claude-Pierre reiterated her claim of a 90 per cent success rate for the clinic and her own conviction that Samantha would be entirely cured. She noted that other patients had been even sicker on arrival, pointing to Caroline as an example. The media were introduced to Dr. Clinton-Baker, who would be monitoring Samantha's medical condition. None of us even thought to ask whether he had any special qualifications to deal with eating disorders, especially in cases as severe as Samantha's.

Harris talked of how both Samantha and her family felt they had exhausted all treatment available in Britain. "They had lost confidence in a system that failed them with one daughter," he said. "They were not going to lose another."

He also talked of his hope that the clinic would soon receive a regular source of funding through the provincial government in B.C. The health ministry had established a special task force to study the clinic as part of a larger, overall study it was undertaking to determine the programs needed to deal with eating disorders across the province.

Harris said he had seen a preliminary draft of the task force report and was pleased with the praise it gave the non-institutional and supportive atmosphere at Montreux. The task force also said, however, that the clinic needed to set out more objective standards by which its work could be measured, and needed to better document its program and results. Harris said the clinic would be happy to make those changes, especially if they could get government funding to pay for a staff member for research. "We've started to do a lot of those things," he said. This was Montreux's first public promise to do a scientific outcome study, a promise unkept over the next seven years.

The overall atmosphere was one of hope and joy. Everyone, from the clinic staff members to the reporters and camera crews, wanted, so badly, for the clinic to work for somebody like Samantha who'd had such a horrible time in the past.

When the cameras left, the staff began the day-to-day routine of work with Samantha, persuading her to eat her six small snacks a day, reassuring her that having an eating disorder did not mean she was "mental," promising her that once she got better, she'd be able to share her experiences with other anorexics and even work at the clinic as a counsellor. Once she began to feel better physically, staff members found Sam to be bright, engaging, and funny. The sense of humour that she'd shown even on the *Povich* shows came out, and Sam and her workers would frequently be heard laughing together. Her interest in music returned, and she would be heard playing the piano or singing. She became fond of several staff members, even having fantasies about eventually marrying one of the male workers she liked the most.

At the same time, the staff realized that she knew more anorexic "tricks" than most of the patients and would try to get away with not eating, even with a staff member only two or three feet from her. Her favourite trick was to hide bits of food in any place she could see, even throwing it out the window. "She was so fast," remembers one of her regular workers. "If you so much as blinked, there'd be food in the potted plants or out the window. You'd think she was reaching up to scratch her nose and she'd be turfing the food backwards over her shoulder and out the window. At the end of a meal, you'd look down and there'd be pieces of muffin and bits of vegetable in the garden."

And always lurking in the background was the media. There wasn't a staff member who didn't know that a huge success with Samantha could be the clinic's "open sesame" to both fame and fortune. Her fame had reached such levels in England, and now, to a lesser degree, in Canada, that her "cure" would be a testimonial to Montreux's success for the whole world.

And Samantha was one of many Montreux patients who responded remarkably well in the first few months of treatment while she remained on 24-hour care, surrounded by Montreux staff every waking moment. When she'd been at the clinic for one month, Harris told the Victoria daily, the *Times-Colonist*, that she was doing "unbelievably well," and was "certainly well out of medical danger." He said Dr. Clinton-Baker was satisfied that she was now medically stable, and, he added, "I think she believes for the first time that she is going to get better."[16]

Just two weeks later, Samantha ate her first meal out in a restaurant—tea at the Blethering Place, a restaurant in the Oak Bay village, a quaint street of shops only about half a mile from the mansion. The restaurant's owner, Ken Agate, was well known in the city for opening up his premises for community events. He also knew David Harris, because Harris's band would sometimes play there as part of the entertainment. The tea turned into a transatlantic media event, with one of the British tabloids, *The Daily Mirror*, sending a reporter and photographer to Victoria to join local reporters in recording the occasion. It also turned into a fundraiser to boost the Save Samantha Appeal and get more donations to continue her treatment. About half the restaurant was taken over by people from the clinic when Samantha showed up for a cup of tea and a muffin.

Spokesperson for the clinic on this occasion was Lori Winstanley, the consultant who sat on the board of the non-profit society. Winstanley said the idea for the restaurant meal-cum-media-event-cum-fundraiser was Samantha's. "Doing this is part of her therapy," she said. Samantha looked obviously healthier than she had on arrival at the clinic, but Winstanley asked reporters not to ask her how much weight she'd gained as it was still "too traumatic" for her to think about recovery in those terms.[17]

The story written by reporter Fran Bowden in the British newspaper *The Daily Mirror* could not have been louder in its praise of Montreux. She described Sam's "winning battle [that] has been an inspiration to fellow-sufferers and has given her the motivation to start a new career to become an anorexic counselor."[18]

Sam is quoted as telling Bowden: "I have something to live for now, to help others like Michaela to love. I want to use my experiences to help sick kids. Then I will feel my suffering and Michaela's death weren't for nothing."

Winstanley gave the latest update on Sam's condition, saying, "Sam looks brilliant. She's very calm and focused."

The story also introduced *Mirror* readers to two other young British women, who would soon become Montreux patients after learning of Samantha's apparent success. One was Jeannie,* a Scottish girl whose weight had plummeted to less than 55 pounds and who was being fed intravenously in hospital. "I saw how Samantha had come on and I realized this clinic was our only hope," said Jeannie's mother. The family of the other girl asked to remain anonymous. The article again encouraged donations, this time not only to support Sam's continued treatment, but also to help pay the costs for Jeannie.

Sam's enthusiasm continued unabated for the next several months. She declared she felt "100 per cent fit," and wrote to her mother: "Mom, you will be so proud of me when you see me. I'm still determined to never starve myself again. It killed my darling Michaela. It's not killing me."

She told of her passion for her new hobby of mountain biking, which she was now allowed to pursue for two hours a day. Much of Sam's rekindled spirit appeared to come from the promise made to her by Claude-Pierre that she could soon start training to be a Montreux counsellor. Although Sam had been in treatment only four months and was still herself an acute-care patient, she said Claude-Pierre had told her she could begin her counselling training just three months later. "Peggy said I'll make a great nurse in January," she wrote. "I really am looking forward to working here."

She'd already begun doing a little work, volunteering to help a newly admitted and very ill patient, Donna Brooks, she said. Samantha was especially attracted to Donna because she looked so much like Michaela, for whom she openly admitted she was still grieving. But, she said in her letters, she seemed to do better than any other staff member in persuading Donna to eat. "Peggy is amazed at how I'm coping, but I feel as if I'm a nurse already," she wrote. "And Donna is just great to be with."

In October, after five months of treatment, Sam made her first visit back home. Claude-Pierre went with her, and part of the time in England was spent making public and media appearances to show the world how well she was doing under the Montreux regime.

Not just Sam's family but virtually all of Britain was ecstatic at her new appearance and her apparent progress. Her weight had increased to about 120 pounds, healthy for her height. Her reunion with her mother was orchestrated to take place on *This Morning*, the Granada TV show that had first publicized her story. There were tears all round as Samantha ran into her mother's arms, looking healthy and happy. Suzy said that the best part was putting her arms around her daughter and not feeling as if she was hugging a skeleton. Even Samantha could not believe the change in herself. "I didn't think I would look at a picture of my [former skeletal] self and say 'Who was that?'" she said on the show. "I looked at it and cried to myself."

In addition to the tabloids, Britain's mainstream newspapers ran stories lauding the work being done at Montreux. The *Telegraph* described Montreux as the program that "has worked where everything else had failed."[19] It described Sam as looking "healthy and tanned," and told of her newly improved attitude that had her wanting to stay on at Montreux and become a counsellor once she had fully recovered. The story also quoted Claude-Pierre explaining her theories about the causes of anorexia and how Sam was now making great progress because her Negative Mind had so little control over her. A small sidebar was headed "The Clinic That Worked." It did include one small note of caution concerning the idea of sufferers from an illness going immediately on to become counsellors. It was important, noted an executive with a volunteer group, that a person be entirely recovered from their own disorder before moving on to try to help others.

The private reality of the trip home did not entirely match the public image. Once again Samantha was caught in the middle of the tensions between her mother and her grandmother. While Suzy wanted to believe Samantha was close to cured, Dorothy was much more doubtful. The two women even appeared to vie for who should appear on TV with Samantha, now that she looked so much better. Even Samantha herself wondered sometimes whether Suzy wasn't becoming a bit too fond of the reflected glory of being the mother of the country's most famous anorexic.

Soon after returning to Victoria, Harris told the media that clinic staff believed Samantha was about halfway through the program. She knew she'd reached a healthy weight, but wasn't yet entirely comfortable about weighing that amount. She was ready, though, for the big move from 24-hour care to partial care. That meant she was allowed to be on her own for at least 8 hours a day and was expected to be able to prepare and eat her own meals. Gradually the amount of unsupervised time she had each day increased to 12 hours and then 16. She moved from the main mansion to a nearby apartment to try living independently.

However, instead of continuing to progress, her improvement stalled. She became less trusting of the promises Claude-Pierre had made her, and that summer she used her unsupervised time to sneak out and buy laxatives again. She said later she believed the staff at Montreux knew she was relapsing into taking laxatives again, but were powerless to do anything about it. There was no more talk of her soon starting training to become a counsellor. In August, her mother, Suzy, came over to Victoria to visit Samantha on a holiday. Out of the blue one night, Samantha begged Suzy to take her back to Britain with her. This time even Suzy had no illusions that Samantha was recovered. It was obvious her mind was very nearly as troubled as it had been when she first came to Montreux. Sam told her mother that everyone at Montreux had been wonderful to her, but she didn't feel "cured" any more. Eventually they agreed Samantha would return to Britain with Suzy for a holiday of her own. Montreux agreed Samantha should go for two weeks, and she even signed a contract promising to return after that time.

Sam knew then that she was never coming back. Just as the British doctors had warned 15 months earlier, there had been no "miracle" treatment in Canada for her. But by then the media attention she had garnered for Montreux had put the clinic on the international map. Her departure attracted scarcely any media attention.

3

The Miracle Show

When Samantha first arrived at Montreux, Peggy Claude-Pierre and David Harris were still waiting for word on whether they'd receive funding from the B.C. government. In their proposal, they had said they would provide their brand of full 24-hour-a-day care for a fee of $500 per day per patient. If the government were to fund six severely eating-disordered patients at Montreux, the clinic would take in more than $1 million annually from those payments alone.

After promising Caroline's parents to look into funding the clinic, health minister Paul Ramsey had ordered the review of the clinic as part of an overall study of services provided for eating-disorder sufferers in B.C. Everyone involved in the field conceded that current services contained major gaps, with patients who were not acutely ill left on waiting lists for weeks or months. Outside the largest cities, almost no treatment programs were available at all. A team of health and social work experts was appointed to undertake the investigation of Montreux. They visited the clinic, met with the management team, talked to family members of patients, and interviewed others in the eating-disorder community.

In June, less than two weeks after Samantha arrived at Montreux, Ramsey made the results of both studies public. He announced a new policy framework for dealing with eating disorders in B.C. and a substantial increase in funding for other programs throughout the province—but no money for Montreux. Their study had shown, he said, that Montreux was not yet at the point where the government would feel comfortable spending taxpayers' dollars there.

The approved "policy framework" noted that residential programs like Montreux would be eligible to receive funding "if they meet the requirements established.... These include cost effectiveness, professional accreditation, licensed facility, and ability to meet standards."

The detailed study of Montreux showed that the clinic had been unable to prove to the ministry that it met any of those conditions. Its proposed daily fee was twice what was being suggested for a residential treatment program to be run through St. Paul's Hospital in Vancouver. Government officials might have been willing to foot the higher bill if they'd been convinced Montreux's treatment was more successful than that found elsewhere. They weren't. They found no outcome studies to back up the clinic's claims of success. They couldn't even find any specific measures by which a patient's recovery would be defined. "In the Montreux program," the study report said, "recovery is defined by the patients themselves according to the weight they have gained and their resumption of life activities. There are no other outcome measures." Neither were there any written care plans for the residents or any documentation of the effects of the treatment. Although few mainstream programs had yet been in business long enough to produce detailed outcome studies, none were saying they offered the exceptional cure rates that Montreux was claiming.

The government officials were also worried that the Montreux staff lacked any formal training or professional qualifications, and that Montreux had established no links with other eating-disorder programs in either hospitals or the community. The report noted that the staff "demonstrated warmth, compassion, and strong personal commitment to their work." However, their lack of training and of membership in any professional association made it difficult to ensure that quality care was being provided. Essentially, they were accountable to no one except Peggy Claude-Pierre.

The investigators noted that other professionals whom they interviewed had found that Claude-Pierre "[did] not demonstrate a thorough knowledge of the literature on eating disorders or current research." Neither did she appear to understand the necessary ethical requirements for confidentiality. Several people had told them, they wrote, about a public meeting at which Claude-Pierre talked about her clients by name, sometimes even discussing their family background.

Even after professionals had warned her about the requirement for confidentiality from a therapist, she'd kept on naming the patients.

The team concluded that Montreux should be considered again for funding only when it could show that it was using trained professional staff to supervise care, was integrating its program within the overall health care system, had proper written standards and policies, and had "developed outcome criteria which are monitored regularly." The report also noted that even to be allowed to continue operating, the clinic needed to obtain a licence under the Community Care Facilities Act.

After the announcement, Claude-Pierre said she wasn't surprised at the government's decision, but was "amazed and bewildered by man's inhumanity to man. I'm saddened and burdened by the many people who won't receive help."

Lori Winstanley, from the board of the non-profit Montreux Society, was more blunt about Montreux's view of the report.

"Our response is somewhat stunned," she told a reporter from the *Times-Colonist*.[20] She argued that the review panel had not taken into account the many strengths of Montreux, including what she insisted was its remarkable success rate. In one of the many contradictory sets of numbers which the clinic issued, she said Montreux had been in existence for 10 years and had treated 460 people. In fact, Claude-Pierre had formally begun her outpatient practice only in 1988, and at the time of the report had been running the residential program for less than one year. It was unclear where Winstanley had obtained her numbers.

In any case, said Winstanley, of those 460 clients, "they're all alive, and 90 per cent of them are totally recovered." She did not say what tracking system had been used to produce those figures, nor what the definition was of "totally recovered."

Not long after the report, though, Montreux found a way to tap into a source of funding that would prove far richer than anything a Canadian government would ever have produced. That source began with the mother of an anorexic who had watched the *Povich* show featuring Samantha Kendall on her way to Montreux. Catherine* was becoming frustrated in her efforts to find what she considered a good treatment program for her daughter, Lynda,* who at the age of 16 was so acutely anorexic that she was, according to her mother, eating only six grapes a day.

Far more than Sam Kendall, Lynda fit the stereotype of a typical anorexic. She and her mother were members of a wealthy and prominent New York–area family. Catherine was a stage actress of some repute in the competitive New York market.

In the year since Lynda had started showing the symptoms of anorexia, Catherine had tried several eating-disorder programs for her, but, she said, the doctors didn't seem to understand the depths of her daughter's problems. She was unhappy with one program that had too much of a behavioural emphasis, and equally unhappy with another where the doctor, himself recovered from an eating disorder, was sympathetic but insisted Lynda had to be responsible for changing herself.

In the spring of 1994, Lynda was hospitalized in a program in Wisconsin, and Catherine was in despair because the doctors there refused to commit her as mentally ill so she could be tube-fed against her will. To Catherine, the doctors' decision was beginning to seem like a prescription for euthanasia, and she wouldn't accept it. No matter what any doctor said, she was not going to sit by and watch her daughter die.

The day of the *Povich* show she had returned home from yet another visit to Lynda in Wisconsin, tired and frustrated from what she saw as another futile effort at advocacy on Lynda's behalf. She flopped down on the couch and began idly channel-surfing through the daytime TV programs. Unexpectedly on the screen appeared the frail body of Samantha Kendall and a photograph of an even sicker Michaela— Samantha's twin who had died. Catherine's attention was immediately riveted to the screen, her determination to find a way to save Lynda renewed. Povich introduced Peggy Claude-Pierre as probably the only person on earth who could save Samantha. As Catherine listened to Claude-Pierre explain her theories and treatment methods, she felt that here was someone who understood, not just what Lynda was going through but the despair of the whole family. She was particularly fascinated by the story of Nicole leaving self-abusing notes around the house, because Lynda had done the same thing. Her notes had explained to her mother that "the man wouldn't let me eat," and insisted that she was worthless. Not surprisingly, Catherine was also buoyed by Claude-Pierre's assertions that her system could cure any anorexic, no matter how severe.

All the same, she wasn't going to entrust her daughter to yet another stranger's care on the basis of just one TV talk show. She needed a way to find out whether the apparent miracles being worked at Montreux were real. Her mind kept coming back to one name—her friend and neighbour, Alan Goldberg.

In the spring of 1994, Alan Goldberg had never heard of Peggy Claude-Pierre or the Montreux Clinic. Eating disorders in general were a foreign world to him. What Catherine believed Goldberg had, however, was an ability to search out the truth. He was a senior producer on ABC-TV's top-rated news documentary show, *20/20*. He had won awards for pieces ranging from inspirational documentaries to investigative reports on issues as complex as the tainted blood system in the U.S. Catherine called him that evening and requested a big favour. She explained what she'd seen on *Povich* and asked if he'd be prepared to use his contacts and investigative skills to check out Montreux.

Goldberg was happy to help his friend out. From what Catherine had said, Montreux sounded like a place that promised to cure people whom mainstream medicine had written off as hopeless. Even more fascinating was the thought that it was curing them with nothing more than kindness, compassion, and unconditional love.

He called Claude-Pierre—and found her story interesting enough that he wanted to make a personal visit to Montreux. Claude-Pierre's ability as a natural storyteller stood her in good stead, and she inserted anecdotes about many of her patients into her explanations of how Montreux's system worked to defeat the Negative Mind. It sounded like some kind of utopia for eating-disorder sufferers. Now he was interested not only for Catherine's sake, but also professionally. He found himself asking if he could come to visit. He wanted to see this place for himself. He would check it out for Catherine, but his reporter's nose for news was already telling him that Montreux also had the potential to be a major story. Claude-Pierre had no hesitation in saying he'd be welcome.

Catherine had told him he'd like Victoria, although they both found it somewhat surprising that a world-class centre had set up shop in what to New Yorkers seemed to be a colonial outpost. Catherine, however, had lived in Victoria for a brief period in her youth and had enjoyed what she considered its quaint charm.

The warm welcome he received from all those at the clinic impressed him, as did the clinic's tranquil setting. Everyone, it seemed, could hardly wait to talk to him—staff, patients, family members, as well as Peggy Claude-Pierre, David Harris, and the other managers. Everyone was telling him the same thing: this was a place where miracles truly did happen, and lives truly were saved. Patients told him their own stories, family members told the stories of their children, staff members told the stories of the clients under their care. Claude-Pierre told him her stories of her own family, of starting the clinic, and of many of the 400 patients she said she'd worked with, emphasizing that virtually all had either been cured or were well on the way to a full recovery.

Everywhere around him, he saw only gentleness—patients being reassured by staff members, hugged by Montreux management every time they saw them, cradled while they were fed as carefully as helpless babies. He became convinced Claude-Pierre was right when she said patients could literally be loved back to health.

It was explained to him that the residential facility was still too new to offer examples of extremely acute patients who had been completely cured by their stay there. The best that could be found were patients who'd been discharged about six months earlier. But he could see amazing improvements already in Caroline and Samantha, compared to the videos taken of them when they'd first arrived.

What Goldberg was not shown was what other staff members saw—what was going on behind the scenes to ensure that the impression he'd take away was indeed 100 per cent positive. Careworkers from those days remember some senior staff members explaining to patients just what they should say in response to the questions that Goldberg would ask them. They remember that if a patient was reluctant to appear on television, Claude-Pierre would herself step in to persuade her how important it was to present a positive image for the TV man. It was, she'd tell them, the most effective thing they could do to share their luck at being at Montreux and help other sufferers get the treatment they needed to recover from their anorexia as well.

Goldberg asked questions outside the clinic and found that not everyone in Victoria shared the same faith in Montreux. However, Claude-Pierre and her staff actually cracked jokes about those who spoke of strange happenings at the clinic and who referred to Claude-Pierre as "the witch doctor." They told Goldberg that the critics just didn't understand anorexia or Montreux. Goldberg figured there couldn't be much merit to the complaints if the Montreux people could be so open and undefensive about them.

On his return to New York, Goldberg was unabashedly enthusiastic as he told Catherine what he'd seen and heard. She immediately began seeking admission for Lynda and began persuading her daughter to allow herself to be stabilized medically so she could travel safely to Victoria.

His chat with Catherine, however, was by no means the end of Goldberg's interest in Montreux. During his visit, he knew he'd been right in thinking that the clinic was ripe for a documentary on its achievements. Before he left, he talked to Claude-Pierre and Harris about the possibility of a return trip, this time with a full crew from *20/20* to spend days or weeks videotaping at Montreux.

Harris and Claude-Pierre were enthusiastic. They promised that the camera crew would have virtually unfettered access to everything and everyone at Montreux, just as he'd had when he came on his own. For a producer of TV documentaries, that sort of access is essential—and highly unusual—in Canadian health care facilities. Most hospitals are bound by provincial legislation governing confidentiality, privacy, and informed consent, meaning access can't be granted to any patients unless they and/or their families have signed the necessary forms, often a difficult thing to get them to do.

When Goldberg returned to the *20/20* offices, he persuaded senior producers at the show that it was time to tell the world about the miracles being worked at Montreux. He began to organize a crew for the return trip to Victoria. The job of correspondent for the piece, the on-air interviewer and personality, fell to Lynn Sherr.

Sherr had 20 years experience in the television business, the last 8 of it with *20/20*. She'd provided on-the-scene analysis of presidential elections and become the network's expert on the Space Shuttle program. But her heart had always been in covering stories involving women's issues and health issues, and it was in these areas that she'd won many of the awards that marked her career—awards for pieces about breast cancer victims, about sexual harassment, about new drugs for schizophrenia and new therapies for the mentally ill. She'd authored a book about the American suffragists and how they starved as a form of protest.

In August, Goldberg and a full camera and sound crew flew to Victoria for taping that, in the end, lasted more than a month. Sherr joined them for only a few days.

Victoria was not nearly so sleepy a city when they returned. It was the month of the Commonwealth Games, and thousands of athletes and supporters from all the countries of the British Commonwealth had gathered for two weeks of friendly competition. In the evenings, as many as 100,000 people would crowd into the area around the Inner Harbour to listen to free concerts and watch nightly fireworks displays. The excitement in the city mirrored Goldberg's as he began work on the Montreux documentary.

Claude-Pierre and Harris were eager to provide the co-operation they had promised. Although someone from Montreux management was always with the crew, filming was permitted, even encouraged. Claude-Pierre was always patient as she explained to them what she was doing and why. All that was required was that the crew follow Claude-Pierre's guidelines in what they could and could not film of the patients and their struggles. Occasionally, Claude-Pierre would suggest they not film a patient going through a particularly difficult time—and they always agreed.

Claude-Pierre apparently never lost her sense of hope and confidence that every one who came through the clinic's doors would one day live a life free from anorexia. Goldberg could see striking improvements in some of the patients he'd met just a few weeks earlier. Samantha was looking better every day, and Caroline was visibly gaining in strength and health.

Newly arrived in the residence was Jeannie,* the girl from Scotland whose parents had sent her to Montreux after seeing Samantha's progress on British TV. Jeannie was so frail that she made even Sam and Caroline look healthy by comparison. Jeannie weighed only 49 pounds when she arrived at Montreux from her home in Scotland. She could hardly stand long enough to be weighed and didn't have the strength to feed herself, even if she'd wanted to. Searching for the right metaphor to describe Jeannie, Sherr came up with the line that she "was so helpless she had to be hand-fed like a baby bird."

Her condition terrified everyone around her, except apparently Claude-Pierre. Even though Jeannie had been at the mansion only a few days, Claude-Pierre was confident enough to go on camera and predict fearlessly, "She'll recover."

"You're so sure," commented Sherr.

"I'm so sure," confirmed Claude-Pierre. "I mean, we're doing everything, we're using every precaution. I can't imagine her not surviving at this point."

Nobody wanted to say the words aloud, but the *20/20* crew members could not help but think that if Jeannie could just survive, she alone would be living proof that Montreux was a place where miracles happened. The crew knew that videotape of Jeannie would bring a lump to the throat of every mother viewing the program. The winding staircase in the mansion, looking like the baronial entrance hall of a British estate, would form the perfect backdrop. They filmed Claude-Pierre carrying Jeannie down the staircase with no more trouble than if she'd been carrying a three-year-old. Jeannie went to be weighed on an ordinary bathroom scale, her weight—up to 57 pounds by then—duly recorded. No one ever asked if it wouldn't have been easier to carry the scale up to Jeannie's room instead of bringing her down. Staff from the time say they never before or after saw Claude-Pierre carrying patients on the stairs.

Claude-Pierre also allowed the crew to film the scene as she provided a weeping Jeannie with some of her first basic counselling.

"I'm not to be loved," Jeannie sobbed. "I'm a horrible, bad person ... I'm worthless."

Claude-Pierre responded in the most tender of voices: "I know you inside out. You're not a horrible, bad person. You're a very, very, very special little girl."

As the days went by and the crew filmed other patients, it grew increasingly clear that Jeannie was going to survive. By the time they were ready to return to New York, they were sure that she was on her way back to health—and that the video taken in her sickest moments would provide some of the most powerful moments in the documentary.

Sam Kendall was a natural for a starring part in the tape, but Claude-Pierre suggested to Goldberg that she be relegated to a more minor role. It was never entirely clear how much this was based on concerns for Sam's well-being or on the fact that Sam was already involved in various media contracts to document her story. In the end, only a brief clip of a healthier-looking Sam appeared, contrasted with a photo of her at her worst shortly before coming to the clinic.

She uttered only a single line, saying that if her twin sister, Michaela, had discovered Montreux in time, "she would have survived. She'd be here today."

One satisfying moment for Goldberg was a brief interview with Lynda, who'd then been a patient for a few weeks. Lynda had reached the point of eating small snacks every couple of hours, and Claude-Pierre was talking to her about her food preferences for her meal plan.

"I like corn... but I don't like yams," Lynda was able to tell her.

Goldberg and Sherr were intrigued by the many frantic calls that came in for Claude-Pierre, calls from sufferers, from parents, and even from doctors in cases where regular treatment did not appear to be working. They decided that following some of these cases, from first contact to eventual admission to Montreux, would provide another powerful piece of the documentary.

One of the callers was Donna Brooks, the 21-year-old from London, England, who would later be befriended by Samantha. Her precise history was somewhat confused, even on the show. At one point she was described as having had anorexia for half her life, at another as having looked like a normal 18-year-old only three years earlier. She had talked to Claude-Pierre on the phone several times by the time the *20/20* crew arrived. Her parents wanted to try Montreux as a last hope, but Donna herself had doubts.

"I don't even know if it will work," she said.

"Sweetheart, I will tell you that it will work or I wouldn't invite you to come," countered Claude-Pierre.

Her confidence was enough to persuade Donna, and a few weeks later, the *20/20* crew was present at the airport as Donna and her mother arrived and met Claude-Pierre in person for the first time. As they greeted each other, Claude-Pierre told Donna that she would "never have to worry again about this silly thing. It's going to go away."

In even more precarious shape was Shannon,* in hospital in Cleveland, Ohio. Harris took the original call from Shannon's mother, and, with the cameras running, told Claude-Pierre of the horrors of the young woman's condition. Claude-Pierre immediately began a rescue mission, talking to the mother, the girl's doctor, and Shannon herself.

From the Cleveland hospital, the doctor warned that while Shannon was so ill she probably would not survive more than another week, the legal system considered her still to be mentally competent and wouldn't force treatment on her.

Claude-Pierre, who had previously treated the doctor with deference, addressing him as "sir," became imploring: "So you're expecting her to die? ... She can live, but I need you to intervene as soon as you can. She's not got very much time, and you're not going to feel better, and I'm not going to feel better if we don't try."

"Well, let me go up there and take a look," the doctor responded.

Several hours later, after much telephone conversation, Claude-Pierre did convince Shannon to accept a feeding tube, in large part by promising her she could come to Montreux as soon as her condition had stabilized. On camera with Sherr, Claude-Pierre was more cautious about Shannon's condition than about any of the others. She said with scientific precision that she doubted they had more than a 4 per cent chance of her surviving long enough to come to Montreux, although it was never clear where that number came from. But the last scene in the documentary showed Shannon—still so weak she needed a wheelchair, but dressed up in a cowboy hat and tassels for the trip—arriving at Victoria for her Montreux stay.

As well as filming the patients, Goldberg and crew also shot hours of tape of Claude-Pierre and of her two daughters, capturing their story in a way that would allow it to rise to mythical proportions among eating-disorder sufferers.

At the end of August, Goldberg and crew packed up their equipment and their boxes of videotapes and returned to New York to begin the long task of post-production editing, of turning the hours of tape into a coherent story. But even before the airplane landed, Goldberg had made one decision—he would try to convince his bosses that Montreux was such an amazing place it deserved an entire hour-long documentary on *20/20*. Most segments on the show are between 7 and 30 minutes long; longer pieces are rare. However, once the senior producers of the show saw some of the dramatic and emotional footage available, they agreed to take the gamble. Goldberg wanted to show viewers the apparent miracles being worked by the Montreux method, but he also wanted to try to make clear Claude-Pierre's views about the cause of anorexia. Although he was aware of the concerns in the report commissioned by the ministry of health, he did not, in the end, include any of that information in the program. No experts from any other treatment facilities appeared on the show to comment on the work Claude-Pierre was doing.

The final version of the script read by Sherr, and also by *20/20* hosts Barbara Walters and Hugh Downs, brought Claude-Pierre close to the image of a saint.

"Lynn Sherr brings you haunting images of unimaginable despair, boundless compassion, and ultimately, salvation," said Downs in the introduction.[21]

Walters called Claude-Pierre "a last hope." Sherr described her as "the voice of comfort and reason," and Montreux as "a very safe place ... a very healing place."

Sherr did point out briefly that Montreux had done no outcome studies on its results, but at the end of the show, she seemed genuinely excited as she told viewers: "Claude-Pierre has treated something like 400 patients in 10 years ... we have found no evidence of failure whatsoever." Again it was unclear where any of the figures came from.

Sounding the only small note of caution was ABC's medical editor, Dr. Tim Johnson. Johnson said all eating-disorder programs would envy Montreux its resources that allowed the clinic to provide true one-on-one care around the clock, and would commend what Claude-Pierre was doing. However, he also noted that "the real experts in the field are very humble about what they do and don't know." Such a brief comment, though, was lost in the outpouring of admiration for the clinic.

No one cast doubt on the claims of a success rate of virtually 100 per cent. No one pointed out that anorexic patients have a high rate of relapse or that signs of improvement—even dramatic improvement—for weeks or months do not necessarily signify recovery. Indeed, many experts suggest that sufferers cannot be considered recovered until they've gone five years with no major relapses. That alone meant that none of Claude-Pierre's residential patients had been out of treatment for long enough to judge her success rate.

Claude-Pierre was again described as "working on her doctorate in psychology" before her daughters became ill, repeating the exaggeration of her academic credentials. The information was never corrected on any of the future *20/20* shows.

The hour-long show was ready to be aired on December 2, 1994. Goldberg knew it was likely to catapult Claude-Pierre onto the world stage in a way he doubted she could even imagine. He warned her to be prepared for an onslaught of people literally dying for her help. She told him she was ready, that this was her destiny.

The night of the broadcast was wildly heady, not only for Claude-Pierre and her family, but also for all the workers then employed at the clinic. Only a few staff remained on duty to care for the patients. Virtually all the rest accepted the invitation of Claude-Pierre and Harris to join them at a trendy restaurant to have dinner and watch the show on a big-screen TV. Most of the staff had been present as the crew filmed for hours in August and September, but even they were amazed and impressed by the glowing review of the clinic. As they watched, they had no idea the impact the show would have on sufferers of eating disorders across North America—and on the clinic itself.

"We literally went from almost total obscurity to being known around the world, all in a single night," says Jane Taylor-Lee, a careworker and team leader at the time. "We were not at all prepared for the reaction it generated. Not at all."

ABC had promoted the show widely, both on its other news and documentary programs and through news releases sent to TV columns in newspapers across the U.S. and Canada. *USA Today* called the hour-long show "a must-see, the entire hour devoted to Peggy Claude-Pierre, a Canadian miracle worker who opens her heart and house to victims of anorexia."[22]

In Victoria, the *Times-Colonist* newspaper published an interview with Goldberg. He said he had originally approached the Montreux story with "a tremendous amount of skepticism," but the program had come together "because of the access we got from Montreux, the nature of the work they do there and the results they get."[23] Despite the skepticism surrounding Montreux in Victoria and B.C., the *Times-Colonist* sounded no notes of caution either.

Thousands of sufferers, their friends, and their families tuned in, hopeful they might learn something that would help them or their loved ones recover. They were not disappointed. But the message many of them received was that the recovery could occur only if they could somehow be one of the lucky ones admitted to Montreux. Even before the show had finished, the switchboard at ABC had lit up with viewers begging for a way to contact the clinic. Claude-Pierre and Harris had agreed previously that the network would give out Montreux's phone and fax numbers to those who called, but they had no idea how many calls the show would generate. For the first few hours the next day, the clinic tried to have staff answering the phone in person, but they soon realized that was a hopeless task. There was no way they could keep up.

"Just about every call was an intake call from someone who wanted to come to Montreux," says Taylor-Lee. "That meant it was an assessment call, which meant each one should take 45 minutes or an hour." If staff tried to do that, though, dozens more calls would back up while they handled the one. Within hours, the clinic resorted to screening all calls through an answering machine.

It became Taylor-Lee's job to take the answering machine tapes home each night, listen to each call, and summarize them for Claude-Pierre the next day. The vast majority of calls were from desperate parents, hoping against hope that their child might be able to gain admission to Montreux and thus, they believed, be cured. Some laid their arguments out with the precision of a legal case, outlining the reasons why their family was the best choice for a new admission. Many more appealed to emotion and sympathy, talking about how many programs their daughter had been in, how little she'd been helped, how dreadful it was to watch her fading away before their eyes, how powerless they felt. A few—the worst, from Taylor-Lee's point of view—said the doctors had already told them there seemed to be little or no hope that their child would survive. If Montreux didn't intervene within a few weeks, they begged, it might be too late. The doctors had warned them that they needed to prepare themselves for their child's death.

However, Montreux, too, was powerless to intervene in the vast majority of cases, even the worst ones. The mansion was already full. Although Claude-Pierre was thrilled at the thought of expansion, the tasks of acquiring and furnishing new space, and hiring and training new staff, were not to be accomplished overnight.

At first, Taylor-Lee assumed she was supposed to respond to all the calls, if only to leave some sort of generic message. She could, she thought, express the clinic's regret that, because of the overwhelming response to the show, Montreux was unable to answer individual queries at this time. However, Claude-Pierre soon made clear to her that that was not the case. There was no point, she told Taylor-Lee, when it wasn't clear whether most of the callers could afford to pay Montreux fees anyway. The show had not pointed out that Montreux was available only to those who could afford to pay the high daily charges, or that there were no guarantees that health insurance companies would cover any stay there. Taylor-Lee was told just to ignore most of the messages, aside from the few that attracted Claude-Pierre's personal interest. Some families left messages of increasing desperation day after day, never receiving an answer at all.

The reaction to the show surprised even Goldberg. Many people called ABC and made their case to Goldberg or Sherr, hoping they'd somehow use their influence with Claude-Pierre to get their child admitted. As well, Sherr's staff found themselves opening piles of mail addressed to her. Some were letters begging for admission to the clinic; others contained cheques made out in trust for the clinic.

The outpouring of support for Montreux was so remarkable that Goldberg decided it was imperative to do a short follow-up the very next week. Barbara Walters told of how, after the show, the clinic had received thousands of calls and faxes from as far away as Saudi Arabia. "We've been inundated, actually," said Claude-Pierre.[24] She talked of having already signed the lease on another house (the mansion just behind the Rockland address, which was to become St. Charles House), but also noted that it would take a year to have another team of caregivers fully trained.

Still, some made it through the sea of faxes and voice-mail summaries to gain admittance to the clinic in the weeks following the show. One was Kristina,* who had attracted Claude-Pierre's attention because of her psychiatrist's personal interest in the Montreux program.

Dr. Craig Pratt was the head of psychiatry at the hospital in the U.S. Midwest where Kristina had been hospitalized 16 times in 1994 alone. He had worked with Kristina but had admitted he was baffled by the anorexia which appeared to him to be more deeply entrenched in Kristina than in any patient he'd ever had before. Pratt was just as impressed by the *20/20* show as Kristina's friends and family were. He urged Claude-Pierre to come and meet Kristina, and also asked whether she would allow him to come to Victoria with Kristina and learn from Montreux how better to deal with acute eating-disorder patients in his own practice.

For an "alternative" clinic trying to gain acceptance with those who practiced mainstream medicine, that was an offer too good to pass up. Pratt, Kristina, and her family were all willing to talk publicly about her struggle with anorexia and their optimism that Montreux would be the place that would cure her. Less than a month after the *20/20* show, Claude-Pierre travelled to the U.S. to assess Kristina in person and meet with Pratt. The meetings yielded not only an admission date just a month later for Kristina, but also a series of front-page articles in the Columbus, Ohio, newspaper.

The articles served several purposes. Not only did they allow Claude-Pierre to explain her theories—and take them several steps further than she had publicly done before—but they also kicked off a major fundraising campaign to keep Kristina at Montreux. This was also the first time that Claude-Pierre publicly challenged several of the key findings of modern research dealing with the risk factors leading to eating disorders. For the first time, she said publicly that anorexia was something that was present from babyhood, suggesting that the symptoms could first appear between the ages of 8 and 12 months. (Kristina had actually been substantially older than most anorexics before her symptoms appeared, well into her twenties.) For the first time also, Claude-Pierre said publicly that childhood traumas "are not relevant to the condition"—another irony in Kristina's case as she had suffered years of sexual and physical abuse while in foster care.

As for Kristina, she was, despite her dangerously weakened physical condition, able to proffer highly articulate descriptions of her fragile emotional state. She described anorexia as "the monster inside of me," and was open about her suicidal thoughts. "I thought the only way to kill the monster was to kill me," she said. "I feel like I am God's mistake, and God is trying to destroy me to cover up his error."[25]

Said Claude-Pierre: "The fact that she isn't dead is remarkable."

Claude-Pierre suggested that the eating disorder had "94 per cent control" over Kristina's life. Just how she came to this conclusion was not explained in any way. It appeared, however, to be the beginning of Montreux's "Life Wellness Scale," in which Claude-Pierre defined her patients' health by how much control the Negative Mind had over their lives. A patient was considered "acute" as long as the Negative Mind was controlling 70 per cent or more of a patient's life. Recovery was reached when the Actual Mind was in control 86 per cent or more of the time.

Dr. Pratt lived up to his promises. When Kristina came to Montreux in January, he accompanied her. While she settled in, Dr. Pratt met with numerous staff members, asked dozens of questions, and spent as much time talking to Claude-Pierre as possible.

The fundraising efforts yielded about $18,000 (US) in donations—no small amount, but a drop in the bucket compared to the $150,000 (US) that her adoptive parents paid for the first seven months of round-the-clock care. The family, convinced that Montreux was the best hope for Kristina, refinanced their home and business office, cashed in their insurance policies, and maxed out their credit cards to pay the bill.

In a follow-up story at the end of August, Pratt described Kristina as "out of physical danger," having reached "a minimal ideal body weight," but still "struggling to maintain that weight."[26] Her adoptive mother described her as "making some real progress," but still thinking she was too fat. She was expected, at that point, to need at least another year of care at Montreux.

She stayed another 11 months, finally returning to Ohio in July 1996. She was much better, she told the reporter, but, "I'm disappointed," she said sadly. "I thought I would be cured."²⁷ However, she added, her counsellors had warned her it would take years to recover entirely. She explained that she still struggled with "the monster" that repeatedly told her that she shouldn't eat, that people would look at her and consider her "huge."

"I still can't look in the mirror and think I'm okay."

Other desperate parents took a different approach to getting admitted to Montreux—they simply arrived on the doorstep, apparently not realizing how much risk the travel itself might pose to their children.

One of those was Robbie,* an 11-year-old boy from New Mexico who had been hospitalized for a severe episode of anorexia just two weeks before the *20/20* show aired. Unlike many patients who had gone through numerous treatment programs, Robbie had been diagnosed only the previous month, and had not tried any forms of treatment before the hospitalization. However, his weight loss had been extremely rapid, and on the night of the show, he was attached to tubes and monitors in hospital because the doctors feared he was so weak he might suffer a fatal heart attack.

It was his terrified mother who watched the show and decided on the spot that the family had to take Robbie there. She and her husband raced to the hospital minutes after the show ended to try to persuade the doctors to discharge their son so they could go immediately to Montreux. They had no idea how much it would cost, where they might find the money, whether Claude-Pierre would accept Robbie as a patient, or even precisely how to get there. They were simply so mesmerized by the show that they could think of no other options.

The doctors did not think Robbie was well enough to be safely discharged, let alone to travel all the way to Canada. The family removed him from the hospital anyway, against all medical advice. For the next three days, they dodged child-protection workers concerned that Robbie was at risk of dying for lack of medical care. On the fourth day, they got on a plane and flew to Seattle, the nearest U.S. airport to Victoria. At stops along the way, they left voice-mail messages from payphones for Claude-Pierre to try to let her know they were on their way. They grew increasingly panicked as Robbie's condition became so severe he was slipping in and out of consciousness.

They had dodged the social workers back home, but at the border, they could not dodge the customs and immigration agents. The agents explained, kindly but firmly, that they could not bring such an ill child into the country until Robbie's admission to Montreux had been confirmed and they could show they had the ability to pay his medical costs while in Canada. They knew they could meet neither condition. Robbie's mother became convinced that her son would die before they made it back to New Mexico.

The customs agent did agree to phone Claude-Pierre for them, and she agreed to travel hastily to Seattle to meet with them. There, she told Robbie that "I've just decided that you will be my next patient." But still, she explained, she would not have room at the clinic for several months. As well, she said, it appeared he was in need of urgent medical attention. She suggested they get him immediate help, then persuade him to accept enough nutrition to keep him alive for three or four months on the promise he'd then be allowed to come to Montreux.

If the TV show had attracted the family, Claude-Pierre in person completely enchanted them. Robbie's mother later remembered Claude-Pierre walking in, saying immediately, "You must be the mama," and hugging her.

"I'll never forget that hug," she said later, "because there was so much confidence and love. I knew we were in the right place."

On Claude-Pierre's advice, the family did go to Seattle's Children's Hospital later that day, where the doctors were so horrified at Robbie's condition that they admitted him on the spot. It took two weeks for his physical health to stabilize enough that they would discharge him to go home to continue treatment. Back in New Mexico, his mother and Claude-Pierre were able to get him to accept a nasogastric tube until a bed could be found for him at Montreux.

It was April when they returned to Canada. This time Robbie was admitted—under the lights of *20/20*'s cameras once again. Based on the overwhelming response to the December program, Goldberg, Sherr, and the rest of the crew had decided it was time to do a longer follow-up program. They would look at the progress of some of the patients from the December show, and put together a feature segment on Robbie. Sherr described Robbie's family as "parents who found Peggy through our first program barely in time to save their little boy."[28]

On the show, Claude-Pierre was seen welcoming the family back, again praising the mother as "a pretty brave lady," and feeding Robbie his first solid food. Helping her was Jeannie, already graduated to outpatient status at the clinic and beginning to work with patients sicker than she, just eight months after her admission.

Jeannie was unquestionably the highlight of the show. The progress she had made in the intervening months appeared to be little short of miraculous. The living skeleton barely able to stand had given way to a healthy-looking young woman able to walk into a fish shop and buy a serving of salmon for herself.

"When we look at somebody like Jeannie, it is a miracle," said Sherr. "Here is a young woman who ... was on the verge of death, and this personality has emerged. She smiles, she laughs."

If the emotional power of the first show had not been enough to convince anorexics and their families of what appeared to be the phenomenal potential of Montreux, the change in Jeannie's condition between the two shows was enough to persuade all but the most hardened skeptics among them.

Again, the show did nothing to strike any notes of caution. No eating-disorder expert was interviewed to point out concerns around possible relapses, or to note that even if Jeannie had been cured, one could not say the same thing would happen to any anorexic who went to Montreux. Instead, the final segment told of the huge rise in popularity of the clinic based on the first show. Sherr noted that Montreux was expanding, that the new house was now open, that the number of patients was now 22, and that more than 80 careworkers were on staff.

Said Claude-Pierre: "After the thousands and thousands of letters we received, I felt so joyous on one hand, but burdened on another.

Suddenly I was in a position of playing God. I had to choose between people who were dying, and that's a terribly difficult choice. It's an impossible choice."

She must have known, though, that this second show, with no less emotional power than the first, could do nothing but return her to that position of having to "play God" hundreds of times over.

4

Taking Anorexia to the Cradle

Among the millions of Americans captivated by *20/20* that night was a young woman in a brownstone in Queens, New York, the mother of a button-cute 2½-year-old boy named Dustin.*

Moira* came from a quintessential New York Italian-American family, a heritage that showed in her luxurious mane of dark hair and her flashing eyes. She and her husband appeared to be an ordinary, middle-class couple. She worked as a clerk in a paint store; her husband was a rep for Publishers' Clearing House. Their flair for the dramatic showed only in their leisure-time activities. Her husband belonged to a group that re-enacted scenes from the Middle Ages. Moira set up her own website, posting a revealing photo of herself and examples of poetry she'd written. Some poems captured her love for her son; others explored sexual feelings more intense than most people would feel comfortable letting the world read.

Dustin's birth as an apparently healthy and normal baby 2½ years earlier had been greeted with rapture by both parents and by the whole extended family. For the first months of his life, they were all convinced he was the perfect baby. His big brown eyes drew admiration from perfect strangers. He hardly ever cried. He was alert and attentive to everything around him. What more could a new mother want?

The first doubts that all was not perfect began to seep into Moira's mind when Dustin was about nine months old. In so many ways he still appeared to be the ideal baby. She found him so bright, talking with what she thought was the vocabulary of a child twice his age. He was fascinated by cars and was rapidly learning the make and model of every vehicle that went down their street.

What he failed to do, however, was eat. When the time came to move from stage-one baby foods to "junior" foods that contained whole lumps of meat or vegetables, he would have none of it. He would clench his teeth, throw his head around, and, if his mother did manage to get a spoonful into his mouth, he would spit it right back out.

Before his first birthday, Moira had a doctor run tests to ensure no physical problem was preventing Dustin from eating properly. The tests showed nothing wrong, and the doctor told Moira not to worry about it, to let Dustin develop at his own pace.

Then came Dustin's first birthday. Like most new moms, Moira was far more excited about the birthday than Dustin, who didn't understand what all the fuss was about. The night before the big day, she waited until Dustin was asleep before decorating the house with balloons and streamers—all with a Mickey Mouse theme since a Mickey Mouse doll was Dustin's favourite toy at the time.

From the moment Dustin woke up, Moira had a sinking feeling that all was not going to go as planned. She was right. Dustin didn't like the balloons. When the other children came, he went to his room instead of playing with them. He didn't want to join in the fun of ripping paper off birthday presents, instead sitting uninterested on the floor while the party guests gleefully opened his gifts. He ignored the potato chips and cookies the others were munching.

Worst of all was the birthday cake. Dustin was sitting in his highchair when the time for cake came, and his mother cut a tiny sliver and put it on a plate in front of him. His only response to that small amount of food was to push himself back as far as he could away from it and to pull at his hair—something he often did when under stress. Moira's sister could not understand Dustin's behaviour. She was convinced that if he could only be persuaded to taste a few delicious morsels, he'd begin to appreciate the joys of eating. So she put her finger into the sweet cream between the layers of cake, and then slid her finger with the cream on it into Dustin's mouth.

That was the end of the party. Dustin screamed so loudly and hysterically that none of the other parents could pretend this was any ordinary temper tantrum. In confusion, they took their children and went home, so that Dustin might calm down.

As Moira remembers it, that was the beginning of the bad period. He developed fanatical obsessions about cleanliness. He'd insist on a complete change of clothing if a tiny spot of dirt or food besmirched what he was wearing. She remembered a day when she and her husband, playing on a glorious autumn afternoon, tossed a handful of fallen leaves on Dustin and into his stroller. He immediately began to cry frantically, refusing to calm down until they had picked off every single piece of leaf, no matter how tiny. When she once tried to put him in a sandbox to play with other children, it "was almost like trying to put a cat in the cat carrier," she remembered later, describing how his arms and legs stiffened and spread out to avoid going in.

He was frightened of almost everything. He was frightened of falling down. He was frightened of hurting himself. Most of all he was afraid of food. Every meal had become a pitched battle. While he'd originally eaten happily any stage-one puréed baby food—meats, vegetables, fruits—he soon would only eat the fruits, and then just applesauce. The only other foods he would accept without a fight were animal crackers and Cheerios.

When Moira took him to her pediatrician, she found he'd nearly stopped growing. From being of average length and weight at birth, he'd dropped in his development to the point where 98 per cent of children his age were both taller and heavier than he was, although he wasn't especially skinny for his height.

The pediatrician suggested serving him Pediasure as a supplement to provide him with more nutrition. But even persuading him to take that liquid was frequently a major battle. Moira and her husband became desperate to find ways to distract Dustin from the fact that he was actually eating or drinking. During meal times, they would dance and sing and put on puppet shows to which Dustin could direct his attention. Sometimes Dustin's dad would literally stand on his head to get his son to eat.

During the next few months, Moira felt like she was fighting a losing battle. Dustin took to keeping either his fingers or his bib in his mouth all the time so he couldn't be surprised with a spoonful of food. His parents sometimes resorted to forcing the food in—sitting on his legs, holding his arms, and pushing on his chin to get him to open his mouth.

Normally, Dustin would never talk about his fears or what it was about eating or dirt that made him upset. He'd chatter happily on about cars or baseball or hockey, but would retreat into silence as soon as the subject of eating came up. But one day in May, Dustin finally said something, something that threw Moira into a complete tailspin. That day, as Dustin was again refusing all food, Moira begged him, as she had a thousand times before, to tell her what was wrong and why he wouldn't eat.

This time he said to her, "Mommy, I have a man under my hair that tells me, 'Dustin, you can't eat.'"

That night Moira sat on the sofa, numbly channel-surfing while wondering how to get help for a 2½-year-old who believed a man was living under his hair. On ABC, up popped the *20/20* update show on Montreux. Moira listened as several patients started talking about the voices in their heads that told them they weren't allowed to eat. Then Claude-Pierre came on, talking about her theory of the Negative Mind and how it can overwhelm someone and lead to an eating disorder. For the rest of the show, Moira was transfixed. It sounded to her exactly like what Dustin had been talking about earlier in the day. As the show ended, she was thinking: "Oh my God, I am not looking any further. This is where Dustin has to go. This is where Dustin needs to be."

Thus far the family hadn't used many of the multitude of resources available in New York City for young children with behavioural or emotional problems. Moira had not been happy with most of the doctors she'd seen in New York, complaining that they patronized her and didn't take her seriously. Dustin had never seen a child psychiatrist. He had never gone to a specialized clinic for children with feeding problems. He had never even had a full psychological assessment with his family—something the experts later said amazed them, because no child would normally be sent to an adult facility before that had been done and other alternatives explored.

Once she saw the *20/20* show, though, Moira made up her own mind. The morning after the show, she obtained Montreux's phone and fax numbers from ABC's offices and sent Peggy Claude-Pierre a fax.

"I prayed the letter would be answered quickly for Dustin was deteriorating fast," she wrote in a letter of support for Montreux later. In fact, however, although Moira was seeing a constant increase in problems around eating, the growth charts painted a different picture. Rather than falling further behind, Dustin was actually beginning to catch up on some growth.

Four days later, Claude-Pierre phoned Moira. For a desperate mom, it was the most reassuring conversation in the world. Claude-Pierre asked a few questions, then told her that she completely understood what Moira was going through. She promised she could help, although at that point there was no talk of Dustin actually attending Montreux. Instead, Claude-Pierre encouraged Moira to call when things got too tough, 7 days a week, 24 hours a day if necessary. It wasn't long before Moira was calling at least once a day, and talking to either Peggy Claude-Pierre or her daughter Nicole.

Over the weeks, Claude-Pierre explained to Moira the theories that she'd developed about the causes of anorexia nervosa, about how some children were born with a predisposition to it, about how they were incredibly sensitive and took the cares of the world onto their shoulders. To Moira, it seemed to fit; she was soon telling Claude-Pierre of incidents she remembered that she thought showed Dustin's unusual sensitivity. She remembered them seeing a news story on TV about a little girl who'd been killed when hit by a car, and Dustin asking her: "Mom, why did that little girl have to die? Why couldn't it have been me?"

Looking back on it, Moira believes it was the support from Peggy and Nicole that allowed her to get through the next few months. No matter how difficult Dustin was being, she could count on them to remind her of his need for gentleness and kindness. "Bring him back to when he was a baby," Claude-Pierre told her. For a while, it seemed to be working, but then Dustin invented a new trick: gagging and spitting up, similar to a much younger baby. Within weeks, it was back to the horrible forced feedings again.

Moira was overjoyed when Claude-Pierre told her on the phone one day that she'd soon be in New York on a business trip and could perhaps find time for a face-to-face meeting. They met late one evening in Claude-Pierre's hotel room.

Even Claude-Pierre's most vehement detractors credit her with considerable ability to make an outstanding first impression, to convince a stranger she's just met that they're the most brilliant, sensitive, amazing person in the whole world. In contrast to many health professionals who pride themselves on their tough, even brutal, realism, Claude-Pierre conveyed nothing but optimism and hope. Like so many others, Moira was captivated by her charisma.

"I felt completely overwhelmed by her kindness, her compassion, her knowledge, and the way she just knew Dustin," she would say. "When the meeting was over and she gave me a hug, I thought to myself, 'Well, that's it. If my son is not going, I'm going,' because she made me feel so great." Somehow, during that single meeting, the decision had been made. Moira and Dustin would travel to Victoria so Dustin could become a patient at Montreux.

Claude-Pierre later said it was Moira's decision alone that Dustin should become a Montreux patient. Clearly, though, it wasn't that simple. After the *20/20* shows, the clinic's waiting list was so long that Claude-Pierre described herself as having to choose between dying patients. She had to agree to Dustin coming into her care.

Gavin,* who became one of Dustin's main workers, remembers Margaret Dobson, associate director at Montreux, describing Dustin as "an experiment" to see if they could successfully apply their theories to preschool-aged children.

That summer, the clinic had received its first residential care licence. Harris had applied for one shortly after the health ministry report the year before, but there had been months of correspondence between the clinic and the licensing officials before the licence was actually granted. Harris had told licensing investigators that none of the clinic patients would require "daily professional care." The officials apparently were not viewers of *20/20* and had not seen the critical condition of many of the patients when they arrived. The licence, when it was granted, covered only the Rockland mansion. It allowed nine patients at any one time. The licence stated that all were to be over the age of 18, and anyone under that age would have to have specific individual approval from health department officials.

The clinic also did not have any set-up for dealing with preschoolers—no toys, no child-sized furniture, no playground equipment. No one on staff had expertise in working with young children. And the family couldn't come anywhere close to paying the standard Montreux fee, even for counselling or outpatient sessions. On the Montreux scale, they had no money.

But if they didn't have money, they did have something else that would prove invaluable to Claude-Pierre almost immediately after their arrival—they had a compelling and unusual story to tell on television. Soon after the *20/20* shows, the *Oprah Winfrey* TV show had contacted the clinic, interested in doing a show on its work.

If *20/20* had put Montreux on the map, it was impossible to say how far a positive piece on *The Oprah Winfrey Show* might take the clinic. *Oprah* is the most-watched television talk show in the world. As many as 20 million people tune in to it each day, and it is carried in 113 countries. Moreover, *Oprah* scripts sound very much like Claude-Pierre talking. Oprah stresses hope and optimism and encourages viewers to believe they can change their lives—and indeed the world. She's devoted to the causes of children, everything from funding scholarships for poor students to pushing the U.S. government to set up a database of known child-abusers.

A major show on *Oprah* would be a coup of unparalleled proportions. Claude-Pierre, though, didn't want to do something for *Oprah* that would look like a repeat of the *20/20* shows. She wanted to come up with something fresh and captivating.

Eventually she proposed to *Oprah* what she believed would be an exciting new angle for the show: a focus on male sufferers, a group she thought was too often neglected in the public portrayals of eating disorders. Even before Robbie and then Dustin came to the clinic, she had had several male patients who could be persuaded to tell their stories publicly. As well, she had Dustin—the highly unusual case of an anorexia nervosa sufferer who was not only male but barely three years old. Dustin and his parents would be among the stars of *Oprah*'s first Montreux show, just 10 weeks after he came to the clinic.

Moira and Dustin arrived in Victoria at the end of October 1995, less than a month after Dustin's third birthday. Soon after his arrival, Claude-Pierre formally diagnosed him with anorexia nervosa, just like the other clinic patients, even though all of them were at least a decade older than he was.

In fact, eating-disorder experts are virtually unanimous in their opinion that preschoolers can't suffer from genuine anorexia nervosa, although they can develop serious feeding problems and fears of food. At the 1999 public hearing called by health authorities to determine whether Montreux should be allowed to retain its operating licence, two child psychiatrists—Dr. Susan Sherkow, retained by Montreux as an expert witness, and Dr. Geoffrey Ainsworth, called in rebuttal by the licensing investigators—both explained that anorexia nervosa is tied inextricably to a fear of gaining weight and becoming fat. No two- or three-year-old child, they each explained, has enough abstract thinking skills or concept of their own body image to develop that fear; hence, they cannot suffer from genuine anorexia nervosa.

Both were clear that, so long after the fact, it was not possible to be certain about the original cause of Dustin's problems. Dr. Sherkow—who actually interviewed Dustin three times in the fall of 1998, a year after he returned to New York—suggested the possibility of Asperger's Syndrome, a form of high-functioning autism. Children with Asperger's Syndrome often have normal, or even above-normal, intelligence and language skills but don't develop social skills in the normal way. Frequently children diagnosed with Asperger's don't like playing with other children, develop obsessive interests in one or two topics, and suffer from bizarre sensory sensitivities, including to the textures of new foods.

Dr. Ainsworth, who didn't have the opportunity to see Dustin or his family in person but had access to much more material about his stay at Montreux, wondered about the possibilities of an obsessive-compulsive disorder—an anxiety disorder in which a person is beset by anxiety-producing thoughts that can often be relieved only by performing rituals over and over. Another possibility he suggested was that of an attachment disorder—a problem that arises when a child has, for one reason or another, been unable to form and maintain a strong bond with a parent or parent figure.

Whatever it was, though, they agreed, it wasn't anorexia nervosa.

Claude-Pierre, however, disagreed. According to her theories, the Confirmed Negativity Condition that can lead to anorexia is something with which children are born, and therefore it can show itself almost from infancy. As she prepared to outline those theories on the *Oprah* show, Dustin was her star example.

Dustin and his mother settled in Victoria, staying in a spare suite at the unlicensed St. Charles House, the expansion site that Montreux had started after the *20/20* publicity. At first, Dustin spent most of the day with Moira but went to the main Rockland mansion for his meals. Claude-Pierre usually fed him, holding him on her knee and telling him she'd protect him from the bad man under his hair as she spooned the food in. Sometimes it was yogurt or instant pudding, sometimes tins of baby-food turkey stew, sometimes tins of Boost, a product formulated only for adults.

Within a few weeks, the production crew from *Oprah* arrived in Victoria to film background pieces for the show, scheduled to be broadcast in early January. They filmed three other male Montreux clients, past and present, discussing their eating disorders and the apparently miraculous cures they'd found with Claude-Pierre.

As well, they filmed Dustin, sitting on Claude-Pierre's lap as she tried, not without difficulty, to feed him a few spoonfuls of instant pudding. He tossed his head around as he tried to avoid the spoon and muttered that he didn't "want to have this."

"I'm afraid it will be scary," he said in a tiny voice.

The stage was set. In mid-January, Claude-Pierre, Harris, Dustin, and his mother all flew to Chicago for the live hour-long broadcast. Dustin's father met them there as well.

If the *20/20* shows had been highly positive towards Montreux, *Oprah* could only be described as gushing. Oprah's viewers had watched her fight her own weight battles for several years, so it was no surprise that she had a special interest in eating disorders. Her show had followed one acutely ill patient, Rudine Howard, since January 1989, through phases of acute illness, apparent recovery, and relapse. Not long before the show on Montreux, Rudine had relapsed again, and this time had succumbed to the disorder. The show about Montreux was Oprah's tribute to her. With the sadness of losing someone to anorexia only a few days earlier, it wasn't surprising that Oprah would be ready to embrace a "miracle cure." It was she who first publicly described Claude-Pierre as "an angel on earth," and Montreux as "a place where miracles happen."

Dustin sat on his dad's lap during the live part of the show; when his case was discussed, shots of him sitting there were interspersed with the tape filmed at the clinic. He had his mother's huge dark eyes and dark hair. He looked smaller and younger than his 39 months, but his cheeks were chubby and he didn't look like a child in the throes of anorexia.

Despite that, Oprah described him on the show as being "on the edge of death"[29] when he came to Montreux, although no medical evidence was presented to back this up. Instead, Oprah talked with Claude-Pierre and Moira about how Dustin was eating only 20 Cheerios a day and drinking a couple of cans of Pediasure before he went to Montreux. His parents glossed over all the other problems they'd noticed. His dad described him as having difficulty "only when you put him down in front of food." All the rest of the time, he said, Dustin was happy, friendly, energetic, and well behaved. His other fears and obsessions were never mentioned.

Claude-Pierre used Dustin as her prize example for her theory of how Confirmed Negativity could be present "virtually from birth," to be cured only by unconditional love.

Oprah was in tears as the show concluded. "Unconditional love can change the world," she said. She wasn't surprised that it alone was enough to bring a total cure, even to those who were only days or weeks away from death.

After the show Moira and little Dustin returned to Victoria and continued the program. Although Dustin was still an outpatient, he was being left for longer and longer periods during the day at Montreux. Instead of going over just for meals, he'd stay after the meals and Claude-Pierre would read to him, or a staff member would let him paint in the art room or play about on the computer. Claude-Pierre had suggested the idea to Moira since, she said, she didn't want him to associate the Rockland site only with the unpleasant activity of eating. He was soon introduced to Louise,* a diminutive 19-year-old British patient, still so ill as to be on 24-hour care herself, but also with a passion for small children and a desire for a career as a nursery school teacher. She quickly became one of his favourite playmates.

When the St. Charles suite was needed for a new patient, Claude-Pierre and Harris found Dustin and his mother an apartment less than a block away in another fine old house that had been converted into several suites. Since the family had come from New York with only the clothes and toiletries for a few months' stay, Montreux also arranged for all their costs of living to be picked up. They found an adult-sized bed for the parents and a child-sized one for Dustin, furniture, dishes, silverware, clothes and toys for Dustin, even food and shampoo. They covered the costs of utilities, and eventually even the rent on the suite. Moira never had to pay a cent.

"I am totally indebted to them," she admitted later.

Claude-Pierre and Margaret Dobson always told her it was worth it to see the improvement in Dustin. The growth charts back up the fact that Dustin was beginning to improve under the regime. During his four months as an outpatient, he gained 2½ pounds, catching up on all he had lost in the previous six months when his feeding problems had been at their worst.

Moira, though, still wasn't happy with his progress. She somehow came to believe he was losing weight, despite what the scales said. He was having horrific nightmares when he returned to their suite for the night. He would wake up screaming and tell his mother he'd dreamed about being tied up and having food stuffed into his mouth. Another repeated nightmare had the man under his hair threatening to kill the family if he let himself eat. Moira didn't find it easy to reassure him, or to persuade him to eat during the parts of the day he was with her. As soon as he showed any signs of anxiety, she'd get emotional or start to cry. That would make Dustin more upset and less willing to eat.

One day, Moira blurted out all her fears and inadequacies to Claude-Pierre, and for a few days they considered possible solutions. Later, no one seemed quite sure whether it was Claude-Pierre or Moira who came up with the idea, but it took hold quickly: Dustin would move to Montreux as a residential inpatient.

No one outside Montreux was consulted. Dr. Charles Medhurst, Claude-Pierre's own family doctor who'd agreed to monitor Dustin's physical care, wasn't even told Dustin was moving into Montreux, let alone asked whether he thought it was a good idea. There was no pediatrician or child psychiatrist to ask, since no contact had been set up for Dustin with any such specialist.

As far as Dustin knew, the morning of March 26, 1996, was just like any other as he left for his day at the clinic. However, while he was there playing, painting, and being fed the inevitable "snacks," the Montreux maintenance staff were moving his bed, his clothes, his toys, every facet of his life, from his mother's apartment to Louise's room at St. Charles House. Claude-Pierre had decided that Louise, the patient who enjoyed being Dustin's "big sister" so much, would make an ideal roommate for him. She had also decided the transition would be easier for Dustin if he wasn't even allowed to say goodbye to his mother.

It wasn't until 8:30 p.m. came, the regular time for Dustin to go home to his mother after supper, that Dustin realized something unusual was happening. Instead of getting his jacket for the quick trip back to his mother's apartment, his worker for the day, Janice, took him upstairs to Louise's room. There he saw his bed and all his possessions already neatly arranged. Janice told him, "Your home is with Louise now." Instead of his mother, it was Louise who cuddled and played with him and helped him get ready for bed.

The Montreux staff breathed a sigh of relief when Dustin appeared to settle into his life at St. Charles House relatively smoothly. It was made clear to the staff that Dustin's presence as an inpatient was not something to be shared with outsiders. Workers were told that since the clinic's licence forbade it to take children, there could be trouble if word got out that he was living there.

Dustin himself posed no obvious problems in his first few weeks in residence. His regular workers found him no more difficult to feed than he had been previously, and he seemed happy with the attention he received from patients, staff members, and visitors. Louise was delighted with her new roommate and enjoyed helping him with meals and with the routine tasks of day-to-day living: getting up in the morning, dressing, having a bath, even changing diapers as Dustin was not yet toilet-trained. She developed a deep and genuine affection for the troubled toddler, and he, in return, became intensely attached to her.

Louise's optimistic side came out when she was dealing with Dustin, but her life had a more tragic side as well. She had been studying ballet seriously when she developed her eating disorder while in her mid-teens. Before coming to Montreux, she had a history of suicide attempts. Although she had already been at Montreux for more than 18 months when Dustin moved in with her, she was still considered an "acute-care" patient, needing a careworker within arm's length of her 24 hours a day. Most of her meals still consisted only of "shakes" of Boost, rather than solid food. Careworkers were instructed to watch her hands at all times because she was likely to try to scratch or cut herself with any available sharp object to try to relieve some of her internal anxiety. She had various obsessions and compulsions of her own, some centred around washing and cleanliness, others around food.

During the first few weeks that Dustin was in residence, he saw his mother frequently on visits or outings to the park or the beach, even on visits to the doctor for the usual childhood sniffles and sore throats. During those first weeks, too, Moira remembered, she was in contact with the clinic as often as two or three times a day to make sure Dustin was doing all right. Every day she was told that he was making progress and eating better. She would usually talk to Louise later in the evening, and Louise would always reassure her that Dustin was safely asleep.

In fact, it wasn't going at all well at night. Dustin would often wake up in the middle of the night with nightmares, just as he'd done while staying with his mother. But as he struggled awake, he knew he wasn't in his usual bed. Instead of crying out for his mother as small children usually do, or even asking for Louise, he would call out a generic, "Worker, worker." It would be up to the night-shift worker who was keeping an eye on both him and Louise to answer and try to reassure him. The commotion would wake Louise up too, and sometimes, when he seemed inconsolable, she would end up taking Dustin into her bed. The staff members allowed it, although they worried that neither Dustin nor Louise was getting enough sleep, and that Louise was showing signs of exhaustion.

Moira also had a new interest in her life. Claude-Pierre asked her if she'd like to become a worker for one of the other patients, a woman named Marie* who was in care at another, smaller house that Montreux ran, a few blocks away on Richmond Avenue. Marie was from New York City as well, and Claude-Pierre thought the two women would have a lot in common. Although her previous job had been as a clerk in a paint store, Moira was soon named as a team leader, a position that held considerable authority in the Montreux structure. The staff member designated a patient's team leader was the one expected to read all the patient logs and staff report forms, and to know exactly what progress a patient was making and what problems might be developing. The team leader was considered the authority on the care of that patient, and was the one the other careworkers were expected to call with questions or concerns. Team leaders were the ones who worked with the counsellors, Margaret Dobson, and Claude-Pierre to develop a food plan and the other "guidelines" that had the virtual force of law in the Montreux system. Most often, they were senior careworkers who had several years' experience and who had developed particularly good rapport with one or two patients. In the case of little Dustin, Claude-Pierre herself was named as his team leader.

However, Moira's lack of experience didn't bother Claude-Pierre when she appointed her to that position for Marie. Moira never got paid in cash for her work. She referred to it as "volunteering," although she did receive payment in kind, since the clinic continued to pay her living expenses as well as treating Dustin for free. More important, though, she said, she found her work with Marie to be very emotionally satisfying. "It took my mind off my pain and suffering," she said. "And it actually helped me to be able to spend time with someone else, and become friends, and make her happy when she was feeling down and blue."

Claude-Pierre didn't consider Moira's lack of training a handicap in dealing with an acutely ill patient, and neither did Moira herself. "The last time I checked, love and compassion and understanding didn't come from a book," she snapped when the issue was raised much later at the licensing hearing.

Moira was about to need more distraction from Dustin's problems. As she and Claude-Pierre talked during the evenings, she began to hear a clear message that Montreux still wasn't entirely happy with Dustin's progress. Claude-Pierre thought that visits with Moira upset Dustin, perhaps because he picked up on the fact that she was sad and missing him.

Separating patients from their parents entirely was a common part of Montreux treatment—but most patients were in their teens, twenties, or even thirties. Claude-Pierre argues in her book that during the acute stage of the illness, patients need a period when they can focus entirely on themselves and their recovery, without ever having to think about their families or how their behaviour is affecting others.

In keeping with this theory, most families agreed not to visit during their child's first weeks or months at Montreux. For many, it would be next to impossible anyway, because of the sheer distances involved. In many cases, even telephone contact, e-mails, or faxes were restricted during the first phase of care. Montreux argued that even this tenuous contact could upset an already fragile patient. Before being admitted, each patient, or a parent for the patients who were still legal minors, signed a contract that specifically removed their rights to uncensored phone calls and mail.

Since separation from family was such a common part of the Montreux program, it was perhaps not surprising that Claude-Pierre began to talk to Moira about the benefits for Dustin if she saw him less. Dustin would be eating well until a visit, Claude-Pierre would explain, but after one, he would seem more upset, have more bad dreams, and be more reluctant to eat. Moira got the message: she quickly came to believe that Dustin might not be cured unless she went along with the plan to give up visits and conversations with him altogether.

Every mother's instinct in Moira cried out against such a plan. She wanted to be able to hold her child, to see for herself how he was doing, to stay a part of his life. She was already missing him terribly and knew that would only become worse if she had no contact at all. Yet, with the help of Claude-Pierre and Margaret Dobson, she managed to persuade herself that such feelings were nothing more than "selfishness" on her part, that she'd be harming her child if she gave in to them.

"I had to stop being selfish," she said. She stressed that Claude-Pierre never forced the complete separation on her, only suggested to her how important it might be for Dustin's future. Claude-Pierre always told her, she said, that if she simply couldn't bear the separation for another minute, she always knew where Dustin was and so could come to see him.

Claude-Pierre provided powerful reinforcements for Moira's decision to accept the separation plan. Every time she saw her, Moira remembered, Peggy would tell her "how strong I was and what a good mother I was for giving up a lot for my son."

Other staff members who worked alongside Moira remembered that she became convinced the separation might be the only way to guarantee her son's survival. Gavin, who became one of Dustin's primary careworkers, recalled that Moira "said that she had been told her son was going to die and that Peggy told her she was the only one that could save her child.... She felt she had to do it because this was her only hope to have her son survive, and that if she questioned too much or wanted to change the program, it would harm the child."

Moira had no one to whom she could turn to ask outside advice about whether such a separation was a reasonable step to take in the case of a three-year-old. If she had, most likely any true expert would have told her no. Two child psychiatrists, Drs. Sherkow and Ainsworth, emphatically denied that they would ever recommend a lengthy separation between a mother and such a young child. "It goes against everything we've been working for [in pediatrics] for the past 50 years," said Dr. Ainsworth. He noted that hospitals that deal with children now make enormous efforts to ensure there are no long separations of children from their families.

But neither Moira nor Claude-Pierre had the benefit of such advice, and in June, Moira reluctantly agreed to what at first was termed a "trial separation." She would have no contact at all with her son, in person or on the phone. The first separation lasted just over a month. Claude-Pierre told Moira it did seem to be helping Dustin make faster progress, and Moira had no independent method to corroborate that. She trusted what Claude-Pierre told her. She agreed to another separation beginning on July 16. She wouldn't see her son again until Dustin's fourth birthday party on October 8.

The importance of the separation in Montreux's eyes was stressed in the new set of guidelines for Dustin that Louise wrote up in August: "Dustin does not see his mother or father at all except for prearranged visits, and there are none planned in the near future."

It wasn't always easy to keep mother and son apart. As Marie's team leader, Moira often found she had to go to the Rockland or St. Charles mansions for meetings or errands, or to take Marie to programs or counselling sessions. The separation was seen as being so important, however, that Montreux management gave Moira a pager that she could use to let management know when she was on her way to one of the other sites. Someone would then make sure that Dustin and his careworker had gone to the park or the beach, someplace where they wouldn't inadvertently run into Moira coming around a corner.

More and more often, that careworker was Louise. In the summer of 1996, Louise was often the primary worker for Dustin every evening plus days during the weekend. Paid staff members were expected to be on shift for only 8 hours at a time, but Louise would end up caring for Dustin for 14 hours a day, sometimes for several days in a row. Although she still was fond of Dustin, she was now also often tired, frustrated with his eating difficulties, and guilt-ridden because she couldn't get him to do better.

Moreover, Louise had her own problems to deal with that summer. In June and July, she was beginning to confront personal and family issues that needed to be faced for her own recovery. Her family had warned her they were about to stop paying for the high-cost treatments at Montreux. Clinic staff were expecting her to make greater progress in her own treatment—to move from shakes to solid food so she would be ready to make the big jump from full care to partial care by the autumn.

And, no matter what Claude-Pierre and Margaret Dobson were telling Moira, no one else was seeing signs of improvement in Dustin's ability to eat. In fact, his regular caregivers were all witnessing what they saw as a frightening deterioration in his condition.

Gavin remembers that in the first months after Dustin came, feeding him was possible with much reassurance and good humour. But by the late spring and early summer, he recalls, the mere sight of the next snack became enough to fill the little boy with "panic and terror." He'd cry about his fear of the "bad man" in his head, about how the man would even play drums very loudly in his head to make sure he didn't want to eat. He reacted the only way he knew how—physically trying to flee from the food as adults might from a poisonous snake. Louise was the best at getting him to eat; sometimes he could accept her persuasions to get a snack down when he wouldn't respond to any of the other workers. But as summer wore on, she too was often totally frustrated by his inability to swallow a single bite without the terror overwhelming him.

His desperation was matched by that of the workers as they tried to find ways to make him take in enough nutrition. Most of them had been convinced by Claude-Pierre that Dustin remained at risk of death if they couldn't get him to eat everything that was on his meal plan for the day.

"We understood that it wasn't about how it appeared, it was about saving his life," Gavin said. Yet to this day there is not a single medical note that suggests he was ever severely medically compromised.

Although meal plans at Montreux were usually inviolable, with Dustin, the careworkers were allowed to try practically anything if they thought he might accept it. For months, his last meal at night would be a bottle of straight cream, sometimes with yogurt or tofu stirred into it, because the workers realized that was one way to get calories into him.

The stress and struggles of eating often also led Dustin to vomit, sometimes after a meal, sometimes in the middle of one. Sometimes he'd say first that his stomach hurt, sometimes he gave no warning at all. On bad days, he would vomit more than half a dozen times. Claude-Pierre's rule, though, was that he was not allowed to avoid eating by vomiting. He would be cleaned up and changed, and then the meal would continue with the workers trying to ensure he got the same amount of nutrition down as he would have if he hadn't vomited. Not only was the nutrition important, Claude-Pierre explained, but if vomiting could be used as a way of avoiding food, the Negative Mind would have won a battle and would be stronger than ever the next day.

Between the vomiting and ensuing cleanup and the struggles to get the food down in the first place, Dustin's whole life became absorbed by the struggles over eating. On many occasions, the time for normal, little-boy play—for bike-riding, and painting, and games on the computer—disappeared. For days on end, practically every waking moment, he was sitting on a worker's knee, being held by a worker on the couch, with the worker trying to get him to eat or drink. There were no more trips to the park or the beach or the petting zoo because there wasn't time in between the efforts to feed him. Often the feeding wouldn't be done even by bedtime, and Louise, sometimes with another worker, would be left trying to get the last bottles of juice or cream down as late as 11:00 p.m. or midnight.

They may have succeeded in completing the food plan for the day, but they had done nothing towards helping ease Dustin's panic. He could no longer take comfort from the workers' reassurances. At the mere sight of food, his eyes would grow wide, and sometimes workers could feel him physically shaking with terror. On some occasions he would get so upset, and scream and cry so hard that the veins in his neck would begin to stand out.

Although Claude-Pierre continued to talk publicly about treating every patient with nothing but "unconditional love," and answering every negative thought with a positive one, virtually every worker who dealt with Dustin admitted that at some time during that long autumn separation, any pretence of gentleness went out the window.

First, the gentle reassurances became firm orders—telling Dustin he had no choice but to eat what was being given him. That escalated to yelling and threats, most often of having to go to see Claude-Pierre. Sometimes that was enough to allow them to get a little food into him. Claude-Pierre still insists that Dustin enjoyed visiting her, and it was more a bribe than a threat. But the workers all agree that the warning about going to see Claude-Pierre was the equivalent of threatening an ill-behaved school pupil with a trip to the principal's office. One day Dustin was told that if he didn't eat, "he'd be living at Peggy's with a tube up his nose."

Nor were the staff above emotional blackmail. On another day, he was told that his mother—who, at that point, he had not been allowed to see for weeks—was "still waiting for him to come back, but he couldn't go back until he was able to eat enough by himself."

And on the days when neither firmness nor threats nor emotional blackmail were enough to get Dustin to eat something, the only answer was to restrain him physically and squirt or spoon the food into his mouth. One adult worker would hold him on a lap or on the corner of a couch, and would grab his two tiny hands in one of their big ones to keep them from frantically thrashing about. Another adult would firmly grasp his head, holding it still and straight so he couldn't twist it away, and a third would then take the spoon or squirt-bottle and force the food into his mouth. During some bad periods, that would be the meal procedure five or six times a day.

The worse things got, the more it seemed his days had become a surreal enactment of his own worst nightmares—big men wrestling him down, making sure he couldn't move, and then forcing food and drink into his mouth. Gavin remembers repeatedly asking for help as to what to do with Dustin on such extra-bad days, but he never got an answer that he could use. "They didn't have any idea either," he concluded sadly.

Although Claude-Pierre has always insisted that she is utterly opposed to force-feeding and would never allow it in the clinic, Gavin remembers at least one day when Claude-Pierre watched their method of feeding Dustin with approval, with Gavin forcibly restraining him and Louise spooning in the yogurt.

More and more often, though, Claude-Pierre wasn't even there to be consulted about Dustin's worsening problems. The deadline was looming for the manuscript of the book she was writing about eating disorders and Montreux, and she was spending increasing amounts of time finishing her writing and diminishing amounts of time at the clinic. The staff members felt as if they were entirely on their own in trying to help Dustin.

At one point, Louise wrote in her journal: "[Peggy] thinks she will have to take Dustin, but can't possibly until the end of the month as her book's deadline is then. So I guess we just keep him going till then."

As the summer wore on, on the very worst days Dustin's last defence would be to clench his teeth together so tightly it was impossible to get the nozzle of the bottle or the spoon into his mouth. In those cases, once he was held immobile, he'd find the staff using another spoon as a lever to pry his teeth open. Sometimes he'd cry out in pain; sometimes his mouth would be left bleeding. At one point Gavin and Louise urged Montreux management to take Dustin to a dentist because they feared they might be damaging his teeth or gums as they forced his mouth open. A few days later they were told he'd gone to the dentist, and they were to continue as before.

"Whatever we had to do to have him eat, we did... it was because his life was in danger," Gavin said, stressing that this was what staff members had been repeatedly told by Claude-Pierre and other senior managers.

By August, Gavin could no longer bear to watch the downward spiral of both Dustin and Louise. Although he hated leaving them both, he resigned from Montreux.

Louise and other workers persevered. But for Louise, too, the strain was getting to be too much. On October 8, Dustin's birthday, he had a party and an hour-long visit with his mother. The short visit, though, only seemed to upset him more, leading Montreux management to believe the best approach was to continue the separation. There are no indications in any records that Moira visited with Dustin again until the clinic's Christmas party more than 10 weeks later.

During the long separation, Louise became Dustin's lifeline, and he began to cling to her frantically. Despite his fights with her over food, he became scared to let her out of his sight. If Louise was there, he didn't want to leave the suite they shared. The workers had to work hard to reassure him that she'd be there waiting for him when he came back. Dr. Ainsworth later noted that these were probably symptoms of a severe separation anxiety, but no one at Montreux seemed willing or able to recognize at the time that this might be the problem.

He began to call Louise "Mom," and sometimes he spread that title around to other female workers he liked, such as Janice. The workers always tried to tell him they were not his mother, that his mother was waiting for him, and that he would return to her, but the behaviour persisted.

Louise, still struggling to cope with her own problems, was frequently becoming overwhelmed with frustration, worry, and guilt over Dustin. Her journal entries show her distressed about Dustin's unpleasant days, fearful that Claude-Pierre would be angry with her for Dustin's problems, and consumed with guilt that she could not help Dustin more.

"I was really, really strict with [a snack]," she wrote one day, "and he screamed, cried and spit out the shake everywhere for the first couple of times … I wanted to make sure he went to bed knowing he was loved still, because everyone had yelled at him who possibly could have done [and probably more!]."

Louise's own counsellor and workers began to write in their reports that they were becoming worried about her stress level and exhaustion.

Dustin's late feedings and nightmares meant she was rarely getting a full night's sleep herself. "Louise feels like she is at the end of her rope and doesn't know what else to do," noted her counsellor after a session with Louise in August.

Louise's own desperation and conflicting emotions boiled over in her journal on October 16 when she wrote at 12:15 a.m. at the end of an exhausting and emotionally draining day: "One of us is on death row— I'm either the executioner or the executee—who knows!!"

She described a day in which Dustin had been so upset he'd already had an hour-long screaming and crying fit, had taken 45 minutes to drink only two ounces, had vomited and wouldn't undress himself to get cleaned up for another two hours, and, when finally released, had fled into the room of two of the other patients and vomited there.

"I think I could be hysterical right now," she noted in her journal at that point.

Things didn't get any better after Dustin went to bed that night. He screamed and threw up twice more even after he was apparently asleep.

Not until early December did Claude-Pierre agree that Louise should no longer be responsible for Dustin's care. By that time she had developed a stomach ulcer, potentially triggered in part by the huge amounts of stress in her life, not the least of which was her effort to help Dustin.

As fall became winter, Moira's frustrations were almost as acute as her son's. The system by which she would be kept regularly updated on Dustin's progress had broken down completely, and she heard nothing about her son for weeks on end. Her pages, which formerly had been answered so quickly, were now ignored.

In desperation, she wrote a note to Claude-Pierre in December, trying to get an answer. "When I paged, it's not to say I don't get upset when I page for three weeks with no reply. Even if you can't call me back, somebody can.... Not knowing my son's progress doesn't help. I go months without any information on him. This alone leaves me in distress... I need to be somewhat part of my son's life."

Claude-Pierre did phone Moira after receiving the note. She apologized, and after that, Moira said, she was updated at least twice a month. However, the updates never included any information about the forced feedings, the struggles to get Dustin to eat, the whole days that were taken up in battles over food. Instead, she was told Dustin was eating new things, was thriving, was happy, was normal, wasn't having bad dreams any more. With no way to check the information, she again felt reassured by Claude-Pierre's promises.

In April, after 18 months in Victoria, Moira needed to return to New York for a month to take care of business and financial affairs. She signed an agreement making Noah and Margaret Dobson the legal guardians of Dustin for the time she would be away. For Dustin, life would continue the same as ever.

When she went to visit Noah to get him to sign the agreement, he had good news for her. Noah told her that as soon as she returned, she was "going to be incorporated into Dustin's meals," because he was doing so well they thought he was now ready to handle that. She returned to New York ecstatic.

But once again, the patient logs describing Dustin's days did not show signs of improvement in his eating or behaviour. The guidelines showed that Dustin's diet was actually slightly more restricted than it had been a year earlier. The fear of eating had transformed itself into a refusal to swallow. Instead of fighting the food entering his mouth, he would take it in but would refuse to swallow it for hours, instead going around with his cheeks puffed out like a chipmunk. His internal struggles sometimes came out as physical aggression towards staff. He would hit and kick them, or become aggressive with other children on the infrequent occasions when he did get to play at the park or the beach.

Moira returned to Victoria on May 16, 1997. By that time, the Dobsons, Claude-Pierre, and Harris were all out of the city on various business trips. Management of the clinic had been left briefly in the hands of Nicole Claude-Pierre and her husband, Justin Williams. Moira settled back into the new apartment into which she had moved, a couple of miles from the clinic. The plan to incorporate her into Dustin's meals had yet to be implemented.

But the time bomb that had been planted when Montreux moved Dustin to in-patient status was about to detonate. For four months, licensing inspectors had been investigating Montreux after receiving complaints from several former staff members. The inspectors had been told of a four-year-old boy who was being kept separated from his mother, living at St. Charles House.

For Dustin, the morning of May 29 started just like any other. He had not been told anything special was going to happen that day. After breakfast, he was taken to the van, just as if it were time for another outing. Instead, he was taken to his mother's apartment. Dustin was discharged to her care with the same abruptness with which he'd left it.

Moira recalls that one day, soon after her return from New York, "I get a knock on the door, and there is Dustin. And he just walked in as though he lived there for the entire time."

What neither Dustin nor most of the staff knew was that on that morning, the licensing team had arrived to do an "unannounced inspection" of the clinic. One of the first things they wanted was a tour and a list of all the patients in residence at Montreux, both at the Rockland site and at the secondary one at St. Charles.

Senior worker Tricia* doesn't remember seeing the inspectors, but she remembers that as soon as she arrived at work that morning, her assignment was changed. Instead of caring for her regular patient, she was to spend the first couple of hours of the morning helping the maintenance man move all of little Dustin's possessions, as he was returning to his mother's care that day.

By the time the inspectors finished their tour of Rockland and moved on to St. Charles House, nothing remained to show that a four-year-old had ever lived there. "No child was found by Licensing," wrote the inspectors in their report to regional medical health officer Dr. Richard Stanwick the next month.

Moira insists that when Dustin returned to her, he was completely cured and ate entirely normally from that moment on. How that could be, when just two weeks earlier workers had been writing of the difficulties of getting him to swallow a single spoonful of yogurt, remains one of the Montreux mysteries.

Meanwhile, after the licensing inspectors had finished touring the two houses, they sat down for a meeting with Nicole, Justin, and scheduling manager Karim Nassar, to discuss some of the allegations that had been made.

All three denied that Dustin had ever been a residential patient at Montreux. They insisted that for the entire time he'd been in Victoria, he'd spent nights with his mother, except for the occasional time when he'd been having a particularly rough day and so had stayed at St. Charles House overnight. As a result, they said, there were no detailed patient logs for Dustin. They were unable, they claimed, to provide a phone number for Moira offhand, although they could probably find it before the end of the day.

When a phone number was provided that afternoon, licensing inspector Kim Macdonald phoned Moira to inquire about Dustin's treatment while at Montreux. Moira told the same story as Nicole and Justin. Dustin, she told them, had been a day patient at Montreux, but had spent the vast majority of nights at home with her. The longest he'd ever stayed there was two nights in a row, she said, and he hadn't stayed there overnight at all for the past six months.

A few days later, Claude-Pierre, Harris, and the Dobsons returned to Victoria; they all told the inspectors the same story.

"It was puzzling," said Macdonald later. The former staff members had been 100 per cent sure that Dustin had been a residential patient, but the inspectors couldn't believe a mother would tell them such blatant lies about her own child. As a result, the licensing inspectors concluded that the allegations about the little boy couldn't be substantiated, so no further action was taken.

Dustin and Moira stayed in Victoria for another few weeks and then returned to New York in time for Dustin to start school in September.

5

Gathering Storm Clouds

Although Dustin's case aroused great concern among many staff members, it was not, in the end, the case that would prove the turning point for Montreux. In the months following the *20/20* broadcasts, the clinic expanded rapidly, with patients mainly from Britain and the U.S. Although Montreux always had some patients it was treating for free, the fee scale alone—soon rising to as much as $925 (US) per day—ensured that many of the patients came from the ranks of the very well-off, some with connections to fame or celebrity. Anthony Andrews, the star of the TV series *Brideshead Revisited*, was one parent who visited the clinic as a possible placement for his daughter.

But of all the rich or famous patients who were to come to Montreux, none had climbed to greater heights of fame—or plumbed greater depths of misery—than Lena Zavaroni. Lena came from the tiny and remote town of Rothesay on the Isle of Bute, a seaside tourist resort off the west coast of Scotland, accessible only by ferry. Her family owned the local fish-and-chip shop there, but their first love was music. Her father, Victor Zavaroni, played the guitar and accordion, while her mother, Hilda, was a singer. Almost as soon as she learned to talk, Lena was singing along with the family.

When she reached school age, she began singing in talent contests in Rothesay, and she won so often that she was politely disqualified from competing in them any more. Instead, she joined her parents in a family act which they called the Zavaroni Family Band, performing in pubs and clubs around the Isle of Bute.

It was in one of those clubs that record producer Tommy Scott, on vacation in Rothesay, first heard Lena. He told her family that her talent was too great to remain hidden away in Bute and convinced Victor to enter her on one of Britain's most popular television shows. *Opportunity Knocks*, hosted by Canadian émigré Hughie Green, was essentially a talent show—a British version of the American show *Star Search*—that sought out rising stars from across the country. An act that won the viewers' polls once would be invited back each week to try to defend the title against all comers.

Lena was dressed up to look even younger than she was, in a minidress and knee socks, as she belted out one of the popular songs from the British clubs, "Ma, He's Making Eyes at Me." Lena and her family were overjoyed when she won the first week she appeared. They were overwhelmed when she just kept on winning and winning—topping the show for an unprecedented five-week run. Lena was on her way to stardom—and at breakneck speed. She was just nine years old.

Her recording of "Ma, He's Making Eyes at Me" peaked at #8 on the British music charts, and she became the youngest person ever to appear on the country's number-one music show, *Top of the Pops*. Through the ages of 10 and 11, she did world tours, appearing with great success in many countries, from South Africa to Japan. She stole the show at a Hollywood charity performance, where she appeared alongside Frank Sinatra and Lucille Ball. She shared a dressing room with Liza Minnelli and sang for President Gerald Ford at the White House and for the Queen at a royal gala.

Rothesay was too small to hold Lena any more. Her manager, Dorothy Solomon, agreed to be Lena's surrogate mother and have Lena live with her in London. Lena was enrolled in the Italia Conte stage school, one of the top performing-arts schools in the world, where she quickly became good friends with another child star, Bonnie Langford. To an outsider looking in, she appeared to be on top of the world. But inside, it was already beginning to overwhelm the small-town girl.

"Everything changed so quickly," she'd later tell reporters.[30] Before coming to London, she'd never even seen an escalator or a traffic light. She'd lived in a simple home, part of a public housing development. Now she was living in a luxurious London flat, with shopping trips to stores like the fabled Harrods. Lena was fond of Dorothy, but she couldn't get used to her new life of luxury. "I was afraid to touch anything [in the flat]," she said. She was homesick for the family from whom she'd been parted so abruptly.

Dorothy, for her part, believed Lena had the voice and the talent to be another Barbra Streisand, and encouraged her with stage performances, theatre concerts, and numerous television appearances, both specials and series. The money and the plaudits just kept rolling in. By 1977, when Lena was 14, she was reputed to be the richest teenager in Scotland. She won a Silver Award in the prestigious Golden Sea Swallow Festival in Belgium for her TV show, "Lena Zavaroni on Broadway."

However, that same year, Lena began to show the first signs of the eating disorder that would plague her life for more than two decades. Although she was actually tiny—she never did grow more than 4 feet, 10 inches tall—the form-fitting costumes popular in musical theatre were enough to make many girls self-conscious about their body image. It didn't help that Lena was rapidly developing a woman's figure, or, as she'd later note, that she was expected to attend a round of celebrity lunches, dinners, and even breakfasts whenever she was away on tour.

Solomon and the teachers at her school wanted her to just "cut out all the little extras" from her diet. Instead she virtually stopped eating altogether. "I only became fanatical about not eating when the pressure became too much," she said.[31]

Once she'd started down the path into anorexia, she found it impossible to turn back. Her weight plummeted. She spent her sixteenth birthday in hospital in Glasgow. From then on, she alternated between times of successful performing and times when she was too ill to work and often had to be hospitalized. She sought a wide variety of treatment options in Britain, ranging from psychiatric help to acupuncture. Sometimes she would gain weight for a short while, but she never truly beat the anorexia.

The stresses in her life seemed intolerable. Her mother began drinking heavily and her parents separated. Lena married a computer consultant, Peter Wiltshire, in the hopes of living a normal life, but the marriage lasted only 18 months. Wiltshire was unable to cope with the demands of living with a depressed and emaciated wife. Only months after they separated, Lena's mother, Hilda, died as the result of an overdose of tranquilizers—an apparent suicide. Lena always believed that she'd inherited her mother's genetic predisposition to depression, and that this had led to her eating disorder as well.

Devastated by her mother's death, and then by a fire that destroyed almost all her show business mementos, Lena moved in with her best friend. Elly Dalziel was another anorexic, a dancer whom she'd met while they were both appearing in a pantomime of *Jack and the Beanstalk*. They called each other Mickey and Minnie (from the Mickey Mouse Show), went to carnivals, and frankly admitted that they didn't want to grow up. Each realized the other was eating almost nothing, but they could not help each other overcome the anorexia.

In 1993, Lena was feeling well enough to do a television appearance—but nothing could hide the devastating toll that the years of malnutrition had taken on her body. Watching at their home, her much-loved cousin Martha and her husband David were horrified by her appearance. Within days, they visited her and persuaded her to move in with them.

The warmth and support Lena received there allowed her to improve. She put on some weight, began talking about a show business comeback, and managed to sing with her father at a family New Year's celebration. But watching her, Martha and David knew she needed more help than they could give her if she was to truly recover.

After they watched the *20/20* show when it aired in England, they became convinced that Montreux might be the place to offer Lena long-lasting hope. Martha joined the parade of hundreds of mothers, fathers, siblings, and husbands who wrote and faxed Peggy Claude-Pierre in the days following the show, frantically seeking to have a loved one admitted to Montreux. At first, Claude-Pierre agreed to meet Lena when she was next in Britain, a few months later. However, within a matter of weeks, it became obvious to Martha and David that that would not be soon enough. Lena was failing again. She was becoming more and more withdrawn and depressed, and again had to be coaxed to eat even the smallest morsel. Despite Martha's best efforts, Lena's weight was dropping rapidly once again and soon had fallen to just 60 pounds.

Desperate, Martha took a photograph of Lena and sent it to Claude-

Pierre. "If you want to help, you've really got to do it now," she said in the attached note.

This time the message got instant results. Less than 24 hours after receiving the picture, Claude-Pierre was making arrangements for Lena to fly to Victoria and be admitted to the clinic. Lena and her family gained new hope from the promises on *20/20* that Montreux was a place that showed no signs of failure, even when dealing with patients as sick or sicker than Lena. They liked the sound of the loving, nurturing environment, the kind of affection that Lena had had to abandon at the age of 10 for the sake of her career. Maybe, they thought, Montreux might succeed where everything else had failed.

Under the 24-hour-care regime at Montreux, Lena did begin to put on weight and stabilize medically. Over the next few months, her weight rose from 65 pounds to a high of 83. Staff members remember her as having a good first few months in the program, apparently co-operating and heading towards recovery.

However, as proved to be the case with so many Montreux patients, the improvement didn't last. She grew increasingly unhappy at Montreux and lost any faith that the program there would provide her with a long-term cure. One of the things that bothered her most was the enforced separation from her family. Like most Montreux patients, she was, in the early days, encouraged to have no contact at all with her father, her sister, or her cousins. Even letters and faxes were not forwarded, especially when Lena was expressing "negativity" in her communications, telling them that she didn't think Montreux was all that had been promised.

Many Montreux patients greeted the separation from loved ones with relief, especially teenagers and young adults who, before coming to Montreux, had found themselves in a struggle to separate psychologically from their parents. Lena, though, was more than 30 years old and had never been closer to her family than in the last few years before coming to Canada. The circumstances reminded her of those troubling times of her youth when she was torn away from parents and family for the sake of her career.

Again, she began talking about her conviction that her root problem was something much deeper than her fear of eating. She was quite sure she was clinically depressed, and again she wondered if she'd inherited a genetic tendency to depression and anorexia from her mother. She began to believe that something must be organically wrong with her brain that it was making her feel so dreadful. Her symptoms, she complained, weren't like the ones that Montreux staff and counsellors talked about with their patients, especially the voices telling them they were fat, ugly, and no good. Virtually all the others said those voices would talk to them—sometimes almost constantly—but Lena wasn't hearing voices.

She'd try to explain to the staff what was going on in her head but never felt she was making much progress in getting them to understand. It was like static, or white noise, she said, a "veil of greyness" that she couldn't get past. And her depression wasn't like the intense sadness that other Montreux patients said they felt. It wasn't that she felt sad or worthless or angry with herself. It was that she couldn't feel anything at all. Even when a clinic staff member was hugging her and reassuring her during a meal, she later said, she couldn't feel the hug or listen to the words past the white noise. On another occasion, she said she felt so removed from the world that she wasn't even sure she was in the room.

"I feel as though I've given away my soul," she said once. "I don't have it any more. I'm dead inside."

She became convinced that the lay counselling which she was receiving at Montreux wasn't enough. The counsellors didn't understand what was going on in her head. She wanted desperately to see a psychiatrist, or a medical doctor, maybe even a neurologist; someone who might be able to figure out what was wrong with her brain. She began asking her counsellors if they couldn't make a referral for her, but they always said no. The "static" and the numbness were just another way that anorexia was exercising its evil voice and power over her, they told her. She'd have to work with them to get past those feelings before she could start to feel better.

She wanted to believe them. Sometimes, for a little while, she did. She'd write notes to Claude-Pierre and her favourite staff members, thanking them for all they were doing for her, for not giving up on her. Sometimes, she'd beg to go home, but then staff would persuade her to withdraw the requests, insisting that she'd never find such a good place to treat her back in Britain. But overall, the terror, the depression, and the unrelenting white noise got worse and worse. Although she'd been eating without too much difficulty when she first came to the clinic, it became a greater and greater trial for her.

Lena had been at the clinic more than a year before she met up with the first staff member who would take her complaints seriously. Gay Pankhurst was newly hired as a careworker but was older than most of the staff and had had more professional training. She'd raised her own daughter and had taken three years of studies in special-needs education. She'd met Claude-Pierre and Harris the night of the first *20/20* show while working at the restaurant where they'd held their party to watch the program.

Like so many others, she'd been impressed with them, and with what she saw on the show. A direct descendant of noted suffragette Emmeline Pankhurst, she considered herself a bit of a rebel and liked the idea of working in a place that was "alternative" and defied all the normal societal and medical stereotypes about anorexia. She applied for a job at the clinic soon afterwards, and about 18 months after the show, Claude-Pierre hired her as a careworker. She'd been there six weeks when she was first assigned to work with Lena for a shift. Within minutes, she was hearing Lena's concerns about her separation from her family and her growing desire to see a psychiatrist or a neurologist.

Gay was sympathetic. Despite her "alternative" mindset, she'd already found herself wondering on a few occasions if some Montreux residents didn't have problems more complex than just an eating disorder, and if perhaps a little more medical input wasn't needed. She asked Lena if she'd made her requests clear to Claude-Pierre, but Lena shook her head. "She just shouted me down," she said.

Gay considered herself too new to make good judgments about such complex issues, but she thought it worth mentioning to the more senior careworkers who were supposed to be supervising her. They sighed. "Quite an actress is our Lena," sneered one. It was just the anorexia talking, they insisted, warning Gay that Lena tried the story on every new worker and it need not be taken seriously.

A little reluctantly, Gay went along with them. Martha came out from Britain to visit, and Lena seemed happier. She was able to prepare and eat her prescribed meals and even nibbled biscotti with her coffee when the three of them went for an outing. When Martha had to return home, though, Lena seemed to sink into an even more depressed mood. Gay had moved on to taking care of some other patients, and it was almost a month before she saw her again.

That night, Gay was working a shift known as "floater," in which a careworker would take turns working with a variety of different patients, so their regular careworkers could take a break to catch up on paperwork, go for a short walk, or even just go to the washroom. Careworkers could also call the floater if they were having a problem with a particular patient and needed a little extra help. Gay was looking forward to seeing again some of the patients with whom she'd worked earlier, especially Lena.

When she went to the suite at St. Charles House where Lena had been staying, however, it was vacant. She found Lena instead at the main Rockland mansion, staying in the attic—a tiny, isolated suite at the very top of the house, often used for the sickest or most disruptive patients. Lena had stopped eating solid food altogether. Montreux management had placed her back on a liquid diet, consisting of nothing more than enhanced Boost shakes, squirted into her mouth from a sports-bottle half a dozen times a day. When Gay found her wandering about the suite, she appeared much sicker, both physically and mentally, than she had just a few weeks earlier.

Again Gay asked about Lena and read what staff members had been writing about her in the patient logbook. Again she was told it was just that Lena was having a much tougher time overcoming the anorexic mindset than some of the other patients were.

November 4 was Lena's birthday. She'd be turning 33. Birthdays were usually cause for celebration at Montreux, even for the sickest patients, and Gay was looking forward to Lena's. Maybe, she thought, a party would, like Martha's visit, be enough to snap Lena out of her dreadful depression for a bit. Gay went a little early to her shift at Montreux that day in the hopes of spending a few extra minutes with Lena at the party. But when she arrived, she could find no indication of a party anywhere. In Lena's attic suite, Gay could see balloons still tied to bedposts and chairs, but the room was dark. Lena was huddled in her bed, apparently sound asleep.

Quietly, so as not to disturb Lena, Gay picked up her logbook and took it to read out in the hallway where the light was brighter. What she read made her feel physically ill. Instead of celebrating her birthday, Gay found, Lena was recovering from a serious overdose of medication that she'd taken the night before in an apparent suicide attempt.

Although Montreux preferred to wean all its patients off psychiatric medications, Lena's problems were so severe that she had continued on some drugs. One was Tegretol, a medication most often used for controlling seizures in epileptics. Lena had originally been prescribed the Tegretol after suffering what appeared to be seizures soon after she'd arrived, but then she'd been taken off it because it was causing problematic side effects with her blood. She hadn't suffered any more seizures, but a few weeks earlier Dr. Clinton-Baker had placed her back on the drug in the hope that it would stabilize her mood.

Now it appeared that for the past two weeks Lena had only been pretending to take her Tegretol each night. She'd put it in her mouth when the staff member gave it to her, but she wouldn't swallow it. Instead, she'd later spit it out and hoard it, apparently planning a final escape from a life that had become completely intolerable to her.

The night before her birthday she'd taken all 15 of the hoarded pills. She'd been complaining of a migraine, and then started vomiting. She'd seemed to be staggering and losing her balance before she'd finally gone to bed and fallen asleep. And then her careworker hadn't been able to wake her up. The worker quickly paged senior management with news of the emergency and, between them, they figured out what Lena had done. They didn't phone 911, but called Dr. David Clinton-Baker, the clinic's medical consultant, who checked her out, concluded Lena would pull through all right, and ordered blood tests done the next day, to be sure there would be no lasting effects.

The worker who took over the next morning described Lena as "right out of it. [She] could barely walk or talk this morning." She again slept through the afternoon shift. "Her pupils were dilated and she wasn't focussing her eyes," noted the worker. "I don't know if she knew who I was."

By the next day, her condition was improved, although she was described as "still detoxifying." But she was considered well enough that her evening worker was prepared to lay down the law. In that night's notes, the worker wrote that she told Lena "how she is going to have to deal with and accept her careworkers being more on top of her. She can't do anything about it, so don't even complain. Also, that she is just going to have to accept that she is in the program and that she is not going anywhere. She needs to be here." The worker added one final line about the conversation: "I don't know if anything got through."

It was obvious that the worker had not even considered that Lena was a 33-year-old woman, not committed under any mental health law, and that she was legally free to leave whenever she wanted to.

"That was when the alarm bells really went off for me," says Gay. "That was when I knew something was really wrong."

Still, she was not sure just what she should do. She tried to see Lena—even if only for a few minutes—every day that she was working, to ensure she was all right. Lena got over the drug overdose, but her depression and resulting unwillingness to eat seemed worse than ever. Her weight started to plunge again.

About a month later, Gay was working with a different patient in the "pink suite," just below the attic where Lena was living. Even from the floor below, she could hear the sounds of loud crashing and banging coming from the attic above, as well as disconsolate wailing and sobbing. As they were going off shift, Gay asked one of Lena's workers what had been going on to cause all the noise.

It had been a dreadful day, the worker replied. It had taken almost four hours for them to feed Lena a single cup of yogurt. She'd become so upset at the thought of eating that not only would she not eat by herself, she had, in panic, also clenched her teeth to prevent staff from feeding her. The worker hadn't been able to do a thing, and had eventually called for help. Jeannie—the star of the *20/20* show who was now working as a careworker—had come, bringing with her a metal spoon. When Lena's panic would not subside enough for her to eat, Jeannie had taken the metal spoon and forced it between Lena's teeth, twisting it and using it as a lever to open her mouth so the food could be jammed in. At one point, Jeannie had just taken the spoon and hit Lena's teeth with it until she opened her mouth in a reflex action.

Gay was horrified. No matter how "alternative" a treatment Montreux might embrace, she couldn't imagine that it would normally include the use of such physical force to make a tiny, terrified patient eat. She was growing increasingly determined that something had to be done.

Three nights later, there was a staff Christmas party. Few of the experienced staff remained on duty; newer staff members stayed at the houses to care for the residents. A worker who'd been there only a few weeks was assigned to work with Lena. Gay was again working in the downstairs suite.

During the evening, Gay got a call on the in-house communication system from Lena's worker, begging her to come up and see if she couldn't help persuade Lena to take some nutrition. Lena was again refusing to eat, and pages to senior management were going unanswered.

When Gay went into the attic, she found Lena sitting on the edge of the bed, quivering and shaking and eyeing the yogurt cup as if it contained poison. Gay sat down on the bed beside her. She could feel the trembling of Lena's bony body. She promised her she wouldn't physically force her to eat, but that she was sure Lena could manage to do it, and that she'd be right there to support and persuade her.

Lena's eyes filled with tears. "Oh Gay, you don't know what they're doing to me here," she said. She still wanted to see a neurologist, and she was still unhappy about the enforced separation from her family. Nearly every time she'd written recently, all she'd done was beg to come home, even though her family couldn't imagine where she'd live, back in England, or what sort of treatment might be provided for her.

But even more now, she complained about repeated struggles to feed her, using the spoon to force her mouth open, banging her on the teeth with it. As well, she said, it seemed just about every minute of her waking hours she was being forced to eat. At bad times, she said, "I'm puking into my own mouth and they're still force-feeding me."

Gay couldn't bear it. For a brief moment, she thought of calling 911, right then and there. It would bring the police to investigate what she saw as the assaults on Lena, she thought, and an ambulance to take Lena to hospital, where she might get the sort of help she really needed. But almost as soon as she thought of the idea, she abandoned it. It would probably cause more problems than it would solve. Other patients, themselves vulnerable, would be terrified by the arrival of ambulances and squad cars. There was no way to tell what would happen to them, or what Claude-Pierre and Harris might do in response.

She told Lena what she was thinking. Lena agreed that "it would be pandemonium" if Gay went about rescuing her that way. Instead, they made a pact. Both would stay quiet for the moment, but Gay would immediately start finding out how to launch a legal complaint about the clinic's operations, and how to make sure Lena wouldn't be held against her will any more.

After a few phone calls, Gay realized that the best officials to complain to were probably those from health licensing, who'd granted Montreux its original licence to operate. Their rules required all facilities to uphold the provincial laws and standards. Even before she talked to officials there, Gay was convinced that no one would think banging a spoon into someone's teeth and refusing to allow them to leave was permissible.

All the same, it took her almost three weeks to launch a formal complaint with licensing. Christmas intervened, and so did a huge blizzard that paralyzed the entire city for more than a week. In the meantime, Gay saw Lena every day, they exchanged small Christmas gifts and cards, and their friendship grew. Only once did Gay see Lena being mistreated again—one day when two staff members were holding her down to get a bottle of sports-drink into her, with one of them threatening, "Do you want me to get the spoon?"

It was a tough time for both of them. Gay wasn't assigned to work with Lena again, but on several occasions Lena managed to smuggle her notes, each increasingly frantic in tone.

"Please, please can you help me soon, I'm desperate," read one. "I can't take this any more. What there [sic] doing to me here is indescribable ... I need professional help ... please get me help now if there is any way in your possible power. Please save my sanity."

By the time Gay had set up an appointment with the licensing officials, it was January. Everyone was in a high state of excitement at Montreux, because the clinic was once again going to be featured on *The Oprah Winfrey Show.* Claude-Pierre and Harris would fly to Chicago, and another group of patients and staff would travel to Vancouver, where they'd be hooked up to the show via satellite. The patient to be featured was Carmen,* who'd first linked up with Claude-Pierre when she was an invited member of the studio audience on the first *Oprah* show a year earlier.

Carmen was 21 and had developed anorexia at the age of 16. Over the next four years she'd lost half her body weight, despite three stints in residential eating-disorder units in the U.S. She could never figure out why she'd become so desperately anorexic. She hadn't, she said, ever had problems with her family or ever been abused.

"I guess that I was just never great at anything, and as I became older, dieting became my specialty," she wrote once on the Internet.

After meeting Claude-Pierre at that first *Oprah* show, Carmen's family had arranged for her to be admitted to Montreux. By the time of the second show, she had been there for several weeks and was prepared to tell the world how much better she was feeling and doing. The key worker going with her would be Jeannie.

It was ridiculous, thought Gay. Jeannie, who'd been jamming the spoon into Lena's mouth, was now going to be the patient-turned-worker hero getting the credit for saving Carmen's life.

On January 6, Gay met for the first time with the region's licensing officials. Greg Dunphy had been serving as the liaison officer to Montreux for the past two years, and Kim Macdonald was the division's nutritionist.

The story Gay told horrified them. If what she related was true, they thought, Montreux could be a clinic with big problems under the surface. On the other hand, it seemed so unlikely. This was a clinic with an international reputation, a place considered a ray of hope for anorexics the world over. Its whole premise was based on unconditional love for the patients. How could it also be a place where patients were treated violently and held against their will?

They decided to visit Montreux that very day. When they arrived, they explained to Margaret Dobson that they needed to talk about Lena. To their surprise, Dobson immediately showed them paperwork indicating that Lena would in fact be going home to Britain in less than a week. The decision to formally discharge her had been made a few days earlier, she explained, and her cousin Martha was heading over from Britain to pick her up. Claude-Pierre had told Lena of the new plans only a few hours earlier. According to Dobson, Montreux had wanted to keep Lena, even as her troubles worsened, believing the clinic was the only place that could help her. But it had now been agreed that Dr. Clinton-Baker, who'd had previous concerns about Lena's condition, would write a letter stating that she "has problems that cannot be dealt with at Montreux"—just what Lena herself had been saying for the previous weeks and months.

Dunphy and Macdonald said they wanted to speak to Lena, alone. At first Lena was very reluctant to talk much, indicating to them that she was concerned about what might happen to her as a consequence. But gradually they were able to reassure her, and she admitted how deeply unhappy she was at Montreux. In the first place, she said, she'd agreed to try Montreux for 12 months at most; now it was 18 months later, she was feeling worse than when she'd first come, and until that very day, there had been no indication of how long she might have to stay.

As well, she suggested, the strict rules that surrounded every aspect of life at the clinic needed to be relaxed for older residents who were accustomed to making some choices about their own lives. She didn't like the fact that staff dictated her reading material and even what television shows she could watch. Not only was she not allowed to leave the building without a staff member, often she wasn't even allowed to leave her tiny attic suite if her careworker of the day didn't think she was in a good headspace.

"It makes me feel like a prisoner," she said. Her desperation had grown so great she'd even thought of trying to drop a letter surreptitiously on the pavement begging for help.

She was upset that all the letters she sent home were opened and censored by Montreux staff, just as all the letters and packages that came for her from her family had been. For the last few months she hadn't even been allowed to talk to her father on the phone because staff considered her too depressed.

Lena readily admitted that in the last few weeks she hadn't been eating all the nutrition prescribed for her in the Montreux meal plan. Usually, she said, she'd take about half of it, and then refuse to eat, clenching her teeth. She told them that the spoon would be used to pry her teeth apart, and also told them that for the last couple of weeks staff had been waking her up every two hours throughout the night, trying to get more nutrition into her. She was being fed as often as seven times a day, she said, and she just couldn't cope with the constant pressure.

Macdonald then gently asked Lena what she thought would've happened if she'd insisted on leaving. "They would never let me leave," Lena replied. "They have physically held me down before."

Montreux's decision to allow Lena to return home alleviated licensing's most immediate concerns. However, Dunphy and Macdonald agreed that the allegations warranted further investigation into Montreux's general policies and procedures—force-feeding, denying clients the right to leave, and denying clients the right to communicate freely with others. Gay had also raised issues concerning the lack of training of many staff, and had questioned whether they even met the most basic licensing requirements, such as having passed a medical exam and a criminal record check.

And then there was the upcoming *Oprah* show.

The more Gay thought about it, the more unhappy she was with the thought of another glowing report on Montreux being shown on TV. It was not only that it seemed the height of irony for such a show to be broadcast within days of a licensing investigation being started. She also knew from past experience that flattering testimonial programs inevitably brought a rush of new clients, many of them critically ill and looking to Montreux as their last possible hope. The last thing the clinic needed at that moment, she reasoned, was the increase in stress that such clients brought.

Gay phoned *The Oprah Winfrey Show* and was connected to one of the producers. She told them she worked at the Montreux clinic and that it might not be the best time to run the Montreux piece. The clinic, she said, "had some things to work out," mentioning the licensing probe.

Gay, however, had no idea of the closeness of the relationship that had developed between Claude-Pierre and the crew at *Oprah*. Almost as soon as she'd hung up, they were on the phone to Claude-Pierre warning her of the disloyalty of one of her staff members. The show's staff did check with the licensing officials, but their investigation wasn't nearly advanced enough for them to be able to confirm whether Montreux had any problems.

Immediately on their return to Victoria, Claude-Pierre and Harris called Gay into the main office at the Rockland mansion. There, they confronted her with making the calls both to licensing and to *Oprah*.

"You know what your mistake was?" asked Harris. "Phoning Oprah. Oprah is our friend. She didn't protect your identity."

They asked Gay to write down answers to questions dealing with how she felt about Montreux, but Gay refused. Instead, she tried to bring up some of the concerns that she'd had about the clinic, and especially about the way Lena had been treated. She told them she honestly believed they weren't aware of some of the things that had been going on recently, especially as Claude-Pierre had been devoting long hours to writing her book and so was much less involved in direct patient care than usual.

However, Gay later said that she soon realized they weren't interested in hearing any criticisms of their clinic. They blamed Lena's treatment on the way she'd behaved and her unwillingness to follow their program. All of Lena's money was gone, they noted, and they'd only been keeping her there out of kindness.

"Don't you understand, Gay?" Harris finally said in exasperation, "She's a psycho."

Even if that were true, Gay retorted, one would think that should make it more essential that she see a psychiatrist, not less so. They wouldn't agree.

Although the official complaint about her was the call to the *Oprah* show, it seemed to Gay that Claude-Pierre and Harris were actually much more worried about her call to licensing officials.

"Don't you know the damage you have caused?" yelled Harris, who was clearly worried that they'd be shut down because of the complaint.

Gay told them she didn't think that would happen, but that she did think some changes needed to be made. However, it soon became apparent to both sides that no agreement was possible. Claude-Pierre and Harris told Gay what she'd expected from the moment the interview began: she was fired.

That weekend, Martha arrived by plane from England, and the next day Lena went home. Before she went, Montreux management insisted that she and Martha both sign what looked like a formal legal document that had been typed on Montreux letterhead.

Entitled "Release," it required Lena to acknowledge that "I am leaving the Montreux Counselling Centre's Specialized Residential Program without their approval and of my own insistence and free will. I understand that, according to Montreux's standards, I have not completed vital aspects of the program. I hereby release Montreux Counselling Centre Ltd. and/or its employees of any responsibility for my well-being."

In another paragraph, it read: "I acknowledge that Montreux has made every attempt within the scope of its abilities—including calling in many other medical professionals—in order to assist with a solution to this problem.... Furthermore, I believe that everyone involved acted in my best interest at all times."

After Lena and Martha signed, Harris and Noah Dobson signed for Montreux. Only then did Martha and Lena leave to board the plane to take them back to Britain. Lena's weight had dropped to 70 pounds, a loss of 13 pounds in six weeks. She weighed only five pounds more than she had when she came to Montreux 18 months before.

On Monday morning, a discouraged Gay returned to the licensing office. She wanted to tell Dunphy and Macdonald about the meeting that had led to her firing. She'd been thinking all weekend about her experiences at Montreux, and she wanted to tell them about all sorts of other problems that she suspected were lurking beneath the surface. Most of all, she wanted them to reassure her that Lena had in fact left the clinic and was back with her family, who'd try to get her the help she needed.

They were able to assure her on that score, but other than that, it was a frustrating meeting for all concerned. Dunphy wasn't happy that Gay had phoned the *Oprah* show. He wasn't sure how many hints she might have dropped about the parts of the clinic program that were under investigation, or how much of that information might have been passed on to Claude-Pierre and Harris. If Montreux management knew too many of the details of the probe, he was afraid they might be able to hamper the investigation by figuring out the "correct" answers to licensing's questions, or even shredding incriminating documents. He'd seen it happen in other investigations.

As for the other problems that Gay wanted to talk about, there were many of them, ranging from major to minor. Some weren't things that she'd seen herself, but only stories that patients or other workers had told her. Gay told story after story while Macdonald desperately tried to take notes and keep them in some kind of logical order.

Just hours later, the *Oprah* show ran as scheduled. Oprah again lauded Claude-Pierre's compassion and her ability to cure anorexics the rest of the world had given up on. Carmen, Jeannie, and others offered their heartfelt testimonials. Although Claude-Pierre didn't herself tout a 100 per cent success rate, Carmen had no doubts. "I think I'm going to get my life back," she told viewers. "I have a chance to go to a place where no one has ever failed."[32]

As the statement was being broadcast, Lena was on her way home. In fact, Lena was not the first patient whom Montreux had discharged as being too difficult for their staff to handle. Only a few weeks earlier, Claude-Pierre and Harris had accepted Clinton-Baker's advice and discharged an American woman named Sylvia.* The concerns about Sylvia were not about her health but rather the safety of staff assigned to work with her. Unlike most eating-disorder sufferers, Sylvia was not compliant or passive, turning all her anger inward. Instead, she attacked staff when she was unhappy with the program. After the attacks had escalated to serious physical violence on several occasions, Clinton-Baker had recommended she be discharged.

However, the *Oprah* show did not mention Lena or Sylvia or the licensing investigation. Claude-Pierre did not contradict Carmen's description. Not a shadow of doubt or concern was displayed on the program.

But that didn't deter licensing investigators. If anything, they became more convinced there were questions that needed to be asked: questions about the feeding methods being used, about mail and phone calls being censored, and about the qualifications of staff.

Macdonald and Dunphy began the painstaking process of collecting files and documentation from Montreux to try to determine the truth about the clinic's operations. The clinic gave them a file detailing much of Lena's stay as well as a variety of staff records and medical records. Reading Lena's files made it clear that the force-feeding that Gay had described was not an isolated incident. Macdonald quickly found at least three occasions in which careworkers had actually written in their daily reports of having to use the "spoon technique" in a desperate effort to get Lena to take some nutrition.

It also didn't take them long to realize that Montreux was having trouble meeting even some of the most basic requirements demanded by the regulations. Most staff didn't have the necessary medical certificates or results of tuberculosis tests on file, and some hadn't had their criminal record checks completed. These were considered relatively minor problems, though, as long as a facility promised to speedily remedy the matter. Indeed, Montreux had quickly produced written policies covering all such matters and promised a speedy follow-up in cases where the policies apparently hadn't been followed.

It was time, Dunphy and Macdonald decided, to interview other Montreux staff members, especially those who had worked with Lena, to ask them how they understood the clinic system to work and especially what rights they believed their patients had. None of the six staff they interviewed said they had personally felt uncomfortable about any part of the program, but they agreed that all mail—both incoming and outgoing—for all residents was screened by staff specifically assigned to the task. Incoming mail, the staff members explained, could be "negative" for the client if they were allowed to read it, and outgoing mail could be upsetting to parents or family if it had been written by a patient who was "in a bad head space." Phone calls were also restricted entirely if a patient was "not in a good head space."

Most of the staff they interviewed also readily admitted that they had sometimes used physical force to prevent residents from leaving. They talked of grabbing clients, of blocking a doorway physically, and of holding them in a bear hug. Most clients, the staff members reported, usually said they wanted to leave when they'd only been in the program a short while. However, the staff said, they knew it was really "the anorexia talking," and not the client, and so, normally, either they themselves, or a more senior staff member, were able to persuade the patient that they didn't truly want to go.

"What would you do," Dunphy asked each staff member, "if a client wanted to phone to get help to leave Montreux?"

Most said they'd talk to the client to persuade them not to make the call and get a more senior person to help in the conversation. But one added that "if the client persisted, [staff] would block the phone." Situations had occurred where clients were "pushed down" in similar circumstances, the staff person added.

A client writing a letter asking to leave wasn't a problem, they noted, because of their policy to screen all outgoing letters. Such letters would simply never be mailed. As for getting stubborn clients to eat, the staff all agreed that the main methods used were encouragement, persuasion, and support. If a client was having a particularly tough time, they said they might "assist" the client by bringing the spoon or bottle right up to their mouths and, if necessary, into their mouths, then encouraging the client to swallow.

When they'd finished interviewing the staff, Macdonald and Dunphy asked Noah Dobson, by now the official manager of Montreux, the same questions. Dobson explained the censoring of mail and phone calls exactly the same way the staff members had. He was more cautious about clients who wanted to leave, saying this should be dealt with by verbal persuasion unless the client was doing something that posed an immediate threat to safety, such as running into traffic. But he went even further than the staff in outlining the steps that might be taken to get clients to eat. A staff member may have to hold them in a bear hug and talk to them, or else eventually "they become exhausted," he said.

These were not the answers that Macdonald and Dunphy wanted to hear. Such procedures were clearly not acceptable in a licensed facility. The mental health laws in British Columbia were very clear on these issues: mentally ill persons could be held in a treatment facility against their will only if they had been formally committed to the facility by two doctors. The doctors had to agree that a committed person was posing an immediate risk of harm, either to him or herself, or to other people.

None of the Montreux patients had been so committed. It was unlikely most would meet the criteria, and in any case, Montreux—unconnected in any way to the rest of the health-care system—was not a facility to which patients could be legally committed.

Macdonald and Dunphy met with Noah and Margaret Dobson the following week to explain this to them. Noah and Margaret agreed the clinic would have to develop a policy so that staff would know what to do in the case of a resident physically trying to leave the building—a system that would ensure the client's immediate safety while making it clear that they would be released as soon as possible.

It was April 2, 1997, when Dunphy and Macdonald sat down with Claude-Pierre and Harris, as well as the Dobsons, to formally review the results of the investigation. The investigators were joined by Lori Frame, who was head of the adult licensing branch. Using their standard procedure, Dunphy and Macdonald explained to the five that they would outline the concerns they had and Montreux would be given an opportunity to respond—either immediately or at a future date, if they wanted more time to consider the issues. After that, the investigators would write up a formal investigation report, with recommendations, which would go to the medical health officer.

The Montreux team appeared fully co-operative. David Harris described the investigation as "a learning opportunity," and said the clinic wouldn't be expanding any further until they had tidied up the operation. They agreed to make all necessary changes to comply with procedures for items like documentation and administering medication. They noted that they'd recently changed their contracts with patients to make specific provision for someone to leave the program within five days of a request to do so. They offered a draft of their new written policy dealing with the physical restraint of patients wanting to leave.

When Macdonald raised the issue about the force-feeding of Lena, the managers were apologetic. It was true, they said, that "some staff had exceeded expectations" in their efforts to get nutrition into Lena. A new policy would be written "with clear limits" as to how far staff could go in trying to get patients to eat. In any case, Harris noted, Lena was "a unique case," and he added that Montreux would not accept another patient like her in the future.

The only outstanding issue was the censorship of residents' mail and phone calls. Montreux management insisted there were "valid therapeutic reasons" for the policy. That might be so, said the licensing investigators, but they still doubted whether it was legal to limit the residents' most basic freedoms, including the freedom to complain to someone impartial if they were unhappy with their treatment. (In the B.C. system, even those convicted of the most heinous crimes are guaranteed the ability to write freely to people like their member of Parliament or the provincial ombudsman.)

Aside from that issue, the investigators were pleased with the way the investigation was going. Like most facilities with which they dealt, Montreux appeared to be willing to co-operate and make the changes necessary to comply with the standards. Licensing staff always preferred to provide education to facilities that were having problems meeting the standards, and to work with them to get them to comply. They didn't like having to play the heavy and adopt a strict enforcement approach, except in the most extreme cases. In their experience, almost all operators wanted to comply and would do the best they could to do so.

But while they were waiting for Montreux to deliver its new policies on feeding methods, on mail censorship, and on physical restraint, they received a phone call that prompted them to begin worrying about the operation all over again. The call was from two more careworkers who'd recently left the clinic's employ and who wanted to come to talk to them. Andrew* and Randi* said they could back up all Gay had told them, and they had other concerns about Montreux as well. On May 15, Dunphy sat down with them to listen to their story.

Andrew and Randi both had degrees in psychology, but neither had much job experience before they began working at Montreux. All the same, they had both become convinced that the reality of life at the clinic didn't match the public image.

Both had worked with Lena and had been uncomfortable doing so.

They were convinced Lena's problems had been more complex than Montreux could handle, but for months, they said, "everyone at Montreux overlooked the situation," and just blamed it on Lena's strong anorexic voice. And both were totally convinced that Lena would never have got to go home if it hadn't been for the licensing office getting involved. Although they couldn't prove it, somehow, they insisted, Montreux had managed to put together that paperwork for Lena from the moment they heard there'd been a complaint.

Randi and Andrew also put a very different spin on the issue of force-feeding, particularly when it came to the most difficult patients like Lena. Far from having "exceeded [Montreux's] expectations," they said, staff who'd been force-feeding Lena had been doing exactly what management demanded. They said they'd been taught by more senior staff how to feed residents, using a bottle, and, if necessary, a spoon, to open the mouth. They'd been told that their job was to make sure the resident took in all the day's prescribed nutrition, even if she was physically fighting against every morsel of it. They'd been told the easiest way was to use two staff: one to hold a resident's arms so they couldn't fight, and a second to spoon or squirt the food into the mouth, and then place a hand over the mouth until the resident would swallow. Just as Lena had described, they said they'd also been told you could put a hand over a resident's mouth to try to prevent them from vomiting up the food.

Many of their other complaints were more general. They were concerned about the competency of many of the staff, including most of those in the senior positions known as "counsellor." A patient's counsellor was, along with the team leader, normally the one who made decisions about all aspects of care, ranging from what outings she should go on to her food plan. But the counsellors, they said, tended to have even less formal training than the ordinary careworkers, most of them being "graduates" of the outpatient program. Randi and Andrew doubted that many, if any, of the counsellors had enough knowledge of nutrition to put together food plans for acutely ill anorexics.

Randi and Andrew were also the first to raise disturbing questions about the true success rate of Montreux. Andrew noted that on the last *Oprah* show, Claude-Pierre had talked about patients needing to stay at the clinic for an average of about eight months. That wasn't their experience, they said. Several of the patients with whom they'd worked had already been at Montreux for more than two years, and didn't seem to be anywhere near ready to return home. Others who had left after a relatively brief stay appeared to relapse and ended up getting readmitted and starting over. Some had relapsed even while they were still receiving counselling from Montreux, and had had to return to one-on-one care. However, the question of the program's success rate was not something that licensing officers were allowed to look at during their investigations. Provided a program met the standards for health and safety, it was up to residents or their families to decide if they were happy with its success rate.

It was also Andrew and Randi who first used the word "cult" to describe Montreux to licensing. "Both feel that Montreux is almost like a cult in atmosphere," Dunphy wrote in his notes of the meeting. They told him that staff were continually told, "It's not a job, it's a lifestyle." The two ex-staff were also worried that the isolation of residents was intensified by the fact that they were not allowed to have any contact with former staff members—even if, like Randi and Andrew, the staff had left of their own volition and in good standing with Montreux management.

Randi recalled a peculiar incident in which staff were talking about an article that had appeared in *Chatelaine* magazine in February, just a few weeks after the *Oprah* program. The article, by Deborah Wilson, recounted many of Montreux's success stories, such as that of Caroline, but also cited some criticism of the clinic, both from professionals and from two former patients.[33] One was Samantha Kendall who'd already been quoted in the British media; the other was Chloe, who, after a couple of years of good therapy, had talked about how she had been held against her will by Claude-Pierre and her staff.

After the article appeared, Randi told Greg that Claude-Pierre had brought out letters which she said were from each of those critical patients, each claiming that they had been made to say bad things about the clinic that weren't true. Randi said she was still unsure just what those ex-residents truly believed.

But, like the success rate issue, the question of the atmosphere at

Montreux was not something that was within licensing's purview.

Randi and Andrew did, however, make some new complaints that were within licensing's jurisdiction and that Dunphy knew needed to be investigated before he and Macdonald could write their report. One was the suggestion that, by keeping another group of equally ill people at the unlicensed St. Charles House, Montreux was far over its licensed capacity of nine residents. The other, far more disturbing, was the story of little Dustin being admitted as a residential patient, kept isolated from his family and often force-fed.

After some discussion, Macdonald and Dunphy decided the best thing to do would be to make an unannounced visit to the clinic, not letting the managers know in advance that they were coming. That, they hoped, would allow them to determine just how many residents were actually living in each mansion.

Macdonald walked through Rockland mansion while Dunphy waited in the lobby. She counted 8 residents, all of them receiving one-on-one care. After that, they walked over to St. Charles where, it became apparent, as many as 15 or 16 Montreux clients were living. However, it was explained to them, many of them were "off-care," living more or less independently and just getting a few counselling sessions a week. And there was, of course, no sign of Dustin.

Within a week, Montreux had sent a letter to the licensing investigators, saying they were sorry they'd been confused about the definition of "providing care," and they'd be happy to license St. Charles House as well, should that be necessary.

By the time of the next formal meeting between Montreux management and licensing, they'd also provided a letter from their lawyer, dealing with the issue of censorship of mail and phone calls. Lawyer Maureen Boyd suggested Montreux could continue the practice, as long as each patient provided an informed written consent for it. "By giving the consent," Boyd wrote, "the patient has waived her privacy interest and has also essentially appointed Montreux an agent for the purposes of written and telephone communication with third parties during the course of treatment."

At the formal meeting, Montreux proudly presented to the investigators a draft of new written policies that would apply to all staff and that dealt with virtually every issue that had been raised. Dunphy was satisfied. It seemed clear to him that Montreux was willing to admit to its mistakes and was acting to resolve them. As long as they kept an eye on the clinic to ensure it was following through on its promises, there would be no more problems, he thought.

He and Macdonald wrote a careful report and presented it to Dr. Richard Stanwick, the regional medical health officer. The report concluded that Montreux had breached more than a dozen sections of the Community Care Facilities Licensing Act and its regulations. However, they recommended no punitive action be taken since the clinic had agreed to tighten up its procedures and policies to avoid any repeat contraventions.

On the basis of the material presented, Dr. Stanwick could see no reason to disagree with their recommendation. He personally delivered to Montreux a letter confirming both the breaches of the legislation and the willingness of the licensing branch to give them a chance to make a fresh start.

For Montreux, it must have seemed as if they'd dodged a giant bullet.

6

Down from the Pinnacle

There could not have been a time in Montreux's history when it was more important to avoid scandal. Peggy Claude-Pierre's book was scheduled for publication less than two months after Dr. Richard Stanwick granted the clinic its second chance. Publisher Random House had already made its plans for the launch of *The Secret Language of Eating Disorders*. It would include more television appearances in both Canada and the U.S., book reviews in dozens of major markets in North America, and a book tour for Claude-Pierre that would eventually span three continents. Every hardcover copy would bear a sticker on the front jacket, saying "As Seen on ABC's *20/20*." That launch—and the potential huge sales and profits—would have been compromised if Claude-Pierre or Random House had had to spend their time defending a clinic that had been publicly censured by the licensing authorities.

As it was, Dr. Stanwick's letter didn't even cause a ripple to mar the book launch. News of it never emerged even into the Victoria community, let alone further afield. A single reporter from Victoria's daily newspaper, the *Times-Colonist*, had in fact heard some disturbing stories that summer about Montreux's operations. Reporter Deborah Pearce spent several weeks looking into the clinic; she had even advertised in her own newspaper, encouraging persons with information about Montreux to come forward and talk to her. Pearce put together a series of articles, but the newspaper did not print them. The darker side of Montreux remained away from public view.

As the hype around the forthcoming book began to swirl, Gay, Randi, and Andrew grew more depressed. They could not believe that licensing had done nothing but give Montreux a slap on the wrist. They could not believe that the investigators had been persuaded that Dustin had been only a day-patient and had in fact never lived with Louise, never been force-fed, never been separated from his parents for months at a time. They could not believe that the investigators had not been able to find the numerous books of notes that they themselves had written and that they knew would back up every complaint they'd made. They knew that Montreux management had told dozens of lies to the investigators, but they couldn't figure out any way to prove it. As far as they were concerned, the decision was proof of what they'd suspected all along—Victoria was a small city in which Peggy Claude-Pierre and David Harris had a great deal of power. Perhaps they really were untouchable, as they'd always implied to the staff and patients at Montreux.

Gay, in particular, found herself having a difficult time. Suddenly, it seemed impossible for her to get a job in the social services field. Friends told her she was being effectively blacklisted at agencies throughout the city, as a troublemaker or worse.

Friends who still worked at Montreux whispered to her that Claude-Pierre and Harris were telling the staff that she had problems that had made her unsuitable to work at Montreux—problems ranging from possible alcohol or drug abuse to emotional instability—without the slightest evidence to back up any such allegations. She was denied unemployment insurance because, the federal agency ruled, Montreux had been within its rights to fire someone who breached confidentiality by going to *Oprah*. She was surviving by running up her credit cards to pay for the basics of life. It seemed that everything she'd put on the line for Lena and the other patients had come to nothing.

By contrast, Claude-Pierre's star seemed to be rising higher than ever. Just two weeks before the book was due to hit the shelves, she scored another huge hit on *20/20*—and this time, she was associated with royalty.

On August 30, 1997, the world was appalled to learn of the death of Princess Diana in a car crash in Paris. Less than three weeks later, as the mourning continued, Claude-Pierre appeared on *20/20* to discuss what the show described as a secret meeting Claude-Pierre had had with Diana in 1995. In that meeting and in further conversations, she said, she had informally helped the princess to deal with her bulimia.

The six-minute piece was, if anything, even more sympathetic to Claude-Pierre than the first *20/20* piece had been. Barbara Walters began by introducing Claude-Pierre as "a remarkable woman," and Lynn Sherr again talked about her "astonishing and very successful approach."[34]

Claude-Pierre described meeting secretly with Diana at Kensington Palace and waxed eloquent about what a wonderful and sensitive young woman the Princess was, and how badly she'd been treated by the rest of the Royal Family—a view of Diana that every audience was eating up that month. Claude-Pierre said she had deliberately decided to be informal with Diana, wearing jeans to their meeting and avoiding calling her "princess." Diana, she said, had responded especially warmly to this approach, apparently pleased to have someone talk to her for herself and not because of the Royal Family.

The show also gave Claude-Pierre the opportunity to reiterate her own views on the causes and correct treatment of eating disorders, and for *20/20* to show yet again some of the particularly emotional scenes from the earlier shows. Sherr even mentioned that it had been some of those scenes that had particularly attracted Diana and motivated her to try to make a connection with Claude-Pierre. At the very end of the piece, Walters mentioned that Claude-Pierre's book about "her unique therapy" was about to be published.

The *20/20* show was not the only place where Claude-Pierre capitalized on the story of her connection with the much-mourned princess. An article in the *Scottish Sunday Mail*—the newspaper that had tracked Jeannie's story and helped raise funds for her Montreux stay—ran a detailed account based on the *20/20* piece but giving the ABC show much more credit for linking the princess with Claude-Pierre than *20/20* itself had done. According to the *Mail* story, Diana had become fascinated by Claude-Pierre and Montreux after watching one of the earlier *20/20* pieces on a video a friend had sent her. She'd started trying to find a way to contact Claude-Pierre immediately.[35]

She had phoned, pleading for the same sort of help that Jeannie had received, and Claude-Pierre had flown to England within days for their first four-hour meeting. Claude-Pierre said she'd hoped to appear alongside Diana later in 1997 at an eating-disorder fundraiser in New York.

The *Mail* reporter asked Claude-Pierre whether telling the world the details of her obviously private meetings with the princess did not pose a confidentiality problem. She replied that she believed the princess's death had released her from any bonds of confidentiality. In fact, she said, she had decided to go public with the story to honour what she called "Diana's courage to go public and her willingness to be a role model for this dreadful condition."

No publisher could have concocted a better launch for a book. Just days after the *20/20* show, Claude-Pierre was starting on her next round of radio, print, and TV interviews—this time to promote *The Secret Language of Eating Disorders*.

The book broke little new ground for anyone who'd been following Claude-Pierre's appearances on *Povich*, *20/20*, and *Oprah*. In it, she outlined again her daughters' history with eating disorders, gave a detailed description of what she now formally named Confirmed Negativity Condition and the Negative Mind, and talked about the need to treat patients with "unconditional love and kindness" and counter every negative thought with a positive one. The theories were amply illustrated with examples and case histories of patients she'd treated and many others who had written her heart-rending letters, even though they had never actually gained admission to Montreux.

One whole chapter dealt with what Claude-Pierre called "Myths and Misconceptions."[36] In it, she tried to dispel not only some unquestionably wrong "old wives' tales," but also some of the mainstream theories on eating disorders, even those backed up by solid scientific evidence. She rejected the idea that anorexics are "selfish...doing it to get back at others," but also completely downplayed any connection between eating disorders and societal or media pressures on girls and young women to be thin or to value their appearance above all else. She rejected the idea that family problems were a factor in the development of eating disorders, except in a few extreme cases. Patients sometimes describe their families as dysfunctional, she said, but that was more likely to be the result of the patient's misperception than any genuine problem in the family.

She downplayed the role of abuse, particularly sexual abuse, in triggering eating disorders. Many scientific studies have in fact shown a higher rate of sexual abuse among eating-disorder sufferers than among the general population. Claude-Pierre agreed that sexual abuse was an "underlying issue" for any victim, but then wrote: "I question whether these issues are directly related to anorexia."[37] Those sexual abuse victims that she had worked with, she said, did not appear to see the abuse as trauma in the same way the rest of the world did. Rather, they felt they'd deserved it, and "were primarily relieved that it had not occurred to someone else." Many counsellors who work with sexual abuse victims say that's not an uncommon attitude among victims, but it is usually an issue that needs to be worked through.

The one time Claude-Pierre ever talked publicly about her own background, that was the attitude she took towards her own abuse. She said she'd been abused at a Catholic girls' school she'd attended, but had constantly been glad that she was the victim rather than someone else; "it was wonderful" that at least she'd prevented someone else from being victimized.[38]

One of the most remarkable "myths" that she said she was trying to dispel was that "anorexia can't be cured; it can only be managed. You'll live with it and die from it."[39] What she did not say was where anyone might have heard such a myth during the late 1990s. In fact, by 1997, virtually no mainstream expert anywhere in the world was suggesting that anorexia was incurable for the vast majority of sufferers; they did say that that in a small proportion of victims, anorexia became a chronic disease, resistant to the best treatments that could be provided. The implication in Claude-Pierre's book was that her methods would in fact cure every case, no matter how severe.

Not surprisingly, many of these comments by Claude-Pierre caused the book to receive short shrift from most professionals in the field. Among the most scathing reviews was that of Dr. Michael Strober, head of the eating disorder program at UCLA. Dr. Strober had long been a passionate advocate for better treatment for eating-disorder sufferers and had stressed the mental torment that victims go through. He had written of an anorexic's extreme sensitivity, of her unwillingness to be a burden on her family, and of her "profound despair and self-loathing"—words that would not have seemed out of place in Claude-Pierre's book.

But Strober condemned Claude-Pierre's suggestions that her theories were in any way new or "revolutionary." The concept she had named "confirmed negativity" had in fact been put forward more than two decades earlier by Hilde Bruch, and with much greater complexity and sensitivity, he said. Worse, however, he argued, was Claude-Pierre's "bold assertion" that her methods would in fact be sure to cure those who were lucky enough to gain admission to Montreux.

"This hope-inspired truly revelatory promise is patently false," wrote Dr. Strober in his review. He stated that he personally knew three patients who had sought further treatment after lengthy stays at Montreux because they remained unwell, and he had heard from his colleagues of other patients who had also found themselves in trouble despite their treatment with Claude-Pierre. "Whatever the virtues of Montreux ... they are invalidated by Miss Claude-Pierre's actions, however well-intentioned her motives may be. The sweeping promise of 'cure' in the absence of a speck of data substantiating the validity of such a promise betrays a potentially dangerous, misguided naïveté that is deserving of the harshest and most unforgiving of criticisms."[40]

Other experts raised similar issues, albeit with somewhat less harsh wording. Among those who worked with anorexics and bulimics, many were concerned by Claude-Pierre's implied promise that she and she alone could offer a cure for every sufferer, still in the absence of any objective evidence to back up her statements. "Ms. Claude-Pierre gives the impression that other available expert treatments are inevitably ineffective," wrote Dr. Blake Woodside of the Toronto General Hospital's eating-disorder program. "This is both untrue and dangerous."[41]

Dr. Joel Yager, of the University of New Mexico eating-disorders program, wrote that Claude-Pierre owed a proper outcome study "to the many thousands of patients and families who've come to invest her center with their fantasies that her program represents some sort of court of last resort." He echoed Dr. Strober's findings that "professionals at many treatment programs in the U.S. and Canada have now seen numbers of patients who have simply not done well in this treatment program or who have had significant relapses shortly after discharge."

He noted that Claude-Pierre "in her public pronouncements has not addressed these issues, so that she leaves the uninformed, either inadvertently or intentionally, with the impression that everyone gets better and stays better. The fact is that they don't. And the fact that the author has been less than forthcoming about these matters is troublesome."[42]

Although some women's studies professors had embraced Claude-Pierre's ideas, other experts who approached eating disorders from a feminist perspective were equally offended by Claude-Pierre's downplaying of sexual abuse and cultural pressures as factors to be considered in dealing with anorexics. If you followed Claude-Pierre's reasoning, wrote Toronto psychotherapist and author Karin Jasper, every sexual abuse victim who did, in fact, have problems dealing with the abuse would be blamed for those problems, rather than the abuser.

Jasper did, however, recognize that the concerns of experts were unlikely to dim Claude-Pierre's star in the eye of the public or the mainstream media. "Its seductive appeal," she notes, "arises from a powerful myth into which the author taps: we have an evil demon, a hapless victim of especially fine character, and a tireless heroine who works wonders with love. Anorexics are extraordinarily caring people who come from extremely loving families. They are caught in the grip of a condition to which they have fallen victim. Enter Claude-Pierre who promises deliverance, then wrestles down the vicious condition while simultaneously feeding them hugs, kisses, and loving words."

"Prepare to hear more about Montreux Centre miracles," she concluded caustically.

She was right. Very few of the experts' doubts and concerns ever made it into the pages of the popular press. There, anorexics or their families who read reviews would again be led to the conclusion that Montreux was a place that performed miracles and saved the lives of those whom no one else had been able to help.

The book was reviewed in prestigious periodicals such as *The New York Times* and *Newsweek*, as well as in numerous local and regional newspapers across Canada, the U.S., and Britain. It spawned a spate of new media visits to the clinic and articles looking at Claude-Pierre's program in more general terms.

Most of the prestigious reviews did note the lack of formal studies to back up Claude-Pierre's claims about the success rates. Several did quote a variety of the experts pointing out that her treatment remained "unproven." But most of them also quoted Claude-Pierre's emotional stories about her own daughters, and cited the testimonials of patients convinced that no other place on earth could have saved their lives.

One of the most positive pieces of publicity came from *Cosmopolitan*, which ran a lengthy testimonial from one of Claude-Pierre's earliest outpatients, Marisa, and what amounted to an excerpt from the book, with no opposing viewpoint whatsoever.[43] Three months later, *Cosmo*—a magazine that describes itself as targeted towards "today's trendy, fun-loving young women," the demographic group most vulnerable to eating disorders—named Claude-Pierre one of its "11 Fun, Fearless Forces" for the year: "Eleven super-inspiring successes who made major headway and headlines."[44] The piece on Claude-Pierre described Montreux as having "extraordinary results—90 per cent of those who complete it recover fully," yet again with not a shred of evidence to back up that statistic. And it included another plug for the book.

Claude-Pierre appeared on the *Montel Williams* talk show in a program that promoted the book more shamelessly than most advertising companies ever would. At the very beginning of the show, Williams told the audience: "If you are at home and you know of a family member who is suffering from an eating disorder, you need to go out and buy this book today. This book will save their life."[45] The show featured testimonials by three of Montreux's patients at the time, including Candace,* a 16-year-old seeing her mother for the first time since she was admitted to the clinic 4½ months earlier.

The only difference in tone between the show and the earlier *20/20* and *Oprah* shows was that Williams implied that it was no longer necessary to be one of the few chosen to actually attend Montreux to receive Claude-Pierre's miracle cure. Every anorexic could now have the same thing, just by having their family, friends, and doctor read the book, and start treating them with unconditional love.

The book also attracted rave reviews from some eating-disorder sufferers, especially on Internet newsgroups and forums which many sufferers read daily. They found that Claude-Pierre's description of the Negative Mind and the awful voices in their heads spoke more truly of their experience than virtually any other book about eating disorders that they'd read.

One 15-year-old sufferer wrote: "Thank you Peggy. You are truly an angel on earth. Your book just might be my tiny light at the end of the tunnel."

Another anorexic, 19 years old, said: "I can honestly say that until I read *The Secret Language of Eating Disorders* I believed I was going to die … Peggy put into words all of my thoughts, feelings, and fears. I have had anorexia/bulimia for 10 years. Thank you Peggy, you have saved my life."

The mother of a child who'd been desperately ill with anorexia described the book as "the most well-written, informative, accurate, and hopeful account of eating disorders available.… The warmth, love, confidence, understanding of this 'angel' of a woman reaches from her pages and envelops the reader. She offers magnificent comfort and support to sufferers and loved ones."

Faced with such testimonials, the few professionals who tried to submit warnings about the lack of proof or scientific reliability in the book received little support. Sufferers and families wrote back to say it was clear from the stories that Montreux's methods worked, and who should need more proof than that? It proved yet again the common fallacy in the public's thinking about medical and psychological issues—that a single emotional anecdote is valued more than a host of scientifically valid and reliable studies. "The problem is that there is nothing more vivid or compelling than sincere personal testimony that something … is true," wrote University of Toronto psychology professor Keith Stanovich.[46] "The vividness of personal testimony often overshadows other information of much higher reliability … a single well-chosen anecdote is worth a thousand statistics in the public mind."

The anecdotes and testimonials provided by Claude-Pierre were seen as even more believable because sufferers and their families so badly wanted them to be true. They wanted to believe there was a "magic bullet" that would cure their, or their child's or loved one's eating disorder, with no risk of relapse or possibility of failure. The sufferers and families who were reading Claude-Pierre's book were buoyed by the sense of hope and optimism the book conveyed.

Soon after the publication, Claude-Pierre began talking about establishing a second clinic, one she would use for training doctors and other health professionals in her methods. The book was soon sold in 20 countries and being translated into more than a dozen languages. Claude-Pierre and the clinic were riding high.

And then the roof fell in. Samantha Kendall died at her home in Britain.

It was enough to make the cauldron of emotions and frustrations that had been simmering among the disenchanted former staff members and patients boil over.

Unable to cope with their feelings of anger and guilt, Andrew, Randi, and some other former workers had already been talking to Lynn Parten, a qualified counsellor in Victoria who specialized in working with eating-disorder victims and was closely associated with the mainstream eating-disorder clinic in town. She had long been suspicious of the claims made on behalf of Montreux, but even she was surprised by some of the stories she heard from Gavin about Dustin's care and treatment, and from Andrew and some of the others. She began asking each of them if she could videotape an interview in which she'd ask them about what they'd found while working at Montreux and their feelings about it. At that point neither she nor the former staff were quite sure what use might be made of the tapes. They all just sensed it would be important to have some kind of record in tangible form.

Then came word of Samantha's death in Britain. She had died of an overdose of over-the-counter painkillers to which she was allergic. At the time of her death, she was just as anorexic, and in just as much mental turmoil, as when she'd first come to Montreux 3½ years earlier. She had actually gone public in Britain two years earlier, wanting to let the world know that Montreux had not worked any miracle cure for her. She knew then that she was relapsing. "I thought I had beaten anorexia, but now it'll probably kill me," ran the sad headline in the *Daily Mail* in 1995.[47]

She had originally told Claude-Pierre she wanted to return to Britain only for a holiday. But once she got away, she had refused to go back to Montreux. Although she had believed the clinic was working for her, once she had progressed enough to be shifted from 24-hour to partial care, she had started skipping meals and taking laxatives. After more than a year at the clinic, her concerns about body image had not diminished. Even as her weight was dropping down to 85 pounds back in Britain, she was saying she'd like to be "thin again."

She found herself confused about the atmosphere of "unconditional love" at Montreux. It had been much more pleasant than the reward-and-punishment schemes she'd experienced in British hospitals previously, and, like so many of Claude-Pierre's patients, she was at first overwhelmed with Peggy's charisma. "She only had to put her arms around you, and you felt like she was an angel," Samantha remembered.

As the months wore on, however, she'd become less trusting and more suspicious of the brand of "love" offered by the clinic, not to mention the promises they were making her. She said Claude-Pierre had promised her a high-paying job at the clinic and her own car once she was finished her treatment, but she wasn't sure it would ever come. She could never be certain, she said, whether the promises were made out of true generosity or out of a sense of obligation because the media attention she'd garnered had been so good for the clinic.

She was upset when Claude-Pierre kept insisting to her, "We're your family now." She never believed that, and never wanted to give up her ties to her mother and stepfather, or to the British Midlands where her roots were—and where Michaela was buried. Even her mother had trouble understanding her homesickness for the most simple, everyday things in Britain. Why, she wondered, would Sam miss the local shops and malls, when she was surrounded by the mountains and beaches of Canada's west coast?

But Sam was homesick, and it all combined to convince her that she never wanted to go back to Canada. Her mother reluctantly accepted her decision, even when Claude-Pierre phoned to warn her that Samantha would probably die if she did not return to Montreux. Sam and her mother both hoped that effective treatment could be found for her in Britain, with Sam in particular pinning her hopes on hypnotherapy.

It didn't work. Over the next two years, she spent time in hospitals, in both medical and psychiatric wards, though still not in the top eating-disorder units. She became paranoid, convinced that everyone in the hospital, and sometimes even friends and family members, wanted either to kill her or to use her to star in pornographic movies. Eventually her mother and stepfather brought her home. Within days, she told them that Michaela had appeared to her in a dream and said it was time for them to be reunited. She'd been home only three weeks when she took the overdose of paracetamol. She weighed less than 65 pounds at the time of her death.

News of her death hit the many Montreux staff members who'd worked with her hard. Sam might have been manipulative and difficult on occasion, but she'd also been bright, lively, and funny. They felt they'd lost a friend. For many, still in their late teens or early twenties, it was the first death of someone to whom they'd felt close.

In addition, though, some had lost something far more valuable to them—they'd lost, for good, their faith in Claude-Pierre and the clinic. For months, they'd been trying to convince themselves that the unorthodox clinic methods, even those they'd watched or participated in, were justified. They were justified because the clinic was succeeding with patients that had failed everywhere else, because it was worth it to save the patients' lives.

Now that justification had disappeared. If the clinic's most famous patient could die, then it was clear that Montreux did not have a 100 per cent success rate, that it could offer no more guarantees than anywhere else. Looking back on it, they realized that Sam had stopped making progress long before she'd returned to Britain. They knew she'd started cheating on the program as soon as she'd had even a few hours a day on her own. Claude-Pierre might be saying that the problem was that Samantha had left before she was officially cured, but they knew that the Montreux program hadn't been helping her even during her last days in Victoria.

Gay, Randi, Andrew, Gavin, and other former careworkers talked to each other. They talked to Parten. They talked to friends they had in the media, friends they had in government. Other disillusioned staff members joined them, as did a few disillusioned patients who still lived in Victoria. They shared stories with those who were still working at the clinic. Together they realized that Claude-Pierre and Harris were doing little to live up to the terms of Dr. Stanwick's letter. On paper, the clinic had written new policies and procedures to deal with issues like force-feeding, but in practice little had changed. They realized as well that, among them, they could perhaps lead the licensing investigators to the evidence needed to take more definitive action against the clinic. It was, they concluded, time to go public.

This time, with the help of Parten and other friends, they would do it in a more organized manner. It was Parten who approached Dr. Stanwick and Steven Eng, the head of licensing for the region. Parten had no personal axe to grind. She could approach as a fellow professional. She explained the help she'd been providing the discouraged and overwhelmed former staff members, and how she had ended up making the videotapes. She personally had become convinced, she said, that Montreux was harbouring more serious problems than those that had been unearthed during the first investigation. From some of the stories she'd heard, she thought it might even be considered criminal activity. She asked Eng and Dr. Stanwick if they'd be willing to watch the videotapes and then decide what licensing should do (even though not all those who'd been taped had been made aware that was the use that was going to be made of them).

Neither Dr. Stanwick nor Eng was entirely surprised to receive Parten's call. Eng and the licensing division hadn't been happy with Montreux's response to the July letter. It hadn't been anything specific they could put their finger on, but Montreux had seemed to be dragging its feet on implementing many of the promised changes, even simple ones like minor physical improvements to the mansion. They agreed to watch the videotapes.

Dr. Stanwick watched for less than 15 minutes. That was all it took to persuade him that a full investigation was warranted. He knew that, depending on the results of that investigation, he could be the person who ended up conducting a hearing into the allegations against Montreux and eventually deciding its fate. That meant that he should learn as little as possible of the evidence as it developed. He asked Eng to watch the rest of the tapes and begin planning the investigation.

At the same time, the former staff members did something they'd been nervous of doing before. They took their story to a reporter.

I had written no stories about Montreux for almost three years at that point. I had been only vaguely aware of the clinic's rise to international prominence and of Claude-Pierre's appearance on shows like *Oprah*.

And so I was taken aback when, on the morning that news of Samantha's death appeared in the B.C. newspapers, I received a phone call from a friend of Gay's, a retired police detective whom I knew from various crime and court stories over the past years. "There's more to this than meets the eye," he told me. "I've been talking a lot to some people who used to work there. This is something you should look into."

I trusted his judgment. We met for coffee that same day. As a detective, he understood well the need for evidence to back up any allegations that might be made in public. He agreed to arrange for me to talk firsthand to Gay and Andrew. He told me about the first investigation, the report of which was available under provincial freedom-of-information laws. And he reminded me of the investigative reporter's motto, known to everyone who followed the story of Watergate or watched Robert Redford and Dustin Hoffman in *All the President's Men*: follow the money. In the case of Montreux, he suggested, that would mean tracing the records of the non-profit Montreux Society as well as the profit-making Montreux Counselling Centres Ltd.

Monday morning found me at the government offices that house the records of legally incorporated companies and societies in B.C. The files yielded a treasure trove of information. The non-profit Montreux Society, it turned out, had been established back in January 1994 when money was needed to pay for the care of Caroline, and, later, Samantha and others. Claude-Pierre and Harris had signed the first form saying a society should be set up, and the official address of the society was the Rockland mansion. However, Claude-Pierre and Harris had never themselves been directors. The three persons listed as directors were a Victoria city police sergeant, a retired senior manager in B.C.'s social services ministry, and the management consultant, Lori Winstanley. Shortly thereafter the society obtained a charitable tax number from Canada's federal income tax department—the key step in allowing donations to be tax-deductible.

The society's name and address appeared prominently in the British media as they collected donations for Samantha later in 1994, and it was officially the first holder of the clinic's licence. According to the British media, it had been a successful fundraising vehicle; stories there said £66,000 ($135,000) had been donated for Kendall alone. But after filing its original incorporation documents, it had never filed another piece of paper with the Societies Act office. That put it in breach of B.C. legislation, which requires all non-profit societies to at least file annual reports, including financial statements and a list of directors.

When the Montreux Society hadn't filed an annual report for 1995, 1996, or 1997, the Societies Act office wrote the directors a letter in June 1997. If the paperwork wasn't brought up to date, they were warned, it would be removed from the registry of recognized societies. No one responded to that letter either, and on September 5, 1997, the Montreux Society for Eating Disorders was officially "dissolved... for failure to file."

Yet two months later, Montreux's electronic voice mail system was still telling callers to "please make donations cheques payable to the Montreux Society," and promising the donations were eligible for tax deductions in both Canada and the U.S. An investigator at Revenue Canada told me they couldn't comment on specific cases, but their policy was clear: it would be next to impossible for an organization to retain its charitable status if it had been delisted as a non-profit society. Neither could a society exist for the sole purpose of raising tax-deductible dollars that would then be passed on to a profit-making corporation, such as Montreux Counselling Centres.

At the same time, Gay and Andrew were prepared to repeat to me, for publication, the same stories they'd told the licensing investigators. They described Montreux's acute-care patients as living practically "under house arrest," and described details of the censorship of mail and phone calls. They also confirmed that force-feeding was not a singular error, as had been implied in the first investigation, but a regular event in the case of those obdurate patients who just couldn't be persuaded to eat any other way.

"Force-feeding was a completely acceptable, okay option," Andrew told me.

The first investigation report also yielded enough details to paint a picture of a clinic that was certainly not always the model of unconditional love, caring, and happiness that had been depicted on *20/20* and *Oprah*.

It was time to ask the various officials what they were planning to do about the allegations. Just asking the question made it clear it would not be so easy to satisfy investigators this time around. Not just licensing officers, but also social workers from the provincial child-protection division, would be involved in the probe. So, at least briefly, would the Victoria City Police. All were prepared to say publicly that they were beginning a wide-ranging investigation into Montreux's operations. The police role was to discover whether any actual criminal breaches of the law had taken place. The child-protection workers were involved because it was their duty to ensure the safety of all children under the age of 19 in B.C., even those who had arrived from outside the country and were staying at a private clinic. And the licensing system remained the main method for the government to exercise any control over the operations and standards of a clinic that received no funding from the public health care system.

On November 19, 1997, a front-page story in *The Province*, the newspaper for which I work, revealed the investigations under the headline "Police probing anorexia centre." The stories told by Gay and Andrew were included, along with the peculiar history of the non-profit society. One part of the story not printed at that time was the case of little Dustin, even though Gay, Andrew, and other former staff members all confirmed the story of his care at Montreux without hesitation. Since the first licensing investigation had ruled that complaint unfounded, it seemed better left unsaid until some documentary evidence became available to prove the case for one side or the other.

Even without it, the other side of the Montreux story was fully in the light for the first time. Other newspapers, radio, and television stations across B.C. and across Canada were soon carrying news of the investigations.

Claude-Pierre and Harris were not in Victoria, or even in Canada, when the story broke. They were in the southern U.S., on yet another leg of the tour to promote her book. Two days after the story was first printed, Claude-Pierre issued a written statement in response. In it, she insisted that the allegations "were dealt with in the past to the satisfaction of the licensing authorities," and added, "I believe that our facility and staff are in full compliance with all regulations and all licensing requirements. Montreux is in good standing with the licensing authorities."

She again stressed the clinic's high success rate, noting that "I know, and others know, that there would be many young people who would not be with us today if we had not tried to help." She did not, however, mention the specifics of the allegations—the restrictions placed on the patients, the force-feedings, or the findings of the first investigation report. She dissociated herself entirely from the problems of the non-profit society, describing it as "an independent group which we apply to for funding individual patients."

Within days of the news becoming public, media outlets were flooded with support letters from more than two dozen grateful patients, parents, and staff members. Many described the mental torment that the victims of eating disorders go through, as well as the misery of treatment in mainstream medical or psychiatric facilities. Many were clearly convinced that Montreux had saved their, or their daughters', lives.

"The bottom line is whether or not my daughter will survive," wrote one father. "She has returned to a near-normal existence (save the regular traumas of being 21), and I thank Peggy Claude-Pierre and her dedicated staff for bringing my daughter back to our world."

"What Montreux has blessed me with is a fresh start and the entrance into a future filled with possibilities," wrote a former patient. "May the world be blessed with more places like Montreux and may humanity prevail as a result."

Esther,* another former patient, who at the time had been discharged just four months, wrote: "Thanks to Montreux I have been blessed with the joy of living, and truly admire and believe in Peggy Claude-Pierre's insight and her principles that form the foundations of the healing process ... Montreux was the very last hope for my survival when I arrived there."

Even as the support letters were pouring in, the investigators were determining how to approach this massive project. They immediately realized it was going to be a much larger and more complex job than the normal investigations they undertook. Normal investigations did not involve allegations that an establishment's management had deliberately and repeatedly lied to officials in previous probes. Normal investigations did not include the medical and legal complexities involved in the treatment of acutely ill patients who had had such restrictions placed on their freedom. Most of all, normal investigations did not involve establishments that had produced dozens of support letters before the questioning had even started, that starred on top U.S. television shows, or that claimed to be associated with Princess Diana.

That, Dr. Stanwick told his staff, was all the more reason why the investigation should be run as normally as possible. Internationally acclaimed centres should not be dealt with any differently than the mom-and-pop daycare operation down the street. The health-and-safety standards applied to every facility in B.C. The question asked in every investigation was whether those standards had been met, and, if not, what changes needed to be made to ensure the clients' health and safety—with the ultimate sanction being closure of a facility altogether. Exactly the same questions would be asked in the Montreux probe.

However, the legal and medical complexities did demand extra consideration. Although Dr. Stanwick could not be directly involved in the investigation, he did agree with Eng that extra resources would be needed to tackle the large and complex task. The provincial ministry of children and families, responsible for child protection, agreed that one of its social workers would remain on the team for as long as necessary, paying special attention to issues surrounding the treatment of children and younger adolescents. The provincial attorney general's ministry was also persuaded to lend an investigator to the team, Gerry Stearns, who brought with her a rare and valuable combination of experiences. She had served for seven years as an RCMP officer, gaining valuable investigative experience, before returning to university to earn her doctorate in psychology. To cover the medical issues, Dr. Stanwick assigned his deputy, Dr. Linda Poffenroth, to provide whatever backup the team needed. Eng, the most experienced investigator in the licensing office, would head the investigation. He would be backed by Macdonald, who already knew the file from the first inquiry and who was the most knowledgeable staff member on questions of nutrition and eating disorders.

The police soon dropped out of the inquiry. They said they could find no evidence of criminal activity. Although the force-feeding and restraint of patients might be technical assaults, it would be hard to attribute a guilty mind to staff members or management who were convinced they were doing it to save someone's life. The detectives concluded it was an issue better pursued through the licensing process or even civil lawsuits launched by former patients or their families.

The licensing investigation, though, just kept on growing. Over the next months, the team would interview almost two dozen complainants, including many whose identity would always be kept confidential. The investigators would also talk to dozens of other staff members, ranging from careworkers to middle managers.

But more than anything else, they read files, cardboard box after cardboard box of files, detailing not only all of Montreux's medical records, guidelines, and food plans for every patient, but every day of every patient's life. The legislation required that licensing investigators have free access to all files, and the team worked out a system with Montreux's lawyers under which they could copy what they needed without taking the originals. The investigators soon realized that the Montreux staff might not have had much professional training, but they did keep copious records. For each acute-care patient, the careworker provided a detailed report on each eight-hour shift—three reports a day per patient, covering exactly what each patient ate and drank, what they did, how well they slept, how they were feeling physically and emotionally. It was in these files that the team would find the heart of their case. No matter what they were being told, the reports told the stories of cases in which patients had been threatened to try to make them eat, had been force-fed, had been suffering medical problems, had been threatening suicide.

They were plowing through still more boxes one day, when Eng gasped aloud. Written on the box that he'd just picked up was Dustin's name. He checked and found it jammed with handwritten reports on the day-to-day care of Dustin—the very files Montreux management had insisted didn't exist. Fascinated and horrified, he and his team pulled out the files and started to read. It was all there—the history of the move to inpatient treatment, the lengthy separations, his deteriorating behaviour. Only the last few months of records were missing, and even those days were covered by staff summaries of Dustin's stay. The story everyone had told them—Justin, Karim, Nicole, Peggy, David

Harris, Noah, Margaret, and even Dustin's mother—had been a complete fabrication. For the first time, the investigators began to look at the possibility that nothing Montreux management said could be trusted.

Finding Dustin's files was the most dramatic moment in the tedious work of reading thousands of pages of logbook entries, but the data in the files also pointed the team to other areas of major concern. In their interviews, several of the former staff members said one of their biggest worries while working at Montreux was that no one at the centre was adequately trained to deal with the potentially lethal physical problems of the clinic's most acute patients. There was no nurse on regular staff, let alone a doctor. Yet at various times, some of the acute patients' families had already been warned by doctors that their physical condition was so precarious they could be within days of death. Some arrived with nasogastric feeding tubes still in place. Some arrived directly from acute-care hospitals. Still, on arrival, the main careworkers for these patients could be Montreux program "graduates" who had not even completed high school. Plans for refeeding them would usually be developed by Claude-Pierre, who kept a library of popular works on nutrition on her bookshelves. Sometimes she'd be helped by Margaret Dobson or the patient's counsellor. None of them had any specialized training at all.

Montreux did have a working relationship with three general practitioners from Victoria, and one of them was always expected to be on call: but they were not involved in developing food plans or other aspects of treating the eating disorder. Dr. David Clinton-Baker had continued his involvement from the earliest days of the clinic. Dr. Mauro Bertoia had become involved because he was the Dobsons' family doctor, and Dr. Charles Medhurst had been Claude-Pierre's own doctor. All three were ordinary family doctors. None had any special training in eating disorders, or in any of the medical specialties normally associated with eating disorders—internal medicine, psychiatry, or pediatrics.

As the team read the files and realized the fragility of some of the patients, they decided they needed to consult with a medical expert about the physical risks for such acutely ill patients. The expert they chose was Dr. Laird Birmingham. Dr. Birmingham was one of the doctors involved in the government-funded eating-disorder program at St. Paul's Hospital in downtown Vancouver, and he had been Caroline's doctor before she moved to Montreux in early 1994. The St. Paul's program remained the central program for treating eating disorders for the entire province; most adult anorexics ill enough to require inpatient treatment in a specialized eating disorder unit would go there. Dr. Birmingham's specialty was internal medicine, meaning his special expertise included the physical problems and complications likely to develop during the course of anorexia or bulimia—problems ranging from blood chemistry disorders to severe osteoporosis.

It clearly would not be possible for Dr. Birmingham to wade through the piles of boxes and files the team had found, so they decided he should review the files of six patients. He'd be given the information Montreux had had prior to the patients' arrival, the results of their first examinations by one of the Montreux doctors, and the notes describing what happened to them immediately after they came to Victoria. He'd then be asked to assess whether they were put at risk in the Montreux system. The six patients included two who'd been at Montreux for more than 18 months at that point, Anna* and Vivian;* one boy, Joshua;* and three girls who were more recent admissions, Angela,* Sharleen,* and Wilma.*

The report that came back from Dr. Birmingham was even worse than the team had expected. Although the six patients had varied in their degrees of acuity, every one of them, he suggested, had been too ill at the time of their admission to be safely cared for in any program that didn't have medical expertise at hand 24 hours a day. Patients at the same level of severity who were admitted to St. Paul's Hospital were placed on an eating-disorder ward that was staffed at the level of an intensive-care ward, because the risk of disastrous—and potentially fatal—complications was so great.

Further, he noted that in at least four of the cases, Montreux had agreed to accept the patient even though they had no recent medical information by which they, or their doctors, could decide whether it would be safe for the patients to stay in a non-hospital setting. The data sent was often months old and didn't include key pieces of information.

One of the six, Angela, had in fact arrived direct from a hospital in her native Germany, with a nasogastric tube that she'd been using for almost three years still in place.

Things didn't get any better once the patients arrived at the clinic. Montreux's policy stated that all patients would be examined by a doctor within 24 hours of their arrival, and all necessary laboratory tests would be done immediately, but the policy was often not followed by Montreux. Dr. Birmingham explained that acute patients were at risk of developing a potentially fatal condition called "refeeding syndrome" when they began to take nutrition after a long period of being malnourished. In refeeding syndrome, the blood chemistry becomes badly imbalanced, which can lead to major heart problems, and even fatal heart failure. Eating-disorder textbooks warn doctors to ensure the blood chemistry is normal before starting refeeding, and to monitor it through lab testing every other day for the first week or 10 days in extremely acute patients. It's also important to start patients with as few as 800 calories a day, then increase the amount as the patient's body is better able to handle it.

In fact, no doctor saw Anna until she'd been at Montreux for four days, and refeeding had been started at a rate of more than 1,400 calories a day. Vivian was actually suffering heart palpitations and chest pain soon after she was admitted. She was given a supplement to remedy blood chemistry problems, but the lab tests weren't done again for another nine days. Sharleen, one of the two patients who had come with up-to-date medical paperwork, had shown some abnormal blood chemistry results on her pre-admission tests. Her blood wasn't checked again until she'd been at Montreux for 3½ months. The investigative team was stunned. Montreux might not only be breaking the licensing rules, it might actually be putting its patients' lives at risk.

The team's last step before putting together its report for Dr. Stanwick was to interview Peggy Claude-Pierre and Noah and Margaret Dobson. All three insisted they have a lawyer present to monitor the questioning. Eng and Macdonald wanted to know what Montreux's response would be to many of the concerns they had. But most of all, they wanted to know how Montreux management planned to explain away the lies they had told about the treatment of Dustin. The answer proved to be simple: they didn't. They tried to bluff it out until the end. None of them was yet prepared to admit that Dustin been a residential patient or separated from his mother. Claude-Pierre told the inspectors "he was an outpatient... he was allowed to stay to have confidence but that wasn't on an ongoing basis... we said that we couldn't take him as a resident. He was underage."

Margaret and Noah Dobson echoed her comments, although they did agree he'd stayed there during the five weeks Moira had spent in New York in April and May. When the interviews were finished, Eng and Macdonald shook their heads in bemusement.

By the end of July 1998, the team was ready to put together an outline of its key concerns to take to Montreux. The law required that Montreux be allowed to respond to all the allegations before the team wrote up a final report with recommendations to Dr. Stanwick. As the correspondence went back and forth, Montreux began making numerous other changes to its policy manual, just as it had done back in 1997. Management wrote a new policy ensuring that patients who were also serving as careworkers met at least the minimum requirements that licensing requires for staff—medical certificates, criminal record checks, tuberculosis tests. The idea of patients providing care was renamed a "practicum" for the patients involved. The clinic began work on a new admissions policy that would try to ensure that proper medical background information was provided on all new patients. They established an external "monitoring committee" to advise management about issues ranging from patient concerns to physical improvements that needed to be made to the mansion. The committee included a school principal whose daughter had been a Montreux outpatient; the mother of the Lawson twins; and Marg Eastman, a registered nurse who had a family member who had received some outpatient counselling from Claude-Pierre more than a decade earlier.

Even as Montreux was delivering the new documents to the licensing team, the team was finding more and more examples of serious problems in the files they were reading. New complainants were coming forward to talk to them, once they were confident their confidentiality would be protected.

Every story the team read and heard only confirmed what they had all begun to believe. Patients' health and safety could not be guaranteed as long as the clinic stayed open. Montreux management couldn't be trusted—the blatant lies they had recently heard around Dustin's year-long stay proved that. Their recommendation to Dr. Stanwick was unequivocal: as medical health officer, he should take action to cancel Montreux's licence to operate. They handed over to him a cardboard carton, filled not only with their report but with three volumes of documents to back up every point they made. Most of the documents were from Montreux's own files.

It wouldn't, of course, be quite that simple. Even though Montreux and the licensing team had been corresponding for months, the clinic was still entitled its day in court before Dr. Stanwick himself. It could tell its side of the story, either through written submissions or by asking for a full public hearing at which witnesses for both sides could be heard at length.

In the meantime, once Dr. Stanwick had received the report, it was up to him to decide whether the allegations were serious enough for him to take action before a full hearing could be held. He spent days poring over the material the investigative team had supplied.

Finally, on December 1, 1998, he rendered his decision. Montreux would be allowed to stay open with the patients then on site until the full hearing was completed, but it would not, in the meantime, be allowed to take any new patients. For the first time, Claude-Pierre and Harris, saying they were acting on the advice of lawyers, had no comment for the media.

7

The Hearing

Despite Dr. Richard Stanwick's wish that the Montreux file be treated like any other, the Montreux hearing would not be like any other ever held in British Columbia. There was no choice but to do this one on a grand scale. Normally only a few hearings were held each year, and they were most often small-scale, low-key efforts attended only by the people involved, maybe a few supporters of one side or the other, and occasionally a lawyer or two. Most were finished in a day or so; a hearing that lasted a week was a rarity.

The Montreux hearing would be different in so many ways. From the beginning, it was scheduled to last for at least three weeks, and it would pit two of the city's top lawyers against each other. Montreux had changed attorneys in the last months of 1998 and was now being represented by Dennis Murray. Murray had moved up the ranks of Crown counsel, rising to the position of deputy solicitor-general for the provincial government. After returning to private practice, he tackled complex and high-profile cases for both Crown and defence. He played a starring role in one true-crime book when he successfully prosecuted Robert Frisbee in a case that came to be known as "the cruise-ship murder." Frisbee had been the valet-companion to an elderly California widow, Muriel Barnett, whom he accompanied on a luxury cruise to Alaska. Soon after the ship pulled out of its stop in Victoria, Barnett was killed when she was hit repeatedly over the head with a full bottle of liquor. The trial involved a wide international cast, intrigue and mystery surrounding codicils to a will, and a diary of Frisbee's written in shorthand. Well-known Canadian mystery author Bill Deverell was part of Frisbee's defence team and later chronicled the trial in his book

Fatal Cruise. Because of his involvement in that trial, Murray was probably the only lawyer in Victoria who had experience with the sort of international media exposure that would follow the Montreux case. His main expertise, however, was in the field of criminal law, not administrative tribunals.

The name of Guy McDannold, who would run the case for licensing, was more likely to be found in tomes of precedent-setting legal judgments than in popular books. Though not nearly so well known to the public as Murray, he was at least as well respected among his legal colleagues. He was considered one of the top municipal and administrative lawyers in the province, and he regularly travelled throughout B.C. to appear on behalf of local governments in cases ranging from zoning bylaw challenges to complex constitutional questions.

Most of all, the Montreux hearing was going to be different because of the amount of media attention—local, regional, national, and international—it seemed bound to attract. Peggy Claude-Pierre's main international supporters, like *20/20* and *Oprah*, had been leaving the story well alone ever since news of the licensing probe broke. However, as the investigation proceeded, it attracted the attention of other media, including *Dateline*, NBC's equivalent to *20/20*. A crew from *Dateline* had journeyed to Victoria in the spring of 1998, and in July an item on the clinic had been included on one of its well-watched Friday night shows. It had been a fight for the *Dateline* crew right to the moment of airing. Montreux had hired a firm of New York lawyers to try to persuade NBC's lawyers that there was no factual basis—and a great deal of legal liability—attached to many of the allegations the crew had heard. In the end, *Dateline* chose to run none of the allegations about little Dustin, because Montreux continued to insist he'd never been a residential patient. The producers made sure the show also included several former patients and parents saying what miracles the clinic had performed for them. The item did, though, make it clear that serious doubts were arising about Montreux's program.

Internationally known correspondent Bob McKeown interviewed several of the former staff members who'd already talked to licensing and they again told their stories. Dr. Stanwick was careful not to pre-judge the case or to provide any details of the allegations, but he went on camera to confirm that a serious and worrisome investigation was being conducted. For the first time since the clinic started attracting publicity, Peggy Claude-Pierre was not available for an interview with the media. She foisted the job of talking to McKeown off onto Noah Dobson, as clinic manager. Despite his best efforts to convince viewers that the complaints were the result of a small number of dissatisfied staff members and people who didn't understand the anorexic mind, he did not come across either as charismatic or as convincing as Claude-Pierre herself.

Tragically, only six weeks after the *Dateline* show aired, its producer, Bruce Hagan, was killed in a freak boating accident over the Labour Day weekend. However, McKeown let Dr. Stanwick's office know that the show was still interested in the outcome of the investigation. So were both of Canada's national TV networks, especially the CBC, whose Hanna Gartner had aired a piece similar to McKeown's as the investigation was ongoing. At one point, even the U.S-based *Court TV* was considering whether the hearing might be worth following.

Medical health officers rarely retain their own lawyers for licensing hearings. However, Dr. Stanwick could see he was likely going to be required to rule on legal questions almost daily. The lawyers were going to dispute everything from the admissibility of certain pieces of evidence to the propriety of questions asked in cross-examination. The media presence meant there'd be questions about disclosure and the confidentiality of patient records. Dr. Stanwick sought the help of lawyer Paul Pearlman. Like McDannold, Pearlman had not attracted much publicity in the wider community, but he was highly respected by his fellow lawyers. His area of expertise included administrative law, and he often served as a mediator or arbitrator in cases ranging from native land claims to labour relations disputes. Moreover, he knew the intricacies of cases that involved balancing the rights to open coverage of a proceeding with the privacy rights of those involved. He'd acted for a municipal police board in a case in which several police officers had been accused of abusing and sexually harassing a female informant. Pearlman had coped with figuring out the rules governing confidentiality and media access at the board's hearing, as well as with the legal manoeuvrings under the Police Act.

After several meetings among the lawyers, it was agreed the hearing would be open and public, but—as in virtually all courtrooms in Canada—the proceedings would not be allowed to be televised. The television cameras would be welcome to shoot video of the set-up and key players each day, as long as the proceedings actually hadn't started; at that point, the tape would have to be turned off. Those who wanted to talk on camera would have to do so outside the hearing room.

The media flocked to the opening day of the hearings, May 3, 1999. The site that had been found to accommodate the crowd was the Oak Room, the banquet room of the Oak Bay Beach Hotel, an attractive country inn–style hotel on the waterfront in the suburb of Oak Bay just east of downtown Victoria. The Oak Bay Beach Hotel was much better known in the region as a place for honeymoons and whale-watching trips than as a conference centre. The owners and staff prided themselves on offering the guests free hot chocolate and cookies before bedtime every night, and it was voted "Best Local Getaway" by the Vancouver Island chapter of the Romance Writers of America. But it could provide all the facilities necessary for the hearing, and was available for the time needed. In fact, on warmer summer days, its acres of gardens sloping down to the ocean proved a popular spot for stress relief for all sides.

When the hearing opened at 9:30 a.m., Dr. Stanwick sat at one end of the room, flanked by Pearlman and a court recorder who would make a transcript of the entire proceedings. At long tables along one wall sat McDannold, backed up by Eng, Macdonald, and Dr. Poffenroth. Opposite him was Murray, alongside his associate who would handle much of the actual questioning, Fiona McQueen. Their support team included both Noah and Margaret Dobson, and David Harris. Spectacularly noticeable in her absence was Claude-Pierre herself. That proved a great disappointment to the many TV journalists, all of whom had been hoping for quotable post-hearing news conferences with her each day. In fact, Claude-Pierre visited the hearing only once before the day she was scheduled to give her own testimony—a quiet Friday afternoon when only the most devoted of the press corps were still in attendance. The others who spoke for Montreux grew tired of explaining that

The Hearing

Claude-Pierre didn't want to "take the attention away" from the rest of the testimony presented at the hearing.

On opening day, I joined a dozen reporters who filled up long tables arranged for them. Behind the press corps were crowded seats for about 50 more spectators. Most days nearly every one was filled with Montreux supporters. Nicole and Kirsten Claude-Pierre attended faithfully most days along with many of the clinic's middle management. The rest of the seats would usually be jammed with parents, staff members, and, often, patients. Some of the patients looked relatively healthy and smiled and chatted in small groups during breaks and at lunch time. Some, such as Carmen and Sheila,* showed a particular interest in the media coverage of the hearing and enjoyed talking to reporters about the reasons for selecting certain pieces of testimony to be included in their stories each day.

Other patients looked so frail it seemed a harsh wind whistling through the gardens from the seafront would be enough to blow them away. Silent and withdrawn, they never seemed to be more than a few feet from their workers for the day. At morning break, some would bring out an apple or a small bag of baby carrots and a water bottle of juice—their snack to ensure they were still eating every 2½ hours. Even with the workers present, the smell of vomit occasionally permeated the women's washroom located just above the hearing room. To many of us it seemed peculiar that Montreux management would allow attendance by patients still so ill they were supposed to be protected even from the negativity found in fictional movies or on the nightly TV news.

The lawyers had agreed that both sides would make their opening statements on the morning of the first day. The differences between their approaches were immediately obvious. Much of the thrust of McDannold's opening was to focus on what the licensing investigation and hearing were not. They were not, he stressed, about anyone's opinion of Claude-Pierre or her theories on the causes of, and best treatment of, eating disorders. They were not about whether a scientific evaluation would show Montreux's success rate to be better or worse than those of other treatment programs. They were not about whether an "alternative" approach to treating anorexia should be compared to a mainstream medical model.

Licensing's focus was required by law to be narrow, he said. Their evidence would look solely at the question of whether Montreux had breached the health and safety standards laid down in the law. Those standards, he said, "are the law in B.C., no matter what the type of program," and "the evidence is overwhelming that Montreux has fallen below those minimum health and safety standards established by the legislature of this province ... in effect, they have put the health and safety of their patients at risk."

In contrast, much of Murray's opening focussed exactly on the topics that McDannold said weren't at issue. He wanted to set the investigative findings in the context of the sort of facility Claude-Pierre and Harris were trying to run. He implied that the case was, underneath it all, a battle between mainstream and alternative medicine, noting that Montreux stresses that it is not a psychiatric or medical or hospital facility, and doesn't want to develop the kind of atmosphere found in one. In illnesses like anorexia, he suggested, "there are varying degrees of invading the dignity of people which are all recognized as necessary and proper adjuncts to helping them." The mainstream medical community thinks nasogastric tube-feeding, for instance, is acceptable in cases of severe anorexia, but Montreux's methods are not. (Witnesses later pointed out that even in the most mainstream hospital, tube-feeding is acceptable only if the patient either agrees to it voluntarily or was legally committed for treatment; it is not something a doctor could normally impose upon a patient against her will.)

He argued that the clinic's success rate should indeed be taken into consideration, claiming that "there is no question that Montreux ... has an exemplary record in terms of helping people to a state of health and well-being ... people who have reached the end of the line." Most of the clinic's patients, he said, have long had "the best of traditional medical treatment" without success. "Montreux's method has to be seen in the context of the desperateness of that state.... What are the alternatives?"

Even the allegations of force-feeding or holding patients against their will had to be seen in the same context, he said. What Montreux did wasn't force-feeding, in his view; it was "gentle persistence," to get the

The mansion in Victoria's tony Rockland district that was home to the residential Montreux Clinic for Eating Disorders.

Montreux lawyer Dennis Murray on the first day of the hearing to look into allegations against the residential clinic.

Regional medical health officer Dr. Richard Stanwick on the opening day of the hearing investigating the Montreux Clinic.

Regional medical health officer Dr. Richard Stanwick (right) with his lawyer Paul Pearlman during the licensing hearing into Montreux's operations.

Guy McDannold, lawyer for health licensing investigators, during the hearing into Montreux's operations.

Guy McDannold (right) holds a quick discussion with Montreux lawyer Dennis Murray during the licensing hearing.

Montreux founder Peggy Claude-Pierre on the day it was announced that health authorities had cancelled the residential clinic's licence to operate.

Peggy Claude-Pierre and her husband, David Harris, at a news conference held by the clinic after it was announced health authorities had ordered the residential clinic closed.

patients to eat. It was essential that the rules allow for such persistence, because if you had to give up every time an anorexic said they didn't want to eat today, "then these people cannot be saved." The persistence might sometimes be "stern," he said, but it was "never abusive."

The patients' requests to leave had to be looked at in the same context, he argued, because almost every patient at some point will want to abandon treatment for the anorexic life. Mostly, those were "fleeting emotional reactions" from which patients could be dissuaded so they could continue on their way to recovery, he claimed.

He did not, in his opening, deal with any of the specific allegations that McDannold had summarized from the investigation. His final conclusion was that "working in difficult circumstances, Montreux contributed to the dignity, health, and well-being of its patients." What problems had arisen, he argued, could easily be worked out to everyone's satisfaction in co-operation with the licensing authorities.

McDannold had anticipated that. He had told Dr. Stanwick that he expected much of Montreux's defence to be, "trust us, we have changed, let us carry on." Indeed, he noted, the centre had been producing new policies for the investigative team just a few days earlier. But, he said, licensing just wasn't buying that any more. The blatant lies about little Dustin had been the last straw.

"We have concluded that Montreux Counselling Centres, Ltd.... either does not intend to, or cannot, comply with minimum standards," he said. "They do not have the skills and abilities to operate a facility in compliance" with the rules. The new written procedures did appear to be an improvement, but "we have no faith that these new written processes actually will be followed in the future." He reiterated the conclusion of the investigation report: licensing could see no alternative to removing the licence to operate and having Montreux closed down as a residential facility.

With that, licensing began calling its witnesses, beginning with Gerry Stearns, the psychologist who'd been seconded to the investigation team from the attorney general's ministry. Stearns, Macdonald, and Eng all summarized their findings from the logbooks: the numerous times they had found staff members recording instances of threats and force-feeding, or of suicide threats or medical problems ignored. Eng told of finding Dustin's logbooks and of the entries in them that showed his growing problems with eating and Louise's growing stress levels. Macdonald and Eng detailed numerous examples they'd found in which feeding methods had reached the point of abuse. Several of them had taken place after the conclusion of the first investigation, when Claude-Pierre had vowed that force-feeding was not something that would ever be allowed at Montreux. With Lena returned to Britain and Dustin back home with his family, Anna appeared to be the patient whose feeding had caused the most problems. One day in November 1997, the patient logs showed it took staff 3½ hours to get her to drink one "shake," while she kept saying, "she was not going to eat another thing, ever!" Two days later, her workers reported she'd been fed from the moment she awoke, and by the end of the shift, "her hair and clothes were covered in shake." A few days later she was "fed for over three hours until 1 a.m.," again ending up "covered in shake" that she'd spat out. Macdonald took pains to note that the logbooks said Claude-Pierre had been paged on these occasions, as well as Anna's counsellor, Kirsten Claude-Pierre, so both must have been aware of what was going on.

Similar logbook entries were found of patients asking to leave the program, but not being allowed to. Both Anna and Vivian—who were rooming together at that point—made repeated requests and demands to leave, but both were still there. Indeed, both were frequently in the hearing room as their cases were discussed. Anna, still frail-looking after three years at Montreux, had become a bit of a favourite with some in the crowd because she regularly brought her cute Jack Russell terrier to the hearings, where he'd sit on her lap and accept copious attention from everyone during the breaks. Vivian, so withdrawn her body sometimes seemed like an empty shell, was one of the few Montreux patients that management did send home one day, realizing it would be too difficult for her to hear details of her history discussed publicly.

The tension in the room grew palpably when it was time for the former staff members to take the witness stand. Almost before they'd started testifying, Dr. Stanwick had to make clear that hisses and boos would result in spectators being asked to leave, or even in having the whole hearing closed to the public. Even so, occasional stage-whispers of "Liar!" would pass through the ranks of staff members during the testimony. In total, five former staff members testified on behalf of licensing, including Andrew and Randi, and Dustin's careworker, Gavin. Joining them on the witness stand were Mark* and Heidi,* both of whom had been longer-term careworkers at Montreux. Mark had been with Montreux from its opening as a residential facility in 1993 until 1997. He had risen to the position of acute-care counsellor, trying to give extra help to some of the sickest patients on their arrival. Gay did not testify. She had a separate court date coming up with Montreux as she had decided to sue the clinic in small claims court for wrongful dismissal. She had given up the whole social services field as a career and gone back to her first love, building and restoring boats.

Each of the five had their own stories to tell. For Heidi it was the day she accidentally witnessed Claude-Pierre herself using physical force to get Anna to eat. The two were on Anna's bed, she testified, and Claude-Pierre was holding a sports-bottle with one hand. With the other, she was holding Anna's chin up to extend her throat as she was telling her, "Swallow, swallow." Heidi remembered, "I felt I had entered into somebody else's secret."

For Mark, it was the day he had to join a desperate effort to keep Brenda,* a highly troubled 16-year-old, from committing suicide by jumping out a third-storey window. Somehow Brenda had slipped out of arm's length distance from her caregiver that afternoon, and by the time Mark came on the scene, she was halfway out the window. From there it would have been a devastating fall straight to the cobblestone pavement below. Jeannie, who, even at a healthy weight, was a much smaller girl than Brenda, was the only staff member present and was clinging to her to prevent her from letting go. When Mark joined in, they were able to pull her back into the bedroom—at which point Mark was amazed to see one of the middle managers videotaping the whole incident. When Mark said he didn't think that would do much towards helping calm the situation, he was told that Claude-Pierre wanted the scene taped because it would provide a good demonstration of how extreme the Negative Mind could become.

For Gavin, it was the day he got a frantic phone call from Claude-

Pierre telling him that his help was needed because Louise—later to be Dustin's primary caregiver—had "escaped." Other staff members had already found her diary, which outlined a detailed suicide plan, including buying Tylenol and razor blades from a drugstore, then overdosing on the whole bottle as well as cutting her wrists. The panicked search by clinic staff did not end in finding Louise, but luckily she herself decided, almost too late, that she didn't want to die. She took a room in a low-class downtown hotel, slit her wrists and took the overdose, but then thought better of it and phoned her mother at home in Britain. The ambulance got to her in time, and only a few days later she was back at the clinic.

The staff members shared other stories in which, they said, the principle of unconditional love appeared to have been abandoned. Both Randi and Heidi testified they'd been at staff meetings where they were told the ways that extremely reluctant patients could be made to eat, including the use of the spoon. They didn't remember Claude-Pierre being at the meetings, but Noah Dobson had been there, they said.

Claude-Pierre had often publicly decried the use of restrictions and punishments in behaviour modification programs in hospitals, but Heidi testified that she'd been ordered to punish young teenage patients for refusing to co-operate with the program. In one case, Carrie,* then only 13, was ordered to stay in her room for three days, and on another occasion, staff took away the sketchbook that was her favourite hobby. Two other girls were kept in their room one night with the heat turned up as high as possible as a punishment specifically ordered by Claude-Pierre.

Even before licensing had finished putting forward their case, it had become obvious that the three weeks that had been allotted for the hearing wasn't going to be nearly enough. Montreux wanted to call many of its patients and their parents, staff members and former staff members, as well as Claude-Pierre, Harris, and the Dobsons. The lawyers put their heads together and concluded that at least another two weeks would be needed. With various participants having unbreakable prior commitments in June, the hearing would now extend through most of the month of July.

The tension turned to eager anticipation among the Montreux supporters when it came time for the clinic to begin calling its defence witnesses. They were convinced that their fellow patients and parents would be able to explain the anorexic mind and why it demanded that things be done differently at the clinic. The reporters were eager too. Most of them were interested to hear what the clinic's defence would be to what looked like incontrovertible evidence, most of it drawn from Montreux's own records.

The testimonials Montreux presented were passionate and heartfelt. A dozen parents took the stand to tell their stories. Their appearance was, almost universally, impeccable. The mothers' makeup was perfect, the fathers wore well-cut suits. The jewellery showed that most of them came from an income group that could afford Montreux's fees. Their stories were remarkably similar. They told of their desperation in trying to get help for their daughters and of the difficulty of finding what they considered good treatment in the conventional medical systems. Some had run the gamut of programs in their home countries; others had tried only a program or two but were unhappy with the rules imposed upon them as well as their children. Some spoke of their despair in trying to find a safe place for their children after U.S. health insurance plans had forced their children out of hospital after only 30 or 60 days, obviously long before they had recovered enough to cope on their own. They spoke in heart-wrenching terms of the torment they could see their children going through, of the relief at finally finding Montreux, and realizing they would be one of the lucky families accepted and that treatment would last for as long as needed. They would never have to search for a program again.

As well, many told of the precarious medical condition that their daughters had reached before they made it to the clinic. Kerry's* father told how, at the age of 12, she'd come direct from another program where she'd been tube-fed for six weeks because she was refusing to eat at all. Shelley's* mom told how Shelley had been in a coma and in intensive care before arriving at Montreux. Sheila's father, a medical doctor himself, talked of bringing Sheila to Victoria in an air ambulance because her condition was so precarious.

In almost every case, the families had learned about Montreux through the media, by watching either the *20/20* or *Oprah* shows or, for some of the later patients, reading Claude-Pierre's book.

"It was like the book was written by someone who had lived with us for 10 years," said Stacey's* father. "I knew immediately that someone understood."

"Call it blind faith or call it what you want," testified Shelley's mother. "This woman was going to save my daughter." Her opinion was based entirely on watching the *20/20* show.

However, despite their passionate defence of the clinic, it soon became apparent that the parents were basing their conclusions more on an innate faith in Claude-Pierre and Montreux than on hard evidence. Whether it was true or not, by the time they arrived in Victoria, many believed they had exhausted all other alternatives. Their perception was that Montreux was the only alternative to death for their daughters.

Consider the case of Sheila, one of the most desperate patients to come to the clinic, even by its own standards. Before coming to Montreux, she had become not only severely anorexic, but also acutely suicidal and an elective mute, speaking to almost nobody. Despite her father's excellent connections with the medical system in the U.S., he had not found a place that would provide his daughter with the long-term care she so clearly needed. Top facilities like Johns Hopkins or the Mayo Clinic would accept her, but their in-patient program would be only 5 to 10 days, and Sheila's father could not imagine who would care for her after that. "There was no other place in the world, literally in the world, that was capable of caring for her," he told Dr. Stanwick. He did know that there could be some risk in placing her in a non-medical facility, he admitted frankly, but by that point, the family had absolutely no alternatives left.

None of the parents expressed any concerns about the concept that Montreux was essentially forcing therapy on their children, whether or not the children wanted it. That was perhaps less surprising when one considered that nearly all the parents who testified were American. Unlike in British Columbia, the laws in many American states governing psychiatric treatment for young people allow parents to force minor children, sometimes up to the age of 21, into therapy or residential treatment for mental illnesses, with the young people themselves having few legal rights.

Most the parents who testified confirmed that they had not spoken to their children in the first weeks or even months that they were at Montreux. That hadn't upset them, they said, because they had understood from the beginning that that was a normal part of the treatment program. Instead, they'd relied on the weekly updates provided for them by Montreux's "family liaison officer"—reports that always ended on a hopeful and optimistic note, even if the patient in question had not had a particularly good week. Jeannie was a favourite family liaison officer because so many of the parents remembered following her high-profile treatment on the two *20/20* shows. Few parents knew what, if any, questions they should be asking. Sharleen's mother admitted, for instance, she'd not been aware that the clinic had not been following up on the abnormal blood-test results her daughter had had just before coming to Montreux. Brenda's mother said the story of her daughter's attempt to jump out the window didn't worry her particularly since no serious consequence had ensued. "Windows were a favourite of Brenda's, I have to say," she added, noting similar problems had occurred in treatment facilities in her native Australia.

The level of warmth and caring they saw when they first arrived at the clinic particularly impressed most of the parents. It seemed so different from the sterile and impersonal atmosphere they had found when admitting their children to the hospital system. They felt that here were people who understood how hard things had been for them and, even more so, for their children. So much understanding and caring translated into a guarantee of safety in their minds. Most had not even asked what the actual qualifications were of those who would be caring for their children.

Most of the parents were convinced that their children were now either cured or were well on the way to being so. As in the 1994 government report, however, it was never clear just what the definition of "cured" was. Kerry's father, for instance, described his daughter now as "fine," although, he admitted, "she does still have some peculiar eating habits." Shelley's mother said Shelley, too, was now cured, although she was seeing a psychiatrist back in her home state. That, it was explained, was not to maintain recovery but rather to see if they could get her "brain chemistry" sorted out.

Nor could any parent speculate how long it might take to complete the cure for those who were described as making progress, but not yet cured. "When she's ready to come home, she'll come home," said the father of Stacey, who'd then been at the clinic for about a year. According to Claude-Pierre's theory, to put forward a target date would be detrimental to Stacey's recovery. Stacey later told a reporter from *Elle* magazine that she expected to stay at the clinic another five or six years.[48]

Of all the parents scheduled to testify, none was so eagerly anticipated as Dustin's mother, Moira. Dustin's story had attracted more attention than any other aspect of the clinic's operations as licensing presented its case. As well, in the week leading up to her appearance on the witness stand, Moira had started posting details of her family's story on the Internet, on a newsgroup designed for eating-disorder sufferers to ask questions and provide support for one another. She told the history of the development of Dustin's eating disorder, of watching the *20/20* show, and of coming to Montreux. She never mentioned her long separations from Dustin or even whether he was a day or a residential patient, but she did say that at Montreux, "my son was treated with love, kindness and compassion—and, when needed, strength that my long journey with him could not give any more.... He needed someone to lean on."

As well, she promised he was now entirely healthy and "eats just like a normal six-year-old boy." Her postings had been picked up in Canadian newspapers, and the day she was scheduled to appear at the hearing, every seat in the room was full long before the appointed starting time. Moira declined to talk to reporters before testifying. She would, she explained, say all she had to say on the witness stand.

She did. Dressed in an electric-blue dress, she turned the heads of the entire crowd as she walked to the table where witnesses sat. After she'd been sworn in, Murray's junior associate Fiona McQueen invited her to tell Dr. Stanwick a little about life with Dustin before they'd come to Montreux. She talked without appearing to draw breath for almost 90 minutes. The monologue stopped then only because Dr. Stanwick took pity on the court recorder and called the lunch break. Lawyers in B.C. courts believe it may have set a record as the longest single answer to a question asked at a trial or hearing.

After lunch, testimony moved on to their stay at Montreux. Moira tried to emphasize that she had been in total charge of Dustin's treatment, that Claude-Pierre had acted only under her instructions, and that she'd endorsed, if not actively initiated, her own long separation from her son. It was a story in complete contradiction not only to the testimony of Dustin's workers, but also to the mounds of Montreux documents, none of which showed her playing any role in her son's care at all. When McDannold showed her the "guidelines" written by Louise for Dustin's care, she admitted she'd never seen them before. She couldn't explain why all of Dustin's documents listed various staff members to call in case of a problem, but none mentioned her. As for her bitter note complaining about being left in the dark about Dustin's care, it was, she said, an outpouring of a single day's frustration and an exaggeration of the problems that had actually occurred.

And when McDannold asked her why she'd told the original licensing investigation that Dustin had been a day-patient only, she—who could remember virtually every individual meal of Dustin's before moving to Victoria—claimed she couldn't remember the conversation at all.

In any case, she argued, it didn't matter. All that mattered was that Montreux had taken her and Dustin in, had charged her nothing for his care, and had given him back to her well and fully recovered from his eating disorder. Only days after their arrival at the clinic, she said, Dustin, then just barely three years old, had said to her, "Thank you for bringing me here, Mommy. Thank you for saving my life." She had brought with her an hour-long video of Dustin at home, made just the weekend before, which she said would show what a normal child he'd now become. However, by the time she'd finished the rest of her testimony, it was too late in the day to have it shown to the hearing with her there to explain it. When Dr. Stanwick watched it a few days later, he noted that the one thing it did not show Dustin doing was eating.

The patients themselves echoed many of their parents' stories, especially about their feelings of hopelessness when they could find no program that would work for them. Sheila was especially eloquent. In the other hospitals she'd attended, she said, "I was locked up, I was tied down, I was given shots, I felt like my body wasn't my own any more. I was really frightened." Before watching a tape of the *20/20* show, she said, "I decided that there was no hope for me. I didn't believe there was any way out of my illness... I arrived feeling like a zombie, feeling like an alien." What Montreux had given her, she said, was "gentleness and consistency," over a long enough time (Sheila was a residential patient at Montreux for two full years) that she was able to heal.

Other patients told similar stories. Deirdre* talked of going through 13 different treatment centres in Britain and getting worse after every stay. Even Anna testified briefly to try to explain that, no matter what the records said, she'd never really been force-fed. It was, she said, just Claude-Pierre's and the clinic's way of helping her undertake the appallingly difficult task of eating. Claude-Pierre, she said, "would raise the bottle in order to help... I needed to hear her say 'Swallow' three times in order to let myself do it." At the time she testified, Anna had been at Montreux for more than three years and was still on 24-hour, one-to-one care.

Brenda testified as well, to explain that her effort to get out the top-storey window wasn't a genuine suicide attempt. "It was an attempt for me to get away from the pain in my head," she said.

The testimony of the patients and the parents taught anyone who was listening many things. It gave a glimpse into the dreadful lives of those who suffer chronic, unremitting anorexia, and of those who love them. It pointed out the huge gaps in treatment services available, especially in the U.S., where managed health care schemes and strict insurance rules often severely restrict how much help an eating-disorder sufferer can receive. It made clear that many doctors and hospitals dealing with anorexia seem, to the patients and their families, to have forgotten the need for humanity and caring, even when dealing with the most difficult cases. It pointed out the inestimable value of hope, the commodity that Claude-Pierre offered in the greatest abundance.

What it did not do, however, was answer those basic questions that were being posed to Dr. Stanwick: did Claude-Pierre and the Montreux staff have the knowledge, expertise, and willingness to operate a clinic that met the minimum health and safety standards for the residents? Were they well enough trained and equipped to handle the severely ill patients that came to them? Did they breach the mental health laws by the way they fed patients and got them to stay when they said they wanted to leave?

The patients themselves had no medical knowledge that could help them answer those questions. Most of the parents didn't either. In the case of those who did, like Sheila's and Carrie's fathers, both medical doctors themselves, they had not been there during the worst moments of treatment, either of their own daughters or of other patients. Nor had they been able to follow the medical care to find out whether necessary precautions were taken or lab tests done on a proper schedule.

It would be up to Montreux's own personnel, and the doctors attached to the clinic, to provide more detailed answers to those questions when the hearings resumed in July.

8

What Montreux Said

The hearing reassembled on a hot morning in July. Before a single witness could be called, however, Guy McDannold leaped to his feet to say an urgent problem needed to be dealt with before any more evidence could be heard. In the days leading up to the resumption of the hearing, he said, one of the former employees who'd testified, Gavin, had been approached and harassed by a pro wrestler–sized private detective who was working on behalf of Montreux. Recalled to the witness stand, Gavin testified that he'd first seen the man five days earlier, watching his apartment building. When Gavin left, the man came up to him and asked him if he knew a person named Gavin. Gavin hastily decided he didn't know himself.

But the next day when he came home from work, he found a message on his answering machine from the same man, saying: "We know where you live ... your friends are in a lot of trouble ... call within 24 hours before you get into more trouble." Nervous and frightened, Gavin instead called the licensing investigators, who put him into immediate contact with McDannold. The next day when he came home, he found a business card slipped under his apartment door. This time the tone was different: "Gavin, please call Mr. Lee. David and Peggy require your help." Instead, he again called McDannold.

Meanwhile, McDannold had been doing a little detective work of his own. He'd found out that the detective, Murray Lee, was a subcontractor, working for another detective agency which apparently had been hired by David Harris. Lee had not been given much information about the case, but told McDannold he'd had instructions to try to contact

Gavin either to see if he'd been previously threatened by anyone or to tell him that Montreux might want him to give evidence for their side. McDannold described that story as "improbable and untrue," given that Gavin had already finished giving his evidence and the Montreux lawyers had had all the freedom they wanted to cross-examine him.

Gavin was the first to admit that the messages might not have been seen as intimidating by everyone. But in the context of all that had been going on surrounding the whole Montreux case, he said, he'd seen it as some type of a threat and "found it extremely worrisome."

McDannold was righteously indignant. The licensing investigators, as well as many of the complainants, had been worried from the beginning about the safety of those who provided evidence to officialdom about Montreux. Now, he said, "those concerns have been seen to be completely substantiated ... I find it completely unacceptable."

The interlude left the Montreux management and lawyers looking flustered and uncomfortable. After a brief break, Dennis Murray returned to admit that it was indeed his client who had hired the investigators—but he insisted that they were never supposed to intimidate or harass witnesses. "There's nothing wrong with a private investigator looking around," Murray contended, especially since Montreux was "facing huge investigational resources against it." However, he said, "it was never intended as a threat" to any of the witnesses. "It was just a dumb thing to do."

When he testified later, David Harris claimed it was actually he and Peggy Claude-Pierre who had been harassed and hounded "for quite some time ... it's clear to us there is something conspiratorial happening." One of their cars had been set on fire, he said, and a different private investigator, whom he didn't name, had been following them for at least six months. They hoped that by hiring their own investigator, they'd be able to find out who was paying that unnamed person, he said, but they'd never expected the detectives to approach any of the witnesses directly. "It was our one and only foray into the private investigation world," he sighed.

McDannold and Murray agreed that no one would approach any of the witnesses, past or present, without first going through the lawyers.

Dr. Stanwick confirmed that would conclude the issue as far as the hearing was concerned. Harris did offer a personal apology to Gavin in the parking lot later.

Once the evidence resumed, among the first professionals to testify on behalf of Montreux were the three doctors who'd provided medical services to the clinic. All three believed strongly that the clinic, overall, was a safe place for the clients and, in many cases, the best place for them, given their mistrust of doctors and hospitals. However, as Dr. Stanwick questioned them about the individual patients who'd been in their care, all three agreed they had not been given some information that they should have known to provide the best care for the patients. Moreover, all three admitted there were things that should have been done differently to ensure the patients were medically safe.

Dr. Charles Medhurst had monitored only three Montreux patients in total, he said, but they included the high-profile case of Dustin as well as that of Joshua, one of the files Dr. Laird Birmingham had reviewed. In Joshua's case, Dr. Medhurst testified, when he first examined the boy, then 13, he found his temperature below normal, his heart rate too slow and his blood pressure too low—all risk signs among doctors who work regularly with eating disorders. However, he didn't think the risk warranted trying to hospitalize Joshua. He later agreed that the lack of earlier medical information in the boy's file could have posed a risk to his health and safety, and concluded, "there's several things I'd change." As for Dustin, Dr. Medhurst said he'd not been involved in the pre-admission screening at all, but noted that when he first saw the boy after he arrived in Victoria, he found him to be undersized but "not medically compromised." Montreux had never told him, he said, that the boy had moved in with fellow patient Louise, nor what Louise's own history was. If he had known all that was going on, he admitted, he might have encouraged them to find a child psychiatrist or psychologist to become involved.

Three of the files that Dr. Birmingham had reviewed were those of Dr. Mauro Bertoia's patients, Angela, Wilma, and Sharleen. Dr. Birmingham, the internist and eating-disorder specialist, had found that it was risky to admit any of the three to a facility like Montreux, given their physical condition, but Dr. Bertoia, the general practitioner, disagreed with Dr. Birmingham on all three cases. He admitted that Angela's case caused him "some trepidation," since she was coming with a nasogastric tube still in place. However, once he met Angela, his fears disappeared, he said, because she appeared medically stable, and the tube-feeding had actually kept her weight to a reasonable level. "I think the risk to her was acceptable," he said, but he later admitted it did concern him that Montreux had developed a food plan for her without ever discussing it with him. He allowed that there were similar problems in both the other cases.

Dr. David Clinton-Baker had been at the clinic the longest of the three and had dealt with the most patients. He told Dr. Stanwick that the admissions process had improved greatly in recent months and years with the doctors much more involved in deciding which patients should be accepted. In the early days, he conceded, patients usually just turned up on the doctor's doorstep, with the doctor having no idea beforehand what information might be available on them or how precarious their condition might be. He would not, for instance, have encouraged the clinic to admit Shannon, the desperately ill woman first seen in hospital in Ohio on the first *20/20* show. Her other physical illnesses, which made her dependent on narcotic painkillers, probably made her unsuitable for a facility like Montreux, he said. Neither would he have recommended taking Sylvia, the patient who had been discharged because of her physical attacks on staff, had he known of her behaviour problems. But he hadn't been consulted in either case, and had made the best of the situation when the two joined the patient roll. However, he argued, it's difficult to have a set of lab readings that decide with certainty whether a person is safe in a place like Montreux. In some cases, he said, those guidelines would have ruled out a prospective patient, "but my experience and judgment tells me this was still the best place for the patient to be." Anna, whose eating had caused such problems even years after her first admission, might have been one of those patients, he suggested, but he later added, "I could have improved my monitoring of this patient... there was room for improvement in her care. There was some risk."

The three doctors all stressed that, in their minds, their job had solely been to provide monitoring of a patient's medical condition, prescribe medications where appropriate or necessary, and treat their patients for the usual illnesses or injuries that were quite separate from the eating disorder. They had had nothing to do with developing food plans for the patients or dealing with the treatment provided for the eating disorder itself. Dr. Clinton-Baker described it as acting like "a consultant," but not taking responsibility for a patient in the way you would if you were a doctor responsible for a patient in hospital. They had not been involved in any discussion of feeding methods or requests from patients to leave. Dr. Clinton-Baker said he'd never looked at the question of whether patients had provided properly informed consent to their Montreux treatment, nor had he explained choices or options to patients. He hadn't seen that as part of his job.

By the time the senior Montreux managers were ready to testify, Murray was leaving more and more of the questioning of the witnesses to Fiona McQueen and was not even in the hearing room for most of the day. He would return only for the questioning of Claude-Pierre herself.

Thus it was McQueen who called Margaret Dobson to the stand to give the first evidence from those who should have known the innermost depths of Montreux's functioning. Dobson explained she had one year of "pre-nursing training" in Scotland before coming to Canada, but would not count as any type of licensed nurse in B.C. Her official title was associate program director, which meant, she explained, that she read the caseworkers' and counsellors' reports, discussed issues with Claude-Pierre, and kept an overall eye on the patients and care staff. She tried to always be there when patients were seeing the doctor, she said, because most of them weren't comfortable talking to a doctor without someone from the clinic there.

As it would be with the examination of all of the managers to come, much of the discussion centred around Dustin, and why the managers had all said previously that he'd never been a residential patient at all. Knowing it would arise in cross-examination, McQueen asked Margaret to explain her previous statements about Dustin. She replied it was "a misunderstanding, but no deceit ... his presence was never hidden."

As soon as it was time for McDannold to begin his cross-examination, he promptly began to read from the transcripts in which she'd told investigators, as late as 1998, that he'd stayed overnight only "on occasion."

"I didn't lie," she continued to insist. "I didn't tell them the facts, but I didn't lie."

As McDannold continued to press the point, she reiterated: "I didn't look at it as a lie. It was somewhat incorrect. This was a very stressful interview. I didn't see the relevance at that point."

She also continued to defend fiercely Claude-Pierre's diagnosis of anorexia nervosa in Dustin and the way the clinic treated him. The separation of the child from his mother had been "mostly Moira's idea," she said, in the hopes he'd eat better if fully separated from her. As McDannold read her entry after entry from Dustin's logbooks, showing his deteriorating behaviour and growing eating problems, she suggested that "I think that was a natural progression of an eating disorder. They get worse before they get better." And, as even more entries were read, she agreed, "It looks like they get worse [but] I don't think it had anything to do with the separation [from his mother]."

Dobson did not admit the hasty nature of Dustin's discharge or how it coincided with the licensing inspection. She testified to it being a "gradual" process of reintegration of Dustin with his family, although that was contradicted by all the other evidence.

McDannold moved on to the question of how patients were persuaded to eat and what happened if they wanted to leave. Was she, he asked, familiar with the provisions of B.C.'s mental health legislation?

Yes, she agreed, she was, but "that doesn't apply to our program." It was the only time during the hearing that the gasps from the licensing team were audible. It was also the first time that the watching reporters, whispering among themselves at break, concluded that Dr. Stanwick would have no choice but to close the clinic. How could any responsible medical health officer deal in any other way with a facility where management said the law didn't apply to them?

Margaret Dobson went on to explain that the whole basis of the Montreux method was that patients "initially always say no [but] they always change their mind."

"When they say no [to food], they mean yes?" asked McDannold.

"Yes," Dobson replied.

McDannold left it at that.

David Harris succeeded Dobson on the witness stand. Harris had originally been the official manager designated under the licence, but in 1997 he had become the general manager of the entire for-profit corporation, including the outpatient counselling practice as well as the residential program. The change had been made after the licensing team complained that Harris was out of town and unavailable too much to function properly as a facility manager.

On the witness stand, he explained how Montreux had set up its financial system on a flat-fee basis, designed to cover all costs of the program and administrative costs, even medical care and extras like music lessons if possible. In some cases they'd work with health insurance companies to persuade them to provide more coverage than usual to cover the "extraordinary situation" of a need for long-term care at the clinic. They were often successful, he added.

Although clinic policy said that patients who were working as careworkers were serving a "practicum" as part of their own healing, Harris confirmed that several were paid as careworkers while still receiving counselling themselves. Some got $380 every two weeks and others $470. It was, he said, "pocket money, so they could be more independent." But in most cases, manager Noah Dobson admitted later, the patients didn't actually receive any cash but rather received a "patient refund" to offset some of the costs of their care.

When McDannold began to cross-examine Harris about a series of problems between licensing and the clinic, ever since it first applied for a licence in 1994, Harris described all of them as a series of "misunderstandings." It was, he said, a misunderstanding when, in the first application for a licence, he'd written that the clinic's clients "would not require daily professional supervision." He'd thought "daily professional supervision" meant having a psychiatrist on site 24 hours a day.

It had been another misunderstanding, he testified, when Montreux continued to house on-care patients in St. Charles House, although the building was never licensed. The misunderstanding, he said, centred on conflicting definitions of "on care" between licensing officials and Montreux's system.

The biggest misunderstanding of all centred on Dustin's care. Harris admitted that what he had said during the 1997 investigation "in fact was not true."

"I was stating our policy more than a fact," he tried to explain. "It's an extension of the reality. It was not a lie."

At another point he suggested that if Dustin had wanted to be back with his mother, "all he had to do was ask" or even walk out the door. A few minutes later he conceded that might have been "a bit of a stretch."

Like Margaret Dobson, Harris said he expected Montreux would still admit the same six patients whose files Dr. Birmingham had reviewed, despite the concerns of the eating-disorder specialist. He did not think the physical risks posed were high enough to deny them admission. He did admit that in Montreux's earlier days they had admitted some patients who had probably been too medically unstable. Jeannie was a case in point. He said that when management had agreed to her admission over the phone, they had believed she weighed about 77 pounds, and when she was taken off the plane weighing only 46 pounds, "it was a terrifying situation for us."

Harris did not repeat Margaret Dobson's suggestion that Montreux was not bound by mental health laws. Rather, he said, it was a question of understanding what the patient really wanted, as opposed to what their anorexic mind wanted them to do, another variation of the "no means yes" theory.

Noah Dobson had moved up from being the clinic's personnel manager to succeed Harris as overall manager in 1997. He made a greater effort to explain the problems that arose when patients wanted to leave, given that most of them weren't from B.C. and didn't have family or a support system in Canada. They would not be safe, he argued, if clinic personnel just allowed them to walk out the front door the minute they asked to leave. He insisted that any "serious" request to leave would be honoured, but it might take several days before a safe discharge could be arranged for them.

In the end, though, it came back down to the no-means-yes theory. He said he'd personally interview any patients who said they wanted to leave, ask them why, and discuss what their other options might be. Too often they said it was because they didn't feel "worthy" to be at the clinic and would change their mind, he explained. Some patients would ask to leave several times a day; but, he contended, they didn't really mean it. He could think of patients who'd made a dozen or more apparently serious requests to get out of Montreux—but they'd never left. "This tends to go hand in hand with our population," he concluded. "They may request to leave... but they may not really want to leave."

In the same way, he said, careworkers, other staff, or even Claude-Pierre may sometimes have to raise their voices or even shout when dealing with a patient in the throes of anorexia. Sometimes it's the only way to break through, he said, and it wouldn't necessarily be verbal abuse of the patient—particularly as it would be the anorexic voice that would be the object, not the patient herself. Noah was adamant, however, that he wouldn't support physical force being used to make a patient eat, and that he'd never been at a staff meeting where such techniques were taught, contrary to what Heidi and Randi had testified. "That did not occur," he insisted.

As for Dustin, Noah was less involved with his care than many of the others, he said, and so wasn't sure just how long he'd actually been a residential patient. "I told *my* truth [emphasis his] which was that I wasn't sure he stayed a day, a week, a month, what have you... no, it wasn't a lie."

Before Claude-Pierre herself could testify, Montreux called one added witness. His name was Bob Enoch, and he was the person whom Montreux wanted to take over as manager of the facility. The Dobsons had announced that, after six years with the clinic, they were resigning their positions there and moving to Ontario, where they had family. Enoch had managed other residential programs on the B.C. mainland and had successfully taken over as administrator of a facility for the head-injured that had run into numerous licensing problems. However, he was the first to admit he knew little about eating disorders—except what Claude-Pierre had already taught him.

What he wanted to do, Enoch explained to Dr. Stanwick, was "devise means to be in compliance [with the licensing standards] while maintaining the unique character of the program." He talked about writing yet more new policies, setting up yet more monitoring committees, and consulting with yet more experts. As well, he said, it was essential that a proper outcome study be undertaken immediately, so the clinic would have scientific evidence to back up its anecdotal stories of how well its patients had done.

He was reluctant, however, to agree that Montreux might have to make major changes in the way it operated, such as substantially increasing the medical expertise on staff, or dealing with the questions of feeding methods and patients' desire to leave. "We're not a hospital and we don't have any intention of transforming ourselves into one," he insisted. And he was comfortable with the clinic's newest admissions policy, which would set up medical parameters for prospective admissions—but then allow every one of them to be thrown out the window if the clinic's "admissions committee" decided it would still be beneficial for an applicant to be admitted.

Enoch made it clear he was not willing to abandon completely the methods that had become known during the hearing as "the illusion of no choice"—efforts made by staff to convince patients that they really did not have any choice about either staying at Montreux or eating, even though legally they undoubtedly did. Enoch said he was looking at "how we can introduce the law and common sense to one another on the subject of anorexia... there must be some way to approach this issue of the refusal of treatment." Perhaps, he thought, the provincial ombudsman or public trustee could help them find a reasonable middle ground.

Then after the lunch break, it was finally the moment everyone had been waiting for—Claude-Pierre's testimony. If the hearing room had been crowded for some of the other key witnesses, like Moira, it was jammed almost beyond capacity that afternoon. Television crews from Vancouver and Toronto scrabbled with the local media to find places. No matter how much Murray and McQueen strived to present Montreux as a team of people working together, everyone knew it wasn't really so. This was Claude-Pierre's clinic, Claude-Pierre's theories, Claude-Pierre's methods. She had the veto on everything that went on there. What she had to say could be vitally important in determining the future of the whole enterprise. Virtually every one of Montreux's staff and patients had come, some patients leaning against their careworkers as if too weak to sit up for a whole afternoon of testimony. A heat wave had hit Victoria, and the air in the room was stifling.

Claude-Pierre made her entrance at the last minute, avoiding the cameras and reporters waiting for her. She was dressed entirely in funereal black, her blonde curls falling softly about her face.

Under gentle questioning from Murray, she outlined yet again the story told on television shows and in her book—the story of her own two daughters. Despite the number of times she'd told it, her voice still broke at the emotional moments, although tears were not actually visible. Many of the patients could be heard crying in sympathy.

It was after Nicole got better, she said, that she resumed her studies, enrolling in the master's program at the Adler Institute in Vancouver. But, she said, the studies were put on hold when she had to decide whether to continue them or to work with an "acutely ill" young girl who turned out to be the family member of Dr. Clinton-Baker. She told of going into hospital and working with patients there and of making speeches to try to increase public knowledge of eating disorders.

"I don't feel myself a hero in this at all," she said, "but rather as a reflection of [the patients'] feelings and thoughts … I certainly don't pretend to know better than anybody else."

In trying to explain Montreux's philosophy, she said that the clinic is, first and foremost, in the business of "delivering hope. These children give up hope, they see no future … they come because they want 24-hour care; they're relieved that someone else will take responsibility for them." Claude-Pierre agreed their success rate was not 100 per cent, but insisted she knew Montreux worked because "people who've been told they can't get better are getting better."

She wasn't much involved with the business side of the clinic, she said, but she knew they sometimes took patients for free, and also insisted they never threw out anyone who'd run out of money. If they did that, she said, "I might as well have never taken that patient at all … I'd be guilty of murder, I think."

She played down the amount of power she had at the clinic, saying she considered herself "a troubleshooter." She'd be the last person someone would call if there was trouble with a patient that couldn't be handled otherwise, she said, but she was adamant she wasn't on top of everything that went on every day, leaving much of that to other clinic managers. Many times she was "overwhelmed" with the rapid growth in the number of patients and staff and couldn't oversee everything herself, she said. "How many kids can you save?"

She echoed Moira's testimony that Moira had been entirely in charge of Dustin's care. "Anything we did with Dustin was at his mother's direction." In fact, she said, Moira had phoned her just before she testified to remind her of that. She quoted Moira as saying: "Peggy, remember I directed this. Everything you did you did under my direction."

As far as the answers to licensing about Dustin, she admitted that "it sounds devious," but "it was never intended to be devious. It was a little boy. I didn't think of him as an issue. I'm sorry if I've done something offensive. I have no defence." Rather, she said, she'd "never thought of Dustin as a residential patient" as far as licensing went, nor did she consider him to be truly separated from his mother. He was "physically" separated, yes, but they were kept aware of each other, so in her mind, the separation wasn't a real one. She remained convinced that he had shown the same signs of negativity and anorexia as all the older patients. "He was manifesting the behaviours and speaking in the same language."

The only specifics she gave of his treatment were that, "he was loved as all our patients are loved. We were in awe of him." And although Louise did stop caring for Dustin because of her stress level, Claude-Pierre still didn't believe that Dustin's behaviour was the cause of any of that stress. "She was very good for him," Claude-Pierre insisted. "She was dealing with little Dustin because she wanted to. That was because of her choice, not mine." It seemed remarkable that a patient still so ill she was on 24-hour care herself would have been seen as capable of making that choice when the Montreux theory said she still wasn't ready to take a shred of responsibility for her own life.

Claude-Pierre told Dr. Stanwick she wished he could talk to Louise so he could understand how good she and Dustin had been for each other. However, Montreux never called Louise as a witness so that wasn't possible. But in the midst of McDannold's cross-examination of Claude-Pierre, the reporters were summoned to the hotel parking lot. There was Louise, prepared to hold a brief press scrum before leaving for Britain on a vacation. At that point she was 24 and had been at the clinic for more than four years. She remained tiny and spoke in a soft voice.

She too stressed that Moira had actually been in charge of Dustin's care, and emphasized that she thought pairing her with Dustin had been good for both of them, but especially for Dustin. "To me, nothing could be worth a little boy's life," she said. "To me, if you abided by the rules, that child should be dead." None of the reporters bothered to point out to her that the evidence had shown Dustin had never been medically compromised.

As for herself, she said, "Objectively, I don't see it as a real negative," although she admitted she became frustrated with caring for Dustin on occasion. The numerous quotes from her own journal and her counsellor's notes were "taken out of context," she said. She was, she claimed, "doing fine" now and was beginning to take correspondence courses to become a Montessori teacher. At that moment, the bus to the airport arrived at the hotel, and Louise boarded it to take her away from the hearing.

The reporters returned to the banquet room. Claude-Pierre was explaining that every part of the treatment of older patients—including stern language or other "firmness"—was done to make it easier for them to eat in the face of negativity in their minds. For example, what Anna had seen as a threat to take her off solid foods and put her back on shakes was not a threat but a way to make it easier for her to eat, since she was having so much trouble with solid foods. "They count on us persisting to save their lives," she said, insisting yet again that the patients really do want to eat, no matter what they say or do at the time. "The patient will say no, but they may show yes," she concluded. "It's not as simple as just a simple no."

The patients crowded around Claude-Pierre as she finished her testimony for the day, all anxious for a hug and a reassuring word. But when the reporters replaced the patients out in the parking lot, Claude-Pierre suddenly became much less outgoing. Instead of talking to the media, she asked her daughter Nicole to fill in for her.

The next day Dr. Stanwick asked Claude-Pierre if she'd have done anything differently.

"I am unbelievably guilty of trying to fix too many kids too fast," she answered. "I hired too many people. The staff didn't have the ability to deal with it all."

Dr. Stanwick again tried to get her to explain how you could tell the difference between a patient who really wanted to leave the program and one who was just having a negative day. "I know the difference," she insisted. "I would respect it if the patients were really insisting on saying no. It basically saves their lives in the end."

But she added softly, "I probably should have done things differently to make things better and safer."

For the first time in the hearing, Dr. Stanwick permitted himself a question outside the strict bounds of evidence he'd been hearing. Why, he asked Claude-Pierre, were so many of the patients, some of them obviously very unwell, attending the hearing? He couldn't think it would be good for them if listening to negativity was hard on them, especially when the person they considered their saviour would be seen as being under attack. Claude-Pierre insisted that it had all been the patients' decision, that they'd wanted to come and hear what was going on.

But almost no patients turned up after that.

Claude-Pierre was not the last witness. That honour fell to the two child psychiatrists who had given expert opinion about Dustin's case. Dr. Susan Sherkow, who had visited Montreux once back in 1998, could not get away from New York, so she testified through a long-distance telephone hook-up. She talked of her three interviews with Dustin. At no time had she seen him eat, she said, but Moira and Dustin had both told her he ate perfectly normally. He still showed obsessive-compulsive symptoms, she said, and was himself clearly worried about his small size and whether he'd be able to measure up. She recognized some hidden aggression in him. She suspected the best diagnosis was Asperger's Syndrome, in which case, she felt, he should be receiving ongoing psychiatric treatment.

When McDannold began his cross-examination, it grew clearer with every question that Dr. Sherkow had not been provided with full details about Dustin's treatment at Montreux. She had not been told he had been living with, and being cared for by, Louise. She knew nothing of Louise's own history. She did not know about Dustin sometimes spending the night in Louise's bed. She did not know that he had had no contact with a pediatrician or child psychologist while in Victoria. She did not know that neither he nor his family had ever had a detailed assessment before moving to Montreux in the first place. With every question, the silence before her answer grew longer, a silence magnified by the fact that it was coming out of a speaker-phone.

It was Saturday when licensing called its rebuttal witness, Vancouver child psychiatrist Dr. Geoffrey Ainsworth. That was the only day when the Oak Bay Beach Hotel room was not available; a wedding reception was to take place there that afternoon. The hearing moved to the boardroom of the Capital Health Region. Not a single Montreux manager turned up to hear Dr. Ainsworth or to help the clinic's lawyers formulate questions for him. Murray and McQueen were on their own. What amazed Dr. Ainsworth most—even more than the enforced separation of Dustin from his mother—was that Dustin had just come from a major city with some of the top medical facilities in the world (and the clinic had accepted him) before a proper diagnosis had ever been established or a proper assessment carried out. The treatment at Montreux had then been prolonged for months longer than any expert would consider normal or acceptable, he testified.

When the lawyers gave their final submissions the next week, neither of them had changed their mind. McDannold's views had strengthened as he'd heard the evidence of the clinic managers. He found the evidence against Montreux to be "overwhelming, the conclusions inescapable ... a repeated and deliberate contravention of community standards." He described the clinic's operations as "dangerous, irresponsible, unethical and illegal," and, he said, "they have no intention of changing their ways." He noted their managers had all said they'd still likely accept the six patients who Dr. Birmingham—with far more medical knowledge—said were at too much risk, and had all insisted they could safely use the "illusion of no choice" without abusing patients' rights.

"They believe they are above the law," he said. "They believe the law does not apply to the Montreux clinic and that is simply unacceptable." At Montreux, he argued, the secret language of eating disorders had become "the secret language of patient abuse."

In the face of the evidence, Murray did not try to argue that Montreux had been innocent of all the allegations against it. Instead, he argued that licensing investigators had essentially had it in for Claude-Pierre and Harris after they learned the truth about Dustin's stay there. "I accept and my clients accept that licensing may well have felt deceived," he said, but that shouldn't have coloured their approach to the whole investigation. After that, he said, they began with a preconceived notion that Montreux was likely to be deceitful and untruthful, which he didn't feel was fair.

As for the possibilities of abuse around feeding issues, Murray argued that "their task is an unbelievably difficult task and they do carry it out with dignity. Staff struggle and struggle to bring out the small part of the patient's actual mind that wants to eat," he said, and "that is where the vast majority of the effort goes ... the overwhelming evidence is that the care and focus is steady, positive, nurturing ... that's what Montreux is all about." And though there were sometimes brutal struggles with the Negative Mind, it would be unfair to characterize that as "verbal abuse," let alone anything worse.

As for accepting Dustin as a residential patient, that, Murray admitted, was "an error of judgment born from a desire to help the little guy."

Instead of cancelling the licence, he urged Dr. Stanwick to allow the clinic to remain open with conditions, if necessary, to ensure safety, but not such that would change its atmosphere. Any conditions imposed, he said, should not be "totally cumbersome and unnecessary. Nor should they take away the fundamental spot on the spectrum that they serve." The patients wouldn't want that either, if it made Montreux too much like the hospitals they'd previously hated, he added.

McDannold shook his head as Murray was talking. His reply was brief. "They still don't get it," he said.

9

Judgment Day

Now it was all up to Dr. Stanwick. It would be his job alone to sort through the hours of testimony and the boxes of documents and decide, in the end, the fate of the Montreux Clinic. In many ways he was an ideal choice for the job. He was a qualified specialist not just in public health, but also in pediatrics. He'd been a full professor at the medical school in his home province of Manitoba, and had kept up his skills there by working at an inner-city community clinic. He still kept up in the field, sat on committees of the Canadian Pediatric Society, and regularly gave presentations to medical conferences. His favourite subject was the many issues where pediatrics and public health overlap—children who are sexually exploited on Canada's streets, young people who die unnecessarily in traffic crashes, toddlers and infants hurt by poorly designed and unsafe products. He sat on a specialized multidisciplinary team that reviewed every single death of a child under the age of 19 in B.C. His pediatric background gave him specialized knowledge of the issues, such as child development, that needed to be considered in the case of little Dustin. He had in fact worked with adolescents who suffered from eating disorders, although he claimed no special expertise in that subject.

In his four years as medical health officer in Victoria, he'd shown he wasn't afraid to make tough decisions when he believed it was necessary for the public good. He'd been on the job in Victoria for only a few days when he'd had to announce that the city water system was the apparent cause of a dangerous outbreak of toxoplasmosis, and he'd never looked back since. Four months before the Montreux hearing started, he'd shepherded through the implementation of the toughest anti-smoking bylaw in Canada. He'd incurred the wrath of bar owners and smoking pub patrons, but he'd persuaded the elected politicians to hang tough and go ahead with the first Canadian bylaw to ban smoking in all indoor public places.

Even the Montreux hearings had been disrupted briefly one morning when protesters on yet a different subject arrived at the hotel. Local environmentalists had hoped he'd say the health risks were too great to allow the aerial spraying of a bacterial insecticide against an outbreak of gypsy moths in Victoria. However, he'd looked at all the studies done elsewhere in the world and decided that no serious risk to human health had ever been proven. The environmentalists were so upset with his failure to stop the project that they dogged him to the hotel with their protest signs. The incident demonstrated clearly one of Dr. Stanwick's strongest principles: that all decisions relating to public health should be based on the best scientific evidence available. It was, he often said, up to the politicians ultimately to consider other factors such as economic pressures or public expectations. His job was to make his recommendations on the basis of the evidence of what would be best for the population's health.

Dr. Stanwick was no stranger to controversy or to the media. Almost 20 years earlier, he'd headed a committee that looked into possibly suspicious deaths of babies in a Winnipeg hospital—at the same time as Toronto nurse Susan Nelles was being investigated for allegedly killing children in hospital there. Even before the 1998 interview on *Dateline*, he'd hit the national and international television circuit more than once, talking about subjects ranging from the smoking bylaw to the flammability of children's pajamas. Locally, it was a rare week when he didn't appear at least once on TV or radio, talking about anything from water-quality problems to rabid bats. Reporters considered him one of the most accessible public servants in the region.

However, he was well aware that writing this judgment would tax all his experience and skills. He needed to put together a decision that would come to the right conclusion based on the evidence; that would explain clearly why he'd reached that conclusion; that would give the losing side no easy grounds for appeal; and that would be understandable to the media and public as well as to the participants in the hearing and to eating-disorder experts.

Meanwhile, Montreux was permitted to continue on as before. It wasn't officially allowed to take any new clients, but its current clients could remain in treatment there. Dr. Stanwick hoped this would allow Montreux to wind down its operations gradually. If he did decide the clinic must be closed, few acute clients would remain who would have to be either transported back to their home countries or receive treatment from the health system in B.C. Both those options would cause disruption to patients and families, something Dr. Stanwick hoped to avoid.

However, it had become clear even during the hearings that Montreux was actually still admitting new patients—but not to the Rockland mansion, the only site that officially came under the health licence. Instead it had found in the law a potential loophole that allowed it to admit new patients to a variety of other apartment blocks strategically placed around the city. The law requires a licence only for facilities that take three or more patients at a time. By installing patients one or two at a time in a variety of physical facilities, they appeared not to need a licence at all. McDannold had argued strenuously at the hearing that extremely ill patients could be put even more at risk if they spent much of the day alone with an untrained careworker in a building where no backup was available. Montreux was still running a centralized operation, he'd contended, with everything from staffing and scheduling to food shopping organized from the main centre. Therefore, it should be required to hold a licence for all its residential care patients, no matter how many sites it wanted to use to house them. But until Dr. Stanwick ruled on that issue, there was no way to prevent clinic management from opening more satellite sites. Throughout 1999, at least half a dozen new patients were admitted that way.

Moreover, many of the patients being admitted to those sites were just as ill as the ones who'd been previously been admitted to Rockland. Kelsey,* a 15-year-old who came with her mother to live in a flat in a four-storey apartment building in 1998, had, like Sheila, been an elective mute when she arrived and also came with a feeding tube still in place. Naomi,* a patient from Japan, came speaking very little English and was so beset by obsessive-compulsive symptoms that she couldn't bear to touch any objects at all, for fear they'd carry germs or dirt. Staff considered it a great victory one night when she agreed to touch the television remote control herself to switch channels. Etta,* a Scandinavian teen, had been guaranteed admission to a top Swedish facility but was still convinced the only alternative to coming to Montreux was death.

Fewer of the patients admitted were from the U.S. or Britain, perhaps because the news coverage there had begun to cast more doubts on the clinic. In addition to Naomi and Etta, new patients arrived from Austria and Switzerland.

Peggy Claude-Pierre still searched out reporters she thought might be favourable to her cause. A freelance column in *The Globe and Mail* in September ran the complete Claude-Pierre defence to all the charges without a single mention of the evidence against the clinic. It described Princess Diana as having become "a friend" of Claude-Pierre's, and said her methods were now replicated "everywhere."[49] All the problems, she said, had come from 5 careworkers whom Claude-Pierre and Harris "refused to promote," 5 careworkers out of a total of 483 who, she said, had ever worked at the clinic. No one was ever quite sure where that number came from. It repeated the *20/20* claim that Montreux patients "are, quite simply, loved back to health," and suggested publicly, for the first time, Montreux's conspiracy theory—that the action against them was all a plot of the provincial government, which feared private clinics intruding into Canada's public medical system.

Claude-Pierre worked with a crew from Australian TV to film a one-hour special about Brenda, the deeply troubled teenager who'd arrived at Montreux as the clinic's first Australian patient three years earlier. The documentary traced Brenda's history from her sickest moments before coming to Montreux to her return to her home country, apparently much healthier and happier, three years later. Even after all the evidence at the hearing, the show still referred to Claude-Pierre as a "clinical psychologist" and dismissed all the complaints as ones relating to the cost of Montreux and its "alternative" mindset.[50]

All the same, after the hearings ended, it wasn't as easy to persuade the media that Montreux was the anorexia sufferers' utopia it had once appeared to be. Articles summarizing both sides of the Montreux story appeared in Canadian, American, and British media in the months before Dr. Stanwick's decision was made.

In August, the 36 million readers of *People* magazine found a three-page spread under the heading "Controversy." Illustrated with cute pictures of Dustin and his family, the article included vehement defences of the clinic from, among others, Sheila's father and Louise. But it also listed all the key allegations from the hearing, implying that Montreux was no longer seen as the "anorexics' Lourdes."[51]

Claude-Pierre made one major television appearance, on another show on ABC, *Good Morning America*. There she joined Moira and Dustin's father to talk about Dustin's case and a little about the licensing investigation as well. Claude-Pierre repeated her contention that the problem was only a few disgruntled staff members. Moira thought the authorities were upset simply because of Claude-Pierre's lack of formal qualifications.

Moira told interviewer Charles Gibson that she was with Dustin in Canada "for the whole time, for the duration he was there ... for two years."[52] She did not mention, and Gibson did not ask, about the weeks and months during that time when she had not been allowed any contact with her son.

However, ABC also brought on to the show an expert child psychologist, Dr. Ramasamy Manikam, director of the Pediatric Feeding Disorders Program at the Maryland Hospital for Children. Dr. Manikam joined the other experts in doubting that Dustin had ever suffered from anorexia nervosa in the first place. And even if the Montreux treatment really was successful, as Moira said, he argued it still might not have been the best way to deal with the child.

Even more dangerous for Montreux were the articles that questioned whether the Montreux treatment really did work in most cases, and whether the clinic really did have the success rates it claimed. In an article for *Elm Street* magazine, published just before Dr. Stanwick's decision, writer Vivian Smith talked to Caroline, Montreux's first famous patient from Chilliwack, who'd been admitted to the clinic in January 1994. Caroline remained convinced that without Claude-

Pierre and Montreux, she would have died in those difficult days. She may well be right. But now, after 5½ years of Montreux treatment, Caroline admitted that she still couldn't bring herself to eat in front of Smith and that she still walked miles every day, to a degree she conceded was not healthy. She didn't know any more when she might actually have "completed" the Montreux program and be considered cured. She told Smith that other Montreux veterans also continue to have problems with eating.[53]

In an article in the U.S. women's magazine *Elle*, reporter Stephanie Mansfield put it even more bluntly. "But," she wrote, "the nagging question remains. Did Claude-Pierre find the elusive cure, or did her enigmatic love therapy merely bring these girls back from the brink of death with no guarantee of lasting, long-range success?"[54]

In Britain, the award-winning daily *The Independent* printed a feature story with the brutally ironic headline, "The Secret Language of Force-Feeding." Reporter Stephanie Nolan talked to Deirdre, who had then been at Montreux almost a year. Deirdre told her "it really is over for me," but then said her best friends and her boyfriend were still all involved with the clinic. And then she added: "Except for food and weight, it's all behind me"—a line that makes virtually no sense given the key symptoms of eating disorders—food and weight.[55]

Perhaps even more difficult for Claude-Pierre and Harris was that, in most cases, they had no control over what the media covered. Gone were the days when the television crews would consider themselves honoured to be allowed to spend days at the clinic, filming everything that went on. Shows like that could not have been produced without Montreux's co-operation. But by the summer of 1999, it didn't matter to the reporters if Claude-Pierre wanted to talk to them or not—and more often than not, she didn't. By now there were plenty of others who would.

The most scathing criticisms of Claude-Pierre and the clinic undoubtedly came from *National Post* columnist Christie Blatchford, who travels the continent for her newspaper, usually writing about the most interesting court cases she can find and giving very personal opinions of the issues raised and the people involved. She has a wicked sense of humour, except to the victims of it. Her Montreux columns were so vitriolic that Montreux insiders dubbed her "the bourbon-drinking bitch."

Blatchford came to Victoria to watch Claude-Pierre testify first-hand and wrote three columns based on her trip to Victoria. At each one, Claude-Pierre, Harris, and Montreux supporters grew more incensed. In the first, she wrote: "Ms. Claude-Pierre is *aggressively* passive, [emphasis Blatchford's], oddly bellicose and earnest at the same time, a delicate little flower built over a frame of steel."[56] She described the Montreux philosophy as one that "appears to be equal parts 24-hour love (sort of a hug-around-the-clock), West Coast psychobabble and ideas borrowed from, as [Claude-Pierre] puts it, sources as diverse as 'gestalt, Freud, and shaman practice' where it's 'red dog versus blue dog, blue dog is the mean one and the one that survives is the one that gets fed.'" It was doubtless not the impression Claude-Pierre was hoping to convey on her opening day of testimony.

On the second day Blatchford focussed in part on the first *20/20* documentary, after Claude-Pierre had confirmed that new staff members watched it as part of their training to work there. "The only imaginable training effect of this video," wrote Blatchford, "aside from perhaps a lesson in bad TV journalism, could be to instill reverence for Ms. Claude-Pierre. It is not an instrument of instruction but a piece of propaganda."[57] She quoted various of Claude-Pierre's quibbles with McDannold over the stories licensing had been told about Dustin, concluding: "By most definitions save Bill Clinton's, that would constitute lying, but not for Ms. Claude-Pierre, who plays furiously with language even as she accuses others of engaging in semantics."

The third day the headline said it all: "Imagine, if you will, a fudging of the facts." She began by noting that the reporters who'd been covering the hearing regularly "privately call it the Twilight Zone. The term is a monumental understatement of what has been happening," singling out for attention "the chasm between the facts as they have unfolded and what Ms. Claude-Pierre claims as truth."[58] She went over much of Dustin's story, pointing out again that Dustin had never been in medical trouble, and concluding that putting him under the primary care of Louise "was a recipe for disaster." As for Claude-Pierre, Blatchford concluded that in looking at Dustin's case, as well as at many other parts of the clinic operation, it was "as plain as the nose on her pretty face...she wouldn't recognize reality if it up and bit her there."

The columns were widely read across Canada, and excerpts were posted on support newsgroups for anorexia sufferers. It seemed unlikely that the family of any sufferer who read them would be rushing off to find the $925 (US)a day which by then it would cost to send their child to Montreux.

Along with moving new patients into the satellite sites, Montreux had also resurrected one of its other ways of raising funds—the non-profit society. After the problems with the society had come to light at the beginning of the new investigation, Revenue Canada had stepped in with an audit to see whether the society should continue to be listed as a charitable group able to give tax receipts. Revenue Canada's opinion had been unequivocal—the Montreux Society would be allowed to remain a charity only if it improved its operations considerably. The first requirement was that it be reinstated as a registered non-profit society and bring its paperwork with both the provincial and federal offices up to date. That necessitated a trip to the B.C. Supreme Court, which the society made in September 1998. They were successfully returned to the rolls of non-profit societies in good standing.

The documents filed as part of its catch-up manoeuvres showed two things: first, that the society had been a lucrative fundraising tool for the clinic itself, especially off-shore, and, second, that despite its lack of paperwork, the society had been expanding its board in the mid-1990s—and a very high-powered board it had become.

The society's most successful year had been 1994, the year of the campaign to raise funds for Samantha Kendall and also the year of the first *20/20* show. That year the society's income was $204,928, of which only $43,578 had been donated by Canadians. The rest was from what Canada's taxman describes as "foreign sources." The next year the total was down somewhat to $125,771, but less than $7,000 of that came from Canadian donations. By 1996 and 1997, the totals declared had fallen off sharply, with the reports showing less than $25,000 received.

In the meantime, the original board of three had expanded to become a board of eight. Each of the five new board members could fairly be described as a mover and shaker in Victoria, with powerful political connections. The society's accountant was the husband of the one of the city's most prominent Conservatives and a past candidate at the federal level. Another member was the wife of the former B.C. attorney general, by then head of B.C. Hydro, the province's major electrical utility. Two parents of former patients had joined—one a well-respected professor at the University of Victoria, the other the wife of a top businessman. Finally a provincial court judge was named in the documents as being a board member. (The judge later said she'd attended only a couple of meetings before deciding it wouldn't be appropriate for her to join the board on a long-term basis.)

However, Harris explained during the hearing that none of the eight were still active in the resurrected society. He testified that the original idea had been that the non-profit society would run the residential program—and indeed it had been the official holder of the health licence from 1995 to 1997. At that time, Montreux asked to have the licence switched over to the profit-making corporation so the society became a less essential part of the operation. About the same time, some board members from the non-profit society resigned, and it seemed better just "to let it lapse." New directors had been appointed in April 1999, he said. When McDannold had shown him the list that was filed as official in late 1998, he insisted that "all those people had resigned some time earlier." He couldn't say why the judge's name was on the list at all, because she'd left the board almost as soon as she'd joined it in 1994. It was, he said, "an oversight" that her name still appeared on the 1998 list.

In fact, society documents show clearly that one of the original three directors—consultant Lori Winstanley—chaired the April 1999 meeting, although she didn't then run for re-election to the board. The documents also make it clear that, far from having disappeared years earlier, some of those former directors, Winstanley and the accountant at least, had spent hours of their time in 1998 working out an acceptable compromise with Revenue Canada. As well as requiring the reinstatement, Revenue Canada was also insisting that the non-profit society couldn't simply serve as a tax-deductible conduit for money actually destined for the profit-making corporation owned by Claude-Pierre and Harris. That, it was clear, was what had actually happened to almost all the money the society had raised previously. Of the total of $360,000 raised between 1994 and 1998, $305,000 had been spent on "financial assistance to patients," paying the bills at Montreux for patients who couldn't afford it on their own or for whom fundraising drives had been started. In the campaign to raise money for Samantha Kendall, for instance, donors had been told to contribute not to the Kendall family or to any type of trust, but directly to the non-profit society. Revenue Canada said the society could certainly help patients pay for treatment for an eating disorder, but the money would have to go to the patient or family, who could then decide whether to spend it for treatment at Montreux or in some other program of their choice. Revenue Canada also wanted greater separation between the clinic and the society; they didn't want the fundraising money being handled only by an employee of the clinic, and suggested that the tax receipts should come from a separate address with a separate signing authority.

At the April 1999 meeting, the society members agreed to those steps. They changed the society's officially listed "purposes" so there was more emphasis on the education of the public and the monitoring of eating-disorder treatment generally, not just at Montreux. They began establishing criteria for the selection of families that might receive donations from the society's funds. Among the proposed criteria were that the patient "is not responding to any form of treatment after repeated tries" and the patient or family "is seeking alternate care." When the new board was set up, the chair was the father of a girl who'd been treated by Claude-Pierre in the early days of her outpatient practice. He was also the manager of the Senator apartment building, the building where Montreux was establishing a number of its unlicensed satellite operations for one or two patients at a time.

Dr. Stanwick could consider none of this, however. As he reviewed the massive amounts of evidence before him, lawyer Paul Pearlman advised him regularly that he could look at only specific breaches of legislation, either the Community Care Facilities Licensing Act and its regulations, or related laws like the Mental Health Act. Any negative finding he made against Montreux had to be backed up by a specific breach of a specific regulation. Originally Stanwick had hoped to deliver his decision early in the fall. But he soon realized there was just too much information to be digested and analyzed. The decision would consume him for almost four months.

It was not a good autumn for Montreux. Two of the clinic's most high-profile patients died of complications arising from their eating disorders. The first was Lena Zavaroni. Despite the best efforts of her family, things had not been going well for Lena since her return to Britain. Her anorexia was just as bad as it had ever been; her depression was, if anything, worse. The huge sums of money she'd made in her show business career were gone too. She was never sure whether they'd gone to pay for her treatment at Montreux, or for the other programs she'd tried, or whether they'd just disappeared somewhere else. But somehow she had gone from being the richest teenager in Scotland to subsisting on welfare benefits of less than £50 a week—about $400 (CAN) a month. She was sometimes helped by a charity established in Britain to aid show business personalities who'd fallen on hard times. She lived in a tiny seventh-floor flat in a public housing complex in a suburb of London to be near her father. Neighbours described her as sweet, but withdrawn and obviously desperately ill. Tormented by her depression, she found herself unable to eat anything and her weight plummeted to only about 55 pounds.

She remained convinced that the root of her problem was biological, and she began to petition the British health care system for a leukotomy, a brain operation in which a neurosurgeon severs the connective tissues that connect the base of the brain with the area in the front that controls things like appetite and depression. It is not so drastic a step as a lobotomy, but it is still rarely used nowadays, as most mental illnesses are treated more successfully and with less risk with psychiatric drugs. But no drugs had helped either Lena's eating disorder or her depression. To be allowed the operation, Lena had to convince a panel of psychiatrists that she had tried every option available without success, and that she was, despite her emotional problems, capable of understanding the risks of such drastic surgery. She did so. One of the doctors involved said later that Lena had convinced the panel that if they said no, she would commit suicide—and this time she would make sure she was successful.

Lena underwent the operation in September at the University of

Wales Hospital in Cardiff, one of the few sites in Britain that did the delicate surgery. In the weeks before she was admitted, she wavered between optimism that it would cure her completely and knowledge of the risk she was facing. When she went to see her friend Elly shortly before going into hospital, Elly whispered to her, "What if you die?"

"Then I'll be at peace," Lena replied.

Immediately after the surgery, it seemed all had gone well. The swelling in Lena's brain went down, and she began to recover full consciousness. However, about two weeks later she developed a blood infection that turned into bronchial pneumonia. Her wasted body was too weak to fight it off, and she died on October 1, her father and sister at her bedside. She was 35 years old and weighed 49 pounds.

Her death was huge news in Britain, where she'd first risen to stardom. Virtually every major newspaper, and radio and TV networks, carried a lengthy obituary. Some focussed on the need to prevent anorexia, others on the dangers of allowing child stars to grow up too fast. Within days, however, some British media had realized that the person known only as Patient 1 in the first licensing investigation report had in fact been Lena.

"Lena's Secret Hell" read the headline in the tabloid *Sunday Mirror*—and the hell was not anorexia or depression, but her treatment at Montreux. The *Mirror* had tracked down Gay and Andrew, who repeated to the newspaper the same story they had originally told licensing investigators. "Tragic Lena Zavaroni was held against her will and force-fed with a spoon jammed between her teeth at a secretive 600 pounds-a-night clinic," the story began.[59] Andrew admitted to the newspaper that he was one of those who'd force-fed Lena. "There would be two of us," he was quoted as saying. "One would hold her down and one would feed her with a spoon or from a bottle. She would struggle." These incidents occurred regularly over a period of months, he added.

The *Mirror* article differed from everything else that had been written about Montreux in one important way: it included no testimonials from any of the patients or parents who were still saying that Montreux was a safe place that was saving lives. Nowhere was there a suggestion that this was a battle between clinic supporters and clinic opponents.

There was no suggestion the clinic even had any supporters left. The *Mirror* didn't publish any comments from Claude-Pierre or other clinic spokespeople, but other media outlets who did ask were told that the problem was simply that Lena had left Montreux too early, before she had completed the program and could be considered cured.

Just six weeks after Lena's death, Montreux was hit with the death of another former patient, Donna Brooks—the young British woman who was seen on the first *20/20* show, talking cautiously to Claude-Pierre on the phone, and then arriving in Victoria with her mother.

"When I bring her through the clinic doors, I'm relieved," Claude-Pierre said as Donna was officially admitted. "I know she'll be safe. I know here's another life."[60]

Donna, however, had not proven to be a Montreux success story. She was never prepared to give up all control over her life to Montreux staff, and she was never convinced that the counselling she could obtain from the clinic's untrained staff was enough to solve her problem. When *20/20* returned to Victoria to do its follow-up program in the spring of 1995, Jeannie and Shannon both gave glowing testimonials as to how much better they were and how wonderful Montreux's therapy had been for them. Donna, however, was conspicuously absent from the show. The only clips to be seen of her were replays of one of her telephone conversations with Claude-Pierre, taped even before she came to Victoria.

By 1996 she'd spent more than 18 months in treatment. Her parents, who owned a farm estate in England, had sold acres of it to pay for her care. But Donna knew she was not making progress in the residential program, and she discharged herself from it. Still, she was not ready to abandon Montreux altogether and return to Britain. She ended up living independently in Victoria, sometimes going to Montreux for outpatient counselling, sometimes trying to get help through a naturopath or herbalist. Neighbours in her apartment building said she still appeared dreadfully unwell, and sometimes they could hear her exercising frenetically in the middle of the night.

Still, when the *Dateline* crew asked Montreux for a list of patients that they considered fully cured after residential treatment at the clinic, Donna's name was on the list. Her name came up at the hearing too, when Dr. Stanwick asked both Noah Dobson and Claude-Pierre about her progress. Dobson implied that she was doing satisfactorily although her way hadn't been entirely smooth after leaving the residential program. Claude-Pierre acknowledged that things were worse than that. She suggested the reason Donna had withdrawn from treatment was that she'd been having intestinal problems and wanted to work with the naturopath to deal with those. "She has regressed," Claude-Pierre admitted, adding she was hospitalized even as the hearing was going on, for the second time that year.

In the autumn, Donna and her family agreed it was finally time for her to return home to Britain. Her family hoped she'd find treatment there that would help her as Montreux never had. However, at that point she was so frail and malnourished that it was impossible for her to make the long flight. She returned to hospital for more than a week in an effort to build up her strength. On November 3, Dr. Clinton-Baker, who'd remained her doctor, cleared her for air travel. She left for Britain two days later, but she never even made it to her own home. She was so ill she was admitted to hospital directly on landing in London. On November 13 she died of pneumonia, an infection she couldn't shake off because she was so weak.

After her daughter died, Donna's mother, Brenda, publicly criticized the clinic for leaving the family in the dark about Donna's deteriorating condition. Brenda said that every time she talked to Montreux, she was told that her daughter was doing fine and had in fact completed the full Montreux program—just as *Dateline* had been told. By the time they finally found out how ill Donna really was, it was too late. If Donna wasn't still in the program, she wondered, why had Montreux staff helped her renew her visa to stay in Canada early in 1999? Montreux said it had been only "as a courtesy," but Brooks noted that if the visa had not been renewed, Donna might have returned home in time to get the life-saving treatment she needed.

Reporters writing about the deaths of Lena and Donna were introduced to a new spokesperson for the clinic, Serena.* Serena had been an acute-care patient under one-on-one care at Montreux only 10 months earlier and was still listed as someone taking "counselling" at the clinic. But once past the acute stage, she had risen in the clinic's hierarchy even faster than Jeannie, and she had assumed Claude-Pierre's role as its official spokeswoman and contact with the media.

She told reporters that, far from being cured, Donna had signed a release similar to Lena's, agreeing that she had not completed the program and was not cured. She was a legal adult, and it was up to her to contact the family after that point, Serena added.

By the time of Donna's death, Dr. Stanwick was putting the finishing touches on his judgment and reviewing the legal technicalities of it with Paul Pearlman. Media outlets across North America had been phoning to ask when, and how, the decision would be released. Many hoped for a few days' notice so they could get crews to Victoria. The day finally chosen for release was December 1, 1999—one year to the day since Dr. Stanwick had first told the clinic to stop taking any new patients.

The time set for the release was 10:00 a.m., and by 9:45 the small lobby of Dr. Stanwick's office was jammed to overflowing with reporters waiting for their packages. Bob McKeown and his crew from *Dateline* had returned to Victoria for the decision. CBC had national reporters there for both television and radio, and its all-news network carried Dr. Stanwick's news conference live. Blatchford had joined the crew from the *National Post*. As well as all the local and regional media, *The Globe and Mail* and CTV both had reporters and photographers on the scene.

Few of the reporters were disappointed. The judgment contained more than enough material for as many news stories as anyone would care to write. Most turned immediately to the last pages to find the answer to the ultimate question: What was to be Montreux's fate?

The last paragraph read: "I hereby order that the licence for 1560 Rockland Avenue, in the name of Montreux Counselling Centre Ltd., be cancelled, effective January 31, 2000." It was the toughest decision that could have been imposed on Montreux.

Dr. Stanwick wrote that "serious breaches" of the legislation and regulations had been proven to his satisfaction. But even more, he cited as reasons for his decision: "Montreux management's lack of honesty in dealing with the Licensing process, including this hearing; their unwillingness to accept responsibility for the clinic's shortcomings; and their unwillingness to change key aspects of their operation to bring them into compliance" with the law.

He sympathized with the parents and patients who had testified on the clinic's behalf, and he noted that "in the majority of cases, treatment was effected through loving and caring kindness, not through actions which would jeopardize a patient's health, safety or dignity." That, though, was not enough to offset what he described as "the serious risk to health and safety" which had occurred in some cases.

The radio reporters rushed off to phone in their stories for the next newscast.

As the reporters had time to peruse the decision more thoroughly, it became clear there were three areas of Montreux's practice that had particularly worried Dr. Stanwick. The first was the question of admitting patients like Anna and Vivian who Dr. Birmingham had warned were not medically stable enough to be treated in a facility with so little medical expertise on hand—either from the front-line staff or from the senior management, who were supposed to be paged in times of crisis. Although one of the greatest risks for highly acute anorexics is heart failure, Montreux had no equipment available to deal with such a crisis. Even if one of the clinic doctors happened to be on the premises, they would be able to do no more than they would in any public building, he noted. And the doctors, who were general practitioners with no special training, couldn't be expected to have the specialized knowledge needed to deal with some of the extremely ill patients who were admitted to the clinic.

The new admission policy was little improvement, Dr. Stanwick wrote, because of the clause, explained at the hearing by Enoch, that allowed the admissions committee to admit anyone it wanted, even those who didn't meet the medical criteria that had been agreed upon. That clause, in Dr. Stanwick's view, "effectively castrates the entire policy." He agreed with McDannold that it would be impossible to have such a policy and not be in breach of the licensing rules.

The second key issue was that of patient rights in the Montreux system, which he described as one of "imposed therapy." Patients were given "the illusion of no choice"—legally they were free to refuse treatment or leave the program, but Claude-Pierre, the clinic staff, and often their families persuaded them that wasn't the case. They had to do what staff said; they had to eat everything that was on their meal plan; essentially they had to give complete control of their lives to Claude-Pierre and the staff. Testimony from staff and managers had made it clear that, for acute patients, it was staff's responsibility to ensure the patient received enough nutrition, not the patient's.

Dr. Stanwick recognized that the whole area of imposing therapy on anorexics, or other victims of mental illness, is one fraught with scientific and ethical questions. "Anorexia is a mental disorder that impairs judgment about treatment, and imposed treatment has the potential to bring about improvement and the first steps towards recovery," he wrote. However, in other cases, imposed treatment leads to the drastic step of taking away a patient's autonomy without any apparent benefit. Such treatment could end up with the patient's being even worse than before. At the least, he noted, most experts say a careful analysis of any individual case must be undertaken before a decision to impose therapy is made.

In any case, Dr. Stanwick ruled, even if the "illusion of no choice" had helped some of Montreux's patients, that didn't, and couldn't, make it legal in British Columbia in a facility like Montreux. "Only if a patient is deemed to be incompetent as a result of a mental disorder, may the decision-making authority be legally shifted to others." In B.C., it requires two doctors to declare a person mentally incompetent. Montreux's doctors could have certified patients—but then they would have had to be transferred to a mental hospital, not allowed to stay at Montreux.

Mental hospitals have the equipment and trained staff to deal with challenging patients, Dr. Stanwick pointed out. Montreux did not, and so, in those cases, to ensure that a patient got all the day's prescribed nutrition staff resorted to verbal abuse, threats, or physical force-feeding. Even the reports of staff yelling and shouting at their charges could be explained if the staff's perception was that they were dealing only with the "Negative Mind," and not the real patient who was sharing the same body. One incident recorded in the logbooks even had Claude-Pierre telling three patients who were being distressingly noisy and difficult to "shut the fuck up," although Claude-Pierre denied this, insisting the comment had come from another patient, the violent Sylvia, who'd been upset by the noise.

Furthermore, Montreux patients who were operating under the "illusion of no choice" did not have the same rights to regular hearings and appeals by an independent body as did those who were legally committed as mentally incompetent.

Dr. Stanwick was impressed by the evidence that had been given by a psychiatrist called by Montreux as one of their witnesses. Dr. Paul Termansen was an expert on suicide whom the clinic had asked to help them develop policies and staff training on reducing the risk of suicide at the facility. But when questioned by Dr. Stanwick, he had also discussed the idea of imposed therapy and what he'd seen when he'd visited the clinic earlier in 1999. He'd talked with three patients, he said, and all three of them found their anxiety level was much less at Montreux than it had been elsewhere. That was a benefit to them, he said, because it reduced the risk of them trying to harm themselves. It probably also made it easier for them to eat.

However, he noted, the therapy the patients had received had not taught them how to recognize the conflicts or stresses that would make them anxious, how Montreux reduced that anxiety, or how they could cope themselves with anxiety in a healthier way than refusing to eat or harming themselves. The logical corollary was that such patients might end up back in trouble in the stressful real world once they left Montreux.

Drs. Birmingham and Termansen both said that even in cases where a patient had been committed for treatment, it was important to move to a voluntary treatment as soon as possible. However, wrote Dr. Stanwick, "the evidence before this hearing suggests that some Montreux patients such as Louise, Anna, and Vivian have been in a state of treatment and dependence for a period of years, during which Montreux staff have struggled with the Negative Mind and made decisions on their behalf."

Dr. Stanwick's conclusion was simple: "Montreux is not above the law and cannot operate outside of the law."

The largest portion of the judgment—almost half of the 147 pages—was devoted to the case of Dustin. Dustin's case, in many ways, provided examples of every concern Dr. Stanwick had about the

Montreux operation: taking on a case without proper medical or psychological assessment; extreme problems in the way both he and Louise were dealt with; lack of consultation with trained professionals throughout; the remarkable number of lies told to licensing investigators; and an insistence by Claude-Pierre and other managers that their way was the right way, no matter what anyone else—or the objective evidence—said.

Quoting extensively from the testimony of child psychiatrists Drs. Sherkow and Ainsworth, Dr. Stanwick concluded that Dustin had never suffered from genuine anorexia nervosa in the first place. No matter what Claude-Pierre and Margaret Dobson said, Dr. Stanwick wrote, Montreux's own documents proved better than their words that Dustin was not getting better in the days he was separated from his mother. "Those documents paint a distressing picture of a young boy whose difficulties around feeding and swallowing remained extreme in April and May of 1997, after more than 13 months of residential care."

Similarly, although Claude-Pierre had testified that she still believed the arrangement in which Louise was a primary caregiver for Dustin had been beneficial for both, Dr. Stanwick rejected that contention as well. "Again," he wrote, "Montreux's own files demonstrate clearly that this was not the case. Louise's records document a pattern of increasing, sometimes nearly intolerable, stress, as her frustration in not being able to help Dustin more grows, to the point it appeared to be affecting her physical as well as emotional health."

One whole section of the report was devoted to detailing the numerous times Claude-Pierre and the other managers had denied that Dustin had ever been a residential patient, and their tortuous explanations of those statements at the hearing. Dr. Stanwick's conclusion was blunt: "I find that Montreux management provided false information to Licensing regarding the care of Dustin, and that they must have known that information to be false." (Moira's evidence about how much control she had over Dustin's care and the separation was more politely described as "unreliable".)

As Dr. Stanwick put together the various pieces of testimony about Dustin, he realized that, even at the hearing, the story that management had told him was still not entirely truthful. Claude-Pierre had testified that Dustin's move back to staying with his mother "wasn't anything that was premeditated. It was something that just seemed to happen." Margaret Dobson also testified about being involved in having Dustin move back to living with Moira.

But Moira's recollection remained that one day soon after her return from New York, "I get a knock on the door, and there is Dustin. And he just walked in as though he lived there for the entire time." That was backed up by the testimony of the staff members who remembered Dustin moving back abruptly on the morning of May 29.

That time frame, Dr. Stanwick realized, made it impossible for either Peggy Claude-Pierre or Margaret Dobson to have been involved in the move. Both were out of town that day, along with David Harris and Noah Dobson. Management of the clinic was in the hands of middle managers, including Nicole Claude-Pierre. Since Moira had returned from her trip to New York just as the others were leaving town, she, Claude-Pierre, and Margaret Dobson hadn't been in the same city for the previous seven weeks.

"I can only conclude," wrote Dr. Stanwick, "that Peggy Claude-Pierre, Noah Dobson, and Margaret Dobson lied, under oath, in giving evidence at this hearing regarding the discharge of Dustin." The ongoing lack of truth around Dustin, he said, had "undermined their credibility" in all the testimony they gave.

By the time Dr. Stanwick's news conference came around, two hours after the report was released, the reporters were loaded with questions and ammunition. Television cameras lined the front row of a dingy room usually used for doctors' training sessions at one of the local hospitals. Quietly at the back stood Gavin and some of the others whose complaints had launched the investigation. This time, their complaints had borne fruit, but they felt no overwhelming joy. Relief was more like it.

Dr. Stanwick reiterated most of the main points in the report, so radio and TV could have them on tape. He explained the lengthy process to those who had not followed it in its entirety, and he reiterated that he had not passed judgment on Claude-Pierre's theories of the causes of, or cures for, anorexia, but only on the way they were implemented at Montreux. Other private clinics had been set up in Canada for treating

eating disorders without coming into conflict with care standards and mental health laws, he pointed out.

The entire process had been complex, intense, and emotionally laden, he said. He remembered again, and gave credit to, the parents who came to tell how desperate they were before finding Montreux. "I can personally say it's been six very difficult months, weighing some very, very challenging issues."

Reporters departed hastily to make sure they got a good seat for the clinic's news conference, scheduled for 90 minutes later.

In contrast to the dingy hospital conference room, Montreux welcomed the press in the banquet room of the Ocean Pointe Resort, one of Victoria's top waterfront hotels. The room was crowded before a single reporter got there. About 70 patients, parents, and staff members mingled, talking in hushed tones. Some, like Brenda's mother and sister, had come from as far away as Australia for the announcement. The crowd burst into applause as Claude-Pierre—again in funereal black—entered the room, accompanied by Harris, lawyer Dennis Murray, and the clinic's new spokeswoman, Serena.

When Claude-Pierre stepped up to the microphone, there was a noticeable hush in the room. Everyone—reporters, patients, and staff alike—wanted to hear every word of what she had to say. Instead, she said, in her softest tones, only a single sentence: "It saddens us greatly that the value of human life could be so trivialized by a political process." Reporters were left shaking their heads at what that was supposed to mean, but Claude-Pierre declined to answer any questions. Murray didn't have anything to say either, leaving Harris and Serena to take the brunt of the dozens of questions.

Serena described the report as "a travesty" and the result of "an inquisition-like process." Harris complained that Dr. Stanwick had "misunderstood" many pieces of evidence and taken all sorts of things out of context, throwing into his responses words like "bias" and "defamation." But when pressed for specifics, both admitted that neither they, nor anyone else at the clinic, had yet read the report.

Still, reporters thought it might be worth trying to pin them down on some of Dr. Stanwick's more serious allegations. As Blatchford said in her column the next day, it was "like trying to wrestle a slippery infant in a bathtub full of Jello."[61] The only result was that they appeared to be trying to back off from what honesty they had finally shown at the hearing. Asked about the lies, especially surrounding Dustin, Harris went back to his old line: "We never intentionally withheld any information." *Dateline*'s Bob McKeown didn't do any better when he tried to get Harris to explain how it could be that they'd been told Donna Brooks was completely cured when she was still appallingly ill, so ill that she'd since died. Neither were there any clear answers as to what Claude-Pierre and Harris might do next. An appeal was one possibility, Harris said. Moving the entire clinic somewhere else was another.

"We will endure. We will endure here if we can work something out," he said. "If not here, then somewhere else."

When the four moved to leave the ballroom, the supporters in the crowd rose to give Claude-Pierre a standing ovation.

Left alone with the reporters and photographers, a host of patients and parents wanted to deliver their testimonials. Some, like Stacey, were already worried about what might happen to them if the clinic did close down entirely. Some wanted to talk again about how much better, and more humane, they'd found the treatment at Montreux than in some of the other hospital-based programs they'd attended. They couldn't understand the legal concepts that meant they might have been tube-fed against their will while committed in hospital, but that it was illegal for Montreux to go as far as it did in getting patients to eat. Led by Harris, they tried to persuade reporters that licensing said it was "force-feeding" if a worker uttered a single sentence like "Come on, you can do it," to persuade a client to eat. No matter whether they'd been at Montreux for months or years, they seemed unable to contemplate the idea of living a normal existence without the clinic being there for them.

McKeown and the *Dateline* crew were among the last to leave the ballroom because of the amount of equipment they had to take down. Suddenly they found themselves surrounded by more than a dozen Montreux supporters, several of them male staff members, and all of them hostile. One would have thought it was McKeown who'd issued the order shutting down the clinic rather than Dr. Stanwick. They wanted to dissect *Dateline*'s first piece line by line, even though it had been shown 17 months earlier. It hadn't been fair, they shouted. It was too sensational, it had paid far too much attention to the staff members who'd complained to licensing and far too little to the stories of those whose lives had been saved. McKeown and field producer Patrick Corbett tried to explain the rules of balanced journalism, in which it's normally expected that both sides of any controversy will be covered. They might as well have saved their breath. They talked for almost half an hour before finally saying they had to get ready for their next interview.

Claude-Pierre might have declined to speak to the assembled media, but she did agree later that afternoon to do a brief interview with the local television station. Reporter Catherine McDonald of CHEK-TV had been one of the few to continue to emphasize the clinic's self-proclaimed excellent record in her stories during the hearing. Talking to McDonald, Claude-Pierre vowed to carry on the program in some way or other, despite the decision. "I can't not," she said.

But Claude-Pierre already had her sights set on higher ground for the one and only major appearance in which she would discuss the decision. The next day she left for New York for yet another appearance with her favourite interviewer, Lynn Sherr for *20/20*.

Meanwhile, the story was covered in nearly every major newspaper in Canada. The *National Post* put it on the front page and then devoted another two full pages inside to it, including an entire column of quotes in which Dr. Stanwick outlined the major problems. Blatchford's column was this time headlined, "They broke the rules, but they still don't get it." When she pointed out that Harris and Serena were stuck trying to answer the questions, Blatchford noted: "They might as well not have bothered in fact, so severe is their collective disconnect from reality."[62] She wrote that Montreux and other clinic managers "came to believe their own sycophantic press clippings, and grew arrogant and zealous ... they decided they were beyond reproach, and rules and retribution."

Blatchford's counterpart at *The Globe and Mail*, Margaret Wente, noted in her column the next day: "The B.C. health authorities have done us two favours by shutting down Montreux. They have reminded us that just about anyone can set up a clinic for eating disorders, and make any claims they want about their success. And they've ensured that Saint Peggy won't get invited on *Oprah* any more."[63]

The other media outlets didn't have a Blatchford or a Wente, but, almost uniformly, their stories stressed the serious weaknesses Dr. Stanwick had found in Montreux's operations far more than the testimonials from patients and parents. In many cases, those patients and parents came out of it all looking so desperate that they were ready to clutch at any passing life raft, including one as riddled with holes as Montreux.

Moira hadn't flown to Victoria for the decision, but *Globe and Mail* reporter Kim Lunman caught up with her in New York. "To me, it's murder," she told Lunman. "Those are my words and that's how I want it printed … you don't know how many kids are out there dying, waiting to get into the clinic."[64] In the same article, Lunman printed many of the quotes from Dr. Stanwick's report, citing how Dustin was misdiagnosed and how serious his feeding problems were after more than a year in care.

In other stories, the testimonials were balanced with comments from one or more of the former staff members, expressing their relief that someone had finally understood what they were trying to say.

"It's been three years of waiting for this," said Gay, praising Dr. Stanwick for the decision. "I know it was hard. I know he was up against a lot of stuff."

The *20/20* piece ran on December 6. Claude-Pierre did more to try to answer the specifics of the charges than she or clinic management had done before or since. Her answers, though, were almost always in contradiction, not just to Dr. Stanwick's decision, but again to many of the clinic's own patient logs. She said she didn't think any of Dr. Stanwick's findings were true, without specifying what was wrong with a single one of them. Asked about force-feeding by Sherr, she asked rhetorically: "How could you force-feed anybody? They would have to swallow."[65] Sherr did not follow up on camera with any questions about the incidents in which Anna was "covered with shake" because she did refuse to swallow, or where Lena had a hand placed over her mouth to prevent her from spitting or gagging instead of swallowing.

Dustin was never force-fed either, she said. Rather, he "opened his mouth the very slightest bit.... This was a child who, as far as we knew, was in dire need. The parents asked for help. And I would do anything I could to save his life. And I did." Again, viewers saw no follow-up questions based on the findings that Dustin had never been medically compromised or on the logbook entries in which his mouth was pried open with the spoon.

Claude-Pierre reiterated her view that any mistakes she and Montreux had made were the result of trying to grow too fast, hire too many staff, "save" too many anorexics. "The problem with me," she said, "is that when a child is suffering, my immediate response is to try to make a difference. Perhaps that's arrogance. I don't feel that it was."

Even as viewers were hearing the allegations in the report put to Claude-Pierre, for much of the time they were seeing pictures taken from the first *20/20* documentaries—the incredible frailness of the girls when they arrived, Claude-Pierre looking soulful as she walked down one of Victoria's beaches. Sherr again talked of the clinic as "a mansion where miracles took place, a safe haven."

"How," she concluded, "could this have happened to a woman many have called a saint?"

10

Struggling for Survival

The climate for Montreux had changed. You could tell by the smattering of letters to the editors that appeared supporting the clinic in the newspapers. This was not the same as in 1997 when, after news of the investigation broke, dozens of supporters flooded media offices with letters of support. Even Victoria's daily, the *Times-Colonist,* printed fewer than a dozen letters, although it's not clear whether they might have actually received more. No one who wrote denied a single one of Dr. Stanwick's major findings. Rather, they mainly argued that Montreux should be allowed some latitude because its approach to treating eating disorders was unique. Dr. David Clinton-Baker wrote a letter, not mentioning that he was one of the clinic's regular doctors for several of the patients who Dr. Birmingham found had been put at risk. He didn't deal with any of the medical issues in the decision that involved him so intimately. Rather, his letter praised the compassion of the staff and defended the concept of having recovering anorexics care for those sicker than themselves. "It is claimed that rules have been broken and that patients' lives have been unnecessarily put at risk," he wrote. "What this statement fails to recognize is that parents have sought out the Montreux treatment because other treatments have failed, and that in fact by not seeking some alternate treatment, their very lives may be put at risk."[66]

Evidence of the changed climate could be seen as well on the Internet, in the chatrooms and discussion groups devoted to eating disorders. After Peggy Claude-Pierre's book was published, most of those who commented on Montreux did so with envy of the few who went there to be cured. Many anorexics around the world had believed it to be a place with no risk of recidivism, with nothing but round-the-clock love. After Dr. Stanwick's decision, Montreux still had its supporters, but many more media-watchers were beginning to realize it had perhaps never been the utopia they'd been looking for. Although far from a scientific sample of opinion, the change in tone in the chatrooms and newsgroups was interesting. Some correspondents to the chatrooms began posting stories of Montreux patients they knew who had not in fact been completely or permanently cured. One talked of a friend who had now returned to the clinic for the third time, having relapsed twice. When the girl had been about to return home for the first time, the correspondent had asked her what she was doing about therapy back in her home city, but was told she wouldn't need any follow-up because she was cured. "In a cocky way, she added, 'I am Montreux. We have a 100 per cent cure rate.' ... A few months after discharge she had to return. And again."

Perhaps the best first-hand analysis came from a correspondent who admitted she'd spent years devoted to Claude-Pierre's theories. She'd believed that, because she could not afford Montreux, nothing else would be able to help. Gradually she realized she was wrong and concluded she would have to take responsibility for changing, and do the work needed to get better. "This revelation sucked and I hated it," she wrote in the chatroom. "I *so* want to believe that [Claude-Pierre] is right. It would make my life so much easier. It would be great if Montreux was Mecca and Peggy an Angel and infantilizing me would make me better. But alas, the more I research that, the more I realize that it is bullshit."

Many of the most strenuous defences of Montreux on the Internet came from those who were still involved, as staff or as parents of patients there. One writer who identified himself as the father of a patient provided a passionate testimonial in which he insisted that his visits to the clinic had convinced him "there are no dark rooms, no force feeding, and none of the bad things that were alleged in the investigation. What there is behind those doors are ... the most kind, loving, and caring people we know. And (surprise!) they know more about treating eating disorders than anyone on the planet. And (surprise!) their methods work. Period." He described Dr. Stanwick and the Capital Health

Region as "a political abomination and an embarrassment to the Canadian government" before admitting he hadn't actually read Dr. Stanwick's report, but had heard about it only from David Harris.

Other postings came from Denise,* who'd come to the clinic as one of its first residential patients at the age of 15. She'd never left, had become a careworker a year before ending her stay as a patient, and, 5½ years later, was still on staff as a careworker and team leader. She talked about how grateful she was that she too had been treated for free, and insisted that the clinic did everything it could to meet licensing requirements. "We were never against them," she wrote. "They were against us from the beginning. The allegations were not true. I've worked with the few who started these allegations. They did not believe in our philosophy."

In an echo of the government's concerns about Claude-Pierre's inability to maintain confidentiality, another staff member went so far as to provide on the Internet the full names of all those who had made allegations against the clinic, even while condemning licensing for allowing the names of any of the patients to slide into public knowledge by entering their files as exhibits.

By far the most bitter debate on the Internet, however, involved Moira. In her first post after Dr. Stanwick's judgment was made public, Moira wrote that Dustin "is doing great. He loves school, has lots of friends, he is in his first Christmas play ... he is happy, thriving and (thank God) healthy." However, just two days later, she stated she wanted him "to be happy and play and live life as a seven-year-old should, but for who he is and how he is. I accept the fact he will be different." It was never clear just what she meant by "different."

Her devotion to Claude-Pierre had not lessened. "Peggy was one of the few where her heart and soul was in the right place," she wrote. "Her kindness, love and endurance was all she wanted to give, and so she did ... I would rather have a world filled with Peggys than the bad, selfish, and hurtful that roam this earth." She said Dustin had told her, "Mom, keep fighting for Peggy like she did for me!"

Several of the correspondents, however, took exception to Moira's decision to publicize Dustin's full name, picture, and story, when he was still not old enough to make a reasonable decision about that himself. That criticism led to a response from Moira, written and posted in all capital letters—the equivalent of shouting in Internet etiquette. "My son does know of his pictures being used, and I allow him to watch all the shows since it is about him and his life," she wrote. Later the same day, though, she tried to downplay the amount of media attention given Dustin. "I only put Dustin on *Oprah* and he really wasn't on the show," she tried to say. Only a few paragraphs later she conceded she'd also participated in the *Dateline* show but that was only because "I love Peggy and support her 100 per cent." (She never did mention *Good Morning America*.)

Her all-capitals conclusion: "One thing I am very proud of is the fact that I gave my son everything, and gave up everything for him, and I would do it again in a heartbeat if he needed me to. And if the person who helped me in that fight needed my help in return, I would do whatever I had to do for them ... again. I regret nothing." She didn't say what it was she had done for Claude-Pierre before, other than giving such passionate testimony on her behalf at the hearing.

Under the legislation, Montreux had exactly 30 days to decide whether it wanted to appeal Dr. Stanwick's decision. One option was an appeal to the B.C. Supreme Court. The court, though, could deal only with any serious legal errors that had been made; it couldn't overrule Dr. Stanwick's findings on the facts of the case. That was why most facilities that chose to appeal licensing decisions went instead to the provincial Community Care Facilities Licensing Appeal Board, a group of lawyers and laypeople appointed by the provincial Cabinet specifically to hear appeals in such cases.

Just one week into the month, a story appeared in *The Globe and Mail*, saying the clinic would need to raise money before it could appeal the decision. Serena was again the clinic spokeswoman, and she said bluntly: "It depends on whether we can get the cash. We don't have anything in the bank account to pay for the appeal."[67] She claimed that Montreux was treating as many as one-third of its patients—then numbered at 34—for free, and the lawyers' fees had already eaten up about $500,000.

Christmas came and went, with no word from Montreux on their future plans. It was December 30 when Paul Pearlman phoned Dr. Stanwick to say he had just received the official word from Dennis Murray:

Montreux was appealing the decision, to the licensing appeal board. It was less than 24 hours before the appeal period would have expired.

Much of Montreux's appeal was based on the structure of the licensing process in B.C. Murray argued that the way the system worked led to a "perception of bias," that perhaps Dr. Stanwick couldn't issue an impartial ruling no matter how hard he tried.

However, in the documents filed with the appeal board, Murray also accused Dr. Stanwick of "actual bias." The decision wasn't fair, he argued, and couldn't be justified on the basis of the evidence that had been presented at the hearing. He complained that Dr. Stanwick had given far too much credibility to former staff members and placed far too little emphasis on the testimonials of grateful parents and patients. Although it didn't bear on the court case, Murray's arguments subtly—and doubtless unintentionally—undermined Peggy Claude-Pierre's claims that her patients would end up entirely recovered, without symptoms and without risk of relapse. The testimonial Murray used as the example of those that had been ignored by Dr. Stanwick was that of Caroline. The lawyer recalled how both Caroline and her father had testified that mainstream medical treatment had not worked for her, and how they were certain she'd be dead without Claude-Pierre and Montreux. But then he also conceded in the appeal documents that Caroline still had some issues around eating and "always would have"—this after almost six years in a program that Claude-Pierre had maintained would provide a complete cure.

Murray also argued that the entire judgment had been coloured by Dr. Stanwick's perception of the honesty—or lack thereof—of the Montreux managers concerning the treatment of Dustin. That, he said, should not have been used to justify a more generalized distrust of Claude-Pierre and Harris and their willingness to deal openly and fairly with licensing in the future. Since the spirit of the legislation was to be "remedial, not punitive," he argued, Dr. Stanwick should have made more effort to find conditions that would have satisfied his concerns but would have allowed the clinic to continue operating.

The allegations of bias led to immediate legal and practical complications. The judgment had given Montreux until the end of January to cease its residential operations. The clinic had been moving its patients out of the Rockland mansion, although most appeared to be moving only into satellite one- or two-person units being set up around the city. Still, the first thing Murray wanted was a stay of the closure order until the appeal was heard, probably three or four months later. It would, he argued, make little sense for the staff, the patients, or their families to have the clinic close down for a few months, have families make alternate care arrangements for their children, in some cases travel thousands of miles—only to have the appeal board grant the appeal and allow the operation to be re-established in its entirety. As well, he admitted frankly, a few months of total closure would probably do Montreux so much harm financially that it might well find it impossible to reopen at all.

However, under the legislation, the person who was required to rule on the request for the stay was none other than Dr. Stanwick himself. The medical health officer who wrote a decision was, in case of an appeal, expected to decide whether there'd be an "immediate risk" to clients' health and safety in allowing a stay, and on that basis decide on the request. But everybody involved—Montreux, licensing investigators, Dr. Stanwick, and all the lawyers—agreed it made no sense for Dr. Stanwick to rule on a stay relating to an appeal in which he personally was being accused of bias. That would be a conflict of interest in any rational mind, everyone agreed.

However, the law didn't make any provision for exceptions. Eventually the lawyers had to go to the B.C. Supreme Court to ask for permission to have someone else hear the request. The judge immediately understood the problem and issued an order, replacing Dr. Stanwick for the hearing on the stay. The person chosen to replace him was Kersteen Johnston, who was director of licensing for the provincial health ministry. Murray wasn't particularly enthusiastic about Johnston as a choice, since she could, in some ways, be seen as Dr. Stanwick's boss. However, no one could think of a better option, and so Johnston took over the role.

By the time the court case was completed, it was the middle of January. Only two weeks remained before the official closure date. The stress and uncertainty were beginning to tell on patients and staff at the clinic. Denise again posted to the Internet: "The part I'm stressed out about is watching the patients go through this. They're so scared of being sent home, going back to live in the tortured lives they used to live.... It breaks my heart to see them like this.... I love [the client for whom she was team leader] dearly; she's like my child even though she's only a year younger than me." (Denise was 21 at the time.)

The first day the lawyers could get together to hear the appeal was Thursday, January 27, only five days before the closure order was scheduled to take effect. Murray reiterated his argument that to deny the stay would effectively deny the appeal, without ever having the merits of it heard. "Don't make us go to the appeal hearing destroyed," he said. He insisted that the clients would be safe at the clinic, and said Montreux was prepared to accept extra monitoring and supervision to ensure no problems arose. In the 24 hours before the hearing began, Murray and Montreux management persuaded Pam Brambell, a nurse with more than 30 years experience, to agree to provide health assessments of the Montreux patients and be on call if the services of a nurse were needed.

The next day, though, McDannold argued that to grant the stay would be "against the public's interest" and would result in further risk to the patients. He astounded the hearing by disclosing that, even while publicly worrying about closing down, Montreux had admitted a new acute-care patient as recently as January 17. The patient, a medical doctor from Switzerland with bulimia, was staying in one of the satellite sites. McDannold revealed that at least three other acute-care patients had been admitted since the hearing ended the previous July. They came from as far afield as England and Sweden, and at least one was a teenager. The total number of patients under Montreux care was now 26, he said, although Stacey was the only one who remained living in the Rockland mansion.

In his judgment, Dr. Stanwick had been clear on the issue of the satellite sites. Up until the decision was delivered, he agreed, Montreux might have genuinely thought there was no legal problem in running an unlimited number of satellite operations, and he would not hold it against them that they had done so. However, he wrote: "The evidence showed clearly that Montreux is a centrally-run operation, no matter how many two-person satellite units it is operating at any specific time

... patients receive exactly the same type of care, delivered by the same providers, no matter at which site they reside.

"If I find that the operation does pose a risk to the health and safety of the nine residents at the licensed site, it does not make sense that Montreux should be allowed to put patients at risk, simply because there are no more than two of them at any one location."[68]

While the community care legislation might be unclear in determining whether a number of satellite operations centrally run require a licence, he noted, the province's Mental Health Act was not. It stated unequivocally that any for-profit facility that treated patients with mental disorders must have a licence.

At the stay hearing, however, Murray said that that issue, too, would be part of the appeal. Montreux was convinced that anyone who had come directly to a satellite site was considered by the clinic to be an "outpatient" and should not be considered part of an operation that required a licence.

Johnston said she would spend the weekend analyzing the information, and would give her decision on Monday, the same day the clinic was supposed to close. Behind the scenes, Montreux management spent part of the weekend working to develop a plan that decentralized the clinic's operations even further. That, they hoped, would allow them to carry on satellite operations even if Johnston ruled against it.

However, the news Claude-Pierre and Harris received on Monday was good. Johnston had decided the clinic should be allowed to stay open until the appeal was decided, and even move patients back to the Rockland mansion. However, Montreux was required to follow both the licensing rules and a series of strict new conditions. She warned Murray that if she found Montreux wasn't obeying the rules, she'd give it as little as 24 hours to shut its doors. In fact, she said, the clinic had to draw up a plan to show her how it would cease operations if it came to that. Johnston also required a significant increase in the medical component at Montreux. A dietitian would have to be a more active part of the treatment team. The registered nurse would have to be on call and perform regular checks of all patients. A new manager would have to be hired, one acceptable to licensing as well as to Montreux. And a doctor recognized by both sides as a genuine expert on eating disorders would have to be brought in as a consultant. His job would be to examine each of Montreux's "on-care" patients to ensure that none was in immediate medical danger. Also hired would be an "administrator," a person who would be paid by Montreux but would report directly to Johnston to ensure that all of the conditions were being met. Johnston also stressed again that Montreux was not to admit any new 24-hour-care patients at all, either to Rockland or to any satellite sites, until that issue too had been dealt with at the appeal.

Claude-Pierre had come to the downtown hotel where the stay hearing was being held. But yet again, she declined to talk to the reporters, leaving that once more to David Harris and Serena. Harris wasn't happy about the conditions, but he supposed the clinic could live with them. "We're fighting for justice and human lives," he said.

Serena was more optimistic. "Basically we're very pleased," she said. No matter what the conditions, the decision allowed the clinic to resume its residential operation and remain open. For her, at least, that was what mattered most.

The next few weeks were harried ones for Montreux staff and management. Patients began to be moved back to the main mansion. The new professional staff had to be hired—ones who were acceptable to Claude-Pierre and also to licensing, not an easy task. An administrator had to be hired and an expert medical consultant found.

Finding the administrator proved the easiest task with the appointment of John Noble. He had had a long career as a civil servant for the British Columbia government, starting off as a social worker in a jail for juvenile delinquents and rising to the post of deputy minister for, at various times, the ministries responsible for welfare, child protection, and health. For a while, he'd actually been Johnston's ultimate boss. Since retiring a few years earlier, he'd worked with a number of non-profit groups and had also undertaken special projects for the government. In one of the largest, he'd co-chaired a commission that travelled around the province to study the entire process of licensing and how it could be improved. No one could deny his experience in the area.

For Montreux, though, Noble had an added advantage—he'd already done some work for them. In early 1999, before the hearing began, clinic management had wanted to try to make some policy changes that would persuade Dr. Stanwick to allow it to take new patients once again. They had briefly hired Noble to help them put the policies together. The attempt hadn't succeeded, but Claude-Pierre and Harris felt comfortable with Noble. They believed he understood what they were trying to do and how important the work was.

Immediately after the stay had been granted, Montreux had again changed lawyers. The case had been taken over by Chris Considine, another of the city's top criminal defence lawyers. Like Dennis Murray, Considine had had books written and TV movies made about, not one, but two of his cases. He had taken on the case of Darren Huenemann, an 18-year-old accused of hiring two younger schoolmates to murder his mother and grandmother so he could acquire a multi-million-dollar inheritance early. Despite Considine's best efforts, the evidence against Huenemann had been overwhelming, and he'd been sentenced to life in prison with no hope of parole for 25 years. The case had prompted both a book and a CBC made-for-TV movie.

He'd also been the lawyer for Sue Rodriguez, an articulate and passionate Victoria-area woman who wanted the right to an assisted suicide as she was dying of Lou Gehrig's disease. Considine took her case all the way to the Supreme Court of Canada. He did not in the end win a legal victory, but the case raised the issue of the right to die on a nation-wide stage. Rodriguez's story was also immortalized in both a book and a TV movie.

It was Considine who began to work with Claude-Pierre, Harris, and Serena to find an acceptable manager and a medical expert on eating disorders who would serve in the consultant's role. Victoria had no doctors who could be considered expert in the sense that Johnston meant. The major programs in British Columbia were based in Vancouver, a 90-minute ferry ride away. The obvious choice for a doctor there was Dr. Birmingham, but Montreux said they would not accept his appointment. After the report he'd provided to Dr. Stanwick, they felt they couldn't trust him, and they couldn't encourage their patients to trust him either. Since virtually every other doctor in Vancouver was a colleague of Dr. Birmingham's, Considine was instructed that none of them would be acceptable either.

Eventually all sides agreed they would have to go farther afield to obtain acceptable expertise of the sort Johnston wanted. For several days, licensing and Montreux negotiated over who might be acceptable. Licensing put forward some names; Claude-Pierre rejected all of them. Montreux suggested several doctors who worked in eating-disorder programs in the U.S. Licensing said they didn't have the high level of expertise needed for the job.

Eventually, exasperated, Johnston said she'd make the decision herself and she didn't care if one side or the other wasn't happy. She chose Dr. Allan Kaplan, who was head of the eating-disorder program at Toronto General Hospital and a full professor of psychiatry at the University of Toronto medical school. It would have been tough to find anyone with a better reputation in the field. He was a fellow of the Academy for Eating Disorders, the worldwide congress of experts in that field, and would within months be elected its president. In 1998 he had been voted by his peers to a group known as "The Best Doctors in America," and his program at Toronto General had won the American Psychiatric Association's Gold Achievement Award. Dr. Kaplan promised to find time within a few weeks to make the trip to Victoria and pay a five-day visit to the clinic.

Despite Dr. Kaplan's reputation, Claude-Pierre was furious with the choice. She complained that he was a psychiatrist with a mainstream medical background who wouldn't be open to alternative theories about the causes or treatment of anorexia. Even worse, he'd already gone public several times, expressing his doubts about Claude-Pierre's self-professed cure rate. He had talked about seeing patients in his practice who had failed in the Montreux program, and, as early as 1997, he had told the *U.S. News & World Report:* "By saying she can cure any patient with anorexia, Peggy Claude-Pierre, by definition, delegitimizes what she does."[69]

Claude-Pierre asked Considine to try to persuade Johnston that Dr. Kaplan wasn't impartial and someone else should be chosen. But Johnston said the time for argument had passed. Dr. Kaplan would soon be on his way to Victoria.

By the time he arrived at the clinic, the nursing team at Montreux was in place as well. Pam Brambell had begun working with dietitian Susan Trefz to prepare the health assessments of the clients. Although Brambell had no specific expertise in eating disorders, she had valuable experience in dealing with children and youth with complex health care needs. One of her regular contracts involved training careworkers who provided round-the-clock care to babies and children with such needs in their own homes or foster homes.

The clinic's plan to hire Bob Enoch as its new manager had not worked out. After the comments made about him in Dr. Stanwick's judgment, Montreux knew licensing would never approve him. Montreux had suggested promoting one of its middle managers from within, but that had been turned down too. Licensing was insisting that the new manager had to have some formal qualifications. A person for the job had to be found quickly. Noah and Margaret Dobson had followed through on their plans to leave town; they were setting up an outpatient counselling practice nearly 2,000 miles away in Ontario. Serena was taking up almost all the slack and handling most of the day-to-day problems at the clinic, but no one believed licensing would accept someone who was still officially a Montreux counselling client either.

After some consideration, the clinic approached Marg Eastman, the nurse who had been sitting on the monitoring committee established in 1998. Eastman's expertise was also in pediatrics; her job with the health region involved dealing with children with asthma and related problems, and with their families. She had a background in training and evaluation, and in writing policies and procedures manuals—all skills likely to prove useful in the Montreux situation.

In the latter days of the monitoring committee, Eastman had insisted that the committee be allowed to review in detail the files of a single patient. That way, she said, committee members could be sure both that they were receiving a full picture of what was going on at the clinic, and also that Montreux staff were properly documenting what they were doing. Eastman had developed some concerns as she went through the file, but nothing that couldn't be easily fixed, she thought. She expected that the gaps in the documentation were the result of having no trained professionals on staff. Since Claude-Pierre and Harris had both said frequently that they wanted to comply with all the necessary laws, Eastman didn't think she'd have an especially difficult job. It would, she believed, be mostly a matter of drawing up proper forms for recording data, training staff how to use them, and developing more practical policies and procedures that could guide staff in their day-to-day decisions.

She went through a gruelling interview with Eng and Macdonald, who asked her dozens of questions about her views on patient rights and informed consent to treatment. The investigators were trying to ensure that the new manager would not continue the practice of imposing therapy on patients who were there voluntarily. They approved of her answers and agreed she could be hired for the job. She asked for, and received, a leave of absence from her regular job, and started reading everything she could find about eating disorders.

By the time Brambell arrived to begin her work at the clinic, Claude-Pierre had decided to move several of the most difficult patients off-care. Anna and her terrier were set up in a basement apartment in the Richmond house. After more than three years on-care, Carmen, who'd starred on the second *Oprah* show, was given an opportunity to try living independently. So was Becca, a 20-year-old who'd also been on 24-hour care for more than two years. Sharleen was listed as being off-care, although she was constantly asking for help and support from Montreux staff and seemed insecure on her own. None of these patients was actually ready for independent living. The move did, though, ensure that Dr. Kaplan and Brambell wouldn't begin by interviewing patients who had been at the clinic for years and still hadn't been able to spend even a day without a careworker hovering over them.

Several of the other patients who had figured prominently in the hearing and judgment were no longer at the clinic either. Vivian's family had taken her home, aware she was still far from well and would probably need hospitalization back in her home country of Israel. Louise had returned to her home in Britain, where she was hoping to continue training as a Montessori teacher. Wilma had returned home to the U.S. after a relatively short, uneventful, and apparently successful stay at Montreux.

Most of the patients who were still listed as being on 24-hour care, and hence the first ones seen by Dr. Kaplan, were newer arrivals at the clinic, including those who had arrived after the hearing concluded.

Dr. Kaplan's main job was to conduct a thorough physical and mental examination of those patients, to ensure that they were not in immediate danger, and to forward his report to Johnston. However, as he spent a week in Victoria, meeting with careworkers and staff members, talking to patients individually, and learning how the Montreux system worked, he began to worry about much of what he was seeing and hearing. He wrote these concerns in a separate report and sent it to Johnston along with the evaluations. When Eng and Macdonald saw its contents, they were so alarmed that they wrote back to Dr. Kaplan, asking if he would be willing to provide more particulars, elaborating on some of his concerns and explaining how Montreux might rectify these problems. In this second, longer report, Dr. Kaplan cited even more examples of problems he'd seen during his visit to the clinic.

Unlike the licensing investigators and Dr. Stanwick, Dr. Kaplan was not constrained by the strictures of the community care facilities legislation. He was free to comment on a variety of issues that he feared might put patients at risk, even if they didn't fall under any specific section of B.C.'s legislation.

The first issue he mentioned in both reports was what he called "the blurring of therapeutic boundaries" between staff and patients. He explained that the standards that apply to any licensed professional require that the limits of a professional therapeutic relationship be carefully defined. Counselling must not be seen as social friendship or the equivalent of family for a patient, he said. Every therapeutic action must be carefully considered to ensure that it is serving the patient's best interests, not the best interests of the therapist or the institution.

"These boundaries are especially critical for clients suffering from eating disorders," Dr. Kaplan wrote in his report to Johnston. "These are extremely vulnerable, impressionable young women, a significant percentage of whom have been sexually abused." Boundary rules might also be considered especially at Montreux, he noted, since none of the staff had the sort of professional training that would give them the tools to think through the ethics and possible consequences of situations where boundaries might become blurred.

During his interviews with the patients, he'd asked them questions about the sort of touching that went on at Montreux—did the staff hug and hold them? Had they always agreed to that? How did it make them feel? What sort of experiences had other patients told them about? He'd also asked more general questions about their experiences with counselling and therapy at Montreux. He asked about patients who became careworkers. Who decided when that should happen? What support did they receive?

It took only a few interviews for Dr. Kaplan to believe that, if Montreux had been staffed by regulated professionals, they would be in regular breach of practice standards around boundary issues. One such standard discourages out-of-office contact between therapist and client. Putting a physical boundary on where therapeutic contact takes place helps in putting an emotional boundary on it. A second therapeutic standard warns of the need for extreme caution in cases of physical contact between therapist and patient, even if the contact is intended to be entirely non-sexual. That standard is especially important in dealing with patients, Dr. Kaplan noted, because they "are very prone to misinterpreting even the most innocent type of contact."

The most obvious problem with out-of-office contact, he'd found, was in the case of a registered clinical counsellor who didn't work full-time for the clinic, but had come on board to give help to some of its more troubled clients. One client told Dr. Kaplan how the counsellor would sometimes take her to Alcoholics Anonymous meetings that he attended because of his personal history of alcohol problems. Kaplan found that positively bizarre. The patient had no history of alcohol abuse herself, and 12-step programs like AA most often have been found to be counterproductive in cases of eating disorders. And attending a meeting where the therapist was essentially a client for his own problems was almost certain to confuse the patient about roles and boundaries. Others talked of the same clinical counsellor—and Montreux's own counsellors—taking them for long walks instead of restricting the therapy to the office. Even that could be enough to blur the boundaries and let the client think of the relationship as one of friendship rather than professional counselling, Dr. Kaplan suggested, although many therapists may make occasional exceptions to that rule when they've thought through the issue and decided it would be in the patient's best interests.

Boundary issues were exacerbated by the Montreux policy of allowing barely recovered anorexics to become careworkers for patients sicker than themselves, Dr. Kaplan believed. Even before their first day of work, they were in a conflict of roles, especially if they were still taking counselling themselves. The practice was likely to lead to risks for both patients and careworkers. Most of the patients-turned-careworkers had no training or expertise that would make them competent in caring for fragile and acutely ill anorexics. "Simply having had the disorder does not in and of itself make someone competent as a caregiver," he wrote.

Some of Montreux's caregivers, he found, couldn't be considered recovered at all. Some still couldn't eat normally. Some did manage to eat but were still obsessed with unrealistic thoughts about body shape and weight. Some of the young women he met at the clinic were so thin he couldn't tell for sure whether they were patients or staff.

Montreux's records were rife with cases in which patients were working as careworkers while still receiving treatment themselves. Senior counsellors like Tessa were beginning to provide counselling while still getting regular help from Claude-Pierre. Jeannie was shown on *20/20* helping Robbie to eat, less than eight months after she'd been admitted only days away from death—even though she later said on *Oprah* that it took at least a year for a person's thinking to change substantially. Denise testified at the hearing that she'd been a careworker for a full year while still receiving outpatient counselling. The story of Louise and Dustin had been told and retold through the investigation and hearing process.

Nothing had changed by the time Dr. Kaplan arrived. One client told him that at least one of her previous caregivers had still not been able to eat normally. "This ... is very confusing to sufferers who are trying to normalize their eating and weight, and see their therapists/caregivers as role models."

The patient-caregivers themselves were at significantly greater risk of relapse than they might otherwise have been, Dr. Kaplan said. Dealing daily with people who are very ill with eating disorders, and who are still trying to deal with issues that the careworker has not entirely resolved either, is stressful for the patient-caregivers, and a risk factor for relapse. Denise was one patient who had admitted to Dr. Stanwick that occasionally, while working as a careworker, she needed a break because she knew the stress was leading her back to disordered eating.

Dr. Kaplan suggested a new policy for the clinic. After someone graduated from the program, there should be a set period of time during which they would not be allowed to work at the clinic at all. If, after that time elapsed, someone still wanted to return, they would have to be able to show that they displayed no symptoms of disordered eating and were fully recovered. The period of time, he added, would probably need to be measured in years, not months or weeks.

One of the issues that set off the loudest alarm bells for Dr. Kaplan was that of non-sexual "therapeutic" touching. From the earliest days of Montreux, physical touch had been a big part of the program, and was seen by Claude-Pierre as innately helpful. In the first *20/20* show, she said, "You know, a dog who is wounded or an animal ... the first thing you do, the natural instinct of any of us is to pick the animal up and to hold it until it feels better, but somehow we don't feel that's right with human beings."[70] In the second, she's seen on the phone with a patient, saying, "Remember I told you I'd come and hug you."[71] And in the show about Princess Diana, she talked again about her and Diana touching each other, noting that "touching is healing."[72] All through the television documentaries she is seen hugging, holding, and caressing the patients. Her book includes a section subtitled "Rocking and Touching," in which those caring for acute anorexics are encouraged to hold the patients on their laps, rock them in a rocking chair, hug and cradle them.

Dr. Kaplan acknowledged that the question of how much non-sexual touch should be allowed in psychotherapy in general had been a controversial one for years. Some ethicists said almost none, particularly between a male therapist/worker and a female patient. Others were prepared to say that some touching could be allowed, even helpful, but only under carefully considered circumstances. Virtually everyone agreed that the patients should always be the ones who were in control, and could stop any hugging or holding if it was starting to make them uncomfortable.

Dr. Kaplan's experience with eating-disorder sufferers had led him to the belief that with that group of patients, more than most, the issue of touch was a delicate one. Many had a history of physical or sexual abuse. Many would be prone to misinterpret, or even sexualize in their minds, what the counsellor thought was a simple expression of unconditional love. Ironically, in her book, Claude-Pierre had also noted how prone acute patients are to misinterpreting what is said and done to or around them. Dr. Kaplan found very few circumstances in which touch would be necessary or helpful in dealing with eating-disorder victims. He agreed with scientific literature that had found it was usually the therapist's needs that were being met by touching, not the patient's.

But Dr. Kaplan found that hugging and holding patients were still often part of the regimen at Montreux, though not as large a part as they'd been in the first years of the clinic. Montreux had a clear policy stating that "there shall be no sexual references, innuendo, or relations between any staff and patient," but no policy dealing with the specific question of physical contact with patients. Several patients told Dr. Kaplan that staff did still sometimes initiate touching, holding, and hugging, even with patients who didn't like it. He summarized the interviews in his report by saying the patients had told him the hugs and the holding were "often unwanted, unsolicited, and made them feel uncomfortable."

Dr. Kaplan warned that hugging and cuddling clients against their wishes was often the beginning of a "very slippery slope" that could lead to improper sexualization of relationships. In his report to Johnston, Dr. Kaplan spelled out one of the major risks of blurring boundaries in a therapeutic relationship—the risk of a therapist taking sexual advantage of a client. "In a significant number of such cases, such behaviour regularly leads to sexual contact with clients," he wrote. The risk has been found to be even higher in cases in which the counsellor "has a past history of the disorder being treated," he noted.

"Such practices, if they are continuing at Montreux, should be stopped immediately," Dr. Kaplan wrote. "Virtually all professional licensing bodies (psychology, psychiatry, social work, etc.) would view such activity negatively and it would be potential grounds for professional misconduct." However, none of the management at Montreux belonged to any licensed professional body; they had no professional licence that could be taken away.

Dr. Kaplan also heard that, not infrequently, untrained male caregivers provided the one-on-one 24-hour care to female patients. That was an especially large problem on the overnight shift, he concluded, when careworker and patient would normally be alone together in a bedroom for the entire shift. This too had been an issue at Montreux since the first complaints had been laid. Staff had mentioned instances in which male workers would cuddle female patients in such a way that, had they seen it in the outside world, they would have assumed they were looking at a boyfriend-girlfriend couple.

"Having a largely untrained male caregiver (or female former sufferer for that matter) with a vulnerable female anorexic alone all night in her bedroom makes me, and should make others, uncomfortable and concerned," Dr. Kaplan wrote.

But when Eng and Macdonald checked the staffing records later, they found that throughout that spring, male careworkers were still regularly being assigned to female patients on the overnight shifts.

No one at the clinic had told Dr. Kaplan of any specific instances of relationships becoming sexualized. Despite that, he believed the risk of such abuse was high. "My clinical feeling is, however, that the conditions at Montreux are ripe for such violations to occur," he wrote. "In fact I think it is almost inevitable that serious boundary violations will occur in the future if they haven't already."

It was enough to make some of the longer-term Montreux employees a little uncomfortable. During the clinic's existence, numerous love relationships—long-term or short-term—had developed among the young adults thrown together in such intense circumstances. Most had been among staff members. However, with so many patients becoming careworkers, and sometimes being both at the same time, it was sometimes hard to say if a relationship was one between two staff members or an improper one involving a client and a staff member. Denise was one patient-turned-careworker who'd later ended up marrying another Montreux worker. Deirdre had told the British newspaper *The Independent* that while she was "off-care" but still receiving counselling, her boyfriend was a staff member and sometimes-careworker at the clinic.[73]

• • •

Only a few weeks after Dr. Kaplan had departed, two Montreux staff members approached Marg Eastman, asking to discuss an urgent problem with her in confidence. The problem, they explained, involved a patient named Marcie.* Marcie had been at Montreux almost four years. She was now assigned to live independently while still receiving counselling from Karen*—another former residential patient turned counsellor with no training at all. Marcie was one of the patients who'd moved to independent living shortly before Dr. Kaplan's arrival, after spending most of her years "on-care."

"What about Marcie?" asked Eastman.

Marcie, they told her, had become romantically involved with Jacob,* a young man who'd quit his job at Montreux just about the time Eastman arrived, and one week before Dr. Kaplan came to the clinic. He'd worked as a driver and also as a relief careworker, especially on the overnight shift. According to Marcie, they had fallen in love and planned to be married in December. Uncomfortably, the staff members told Eastman they believed the relationship had probably started during the past winter, while Jacob was still employed at the centre and Marcie was still a patient on residential care.

Eastman was flabbergasted. She could see no explanation that didn't involve an outrageous violation of professional ethics by Jacob, and by anyone else who knew about the problem earlier. She knew she had no choice but to report the incident to licensing and filled out the appropriate form. Marcie asked to talk to Eastman too—she wanted to be formally discharged from Montreux's residential program so, she thought, she'd be free to pursue her relationship with Jacob.

But when she came in to talk, she made it clear she was angry about what was happening. She accused the other staff members of "gossiping" about her and making trouble. And she insisted her romantic relationship with Jacob had started after she had moved out of the Rockland facility. From what she said, Eastman knew she had to be aware that a report had gone forward to licensing. And that information, being kept as secret as possible around the clinic, could have reached her only through her counsellor, Karen. Now Eastman didn't just have a staff member who'd broken all standards to become romantically involved with a patient; she also had a counsellor who obviously didn't know a thing about maintaining confidentiality, even in the most delicate circumstances. Eastman signed Marcie's discharge papers and didn't even bother trying to explain to her that the situation was not much improved even if the full-blown relationship had flowered when she was officially "off-care."

The staff members who'd originally talked to Eastman had dropped another hint that made her even more nervous about the situation. This was not, they'd said, the first time that Jacob had become romantically involved with one of the clients. They told her they believed he'd been involved at least twice before. For one thing, he was the staff person who'd been Deirdre's "boyfriend" while she was still a counselling client. Kim Macdonald, who received Eastman's incident report, immediately obtained and checked Jacob's personnel file and also the schedules for the last weeks he was working for the centre.

Even Macdonald was shocked by what she found in the personnel file. Jacob had first joined the clinic staff more than four years earlier, hired in large part because his sister was a counsellor there. He'd been on staff only a few months when he'd been caught kissing and trying to begin a relationship with a patient who was still in her teens at the time. At first he'd tried to deny the accusation and brazen it out, but eventually he'd confessed to his sister, and then, with many apologies, to Claude-Pierre. It appeared the clinic had taken the right action at that time: Jacob was immediately fired.

However, a few months later, that patient returned to her home in the U.S., apparently one of Montreux's success stories. Jacob and his sister both began to let it be known around the clinic that he was adamant he'd learned his lesson, that he'd been filled with remorse when he'd realized the danger he'd put the clinic in, that working for Montreux had been "his dream job" and he'd never be so stupid as to throw it away again.

Their contrition bore results. Less than nine months after he'd been fired, Jacob was back on the Montreux staff list.

If Montreux management was aware of the relationship between Jacob and Deirdre, it wasn't obvious from the files. Certainly no action had ever been taken as a result of it. As Macdonald reviewed the staff schedules for the early part of the year, she realized that the clinic had clearly been in a compromised position. On several occasions during January and February, while Marcie was still on 24-hour care, Jacob had spent at least part of the night in her room in his job as relief careworker.

From the logs of the days when Jacob was acting as driver, Eastman learned that Jacob was showing a lot of interest in Marcie before he quit his job. In one entry, which recorded a trip in which he'd given her a ride in the van, he'd written beside her name "object of my affection." On another occasion, another staff member had been sent to see if Marcie was at Jacob's—even though Montreux policy did state unequivocally that staff members must not take patients to their own homes.

There was nothing Eastman could do. Jacob had quit working for Montreux 10 weeks earlier. Marcie had discharged herself from care.

Their romance had been flowering during the very week that Dr. Kaplan was at the clinic, worrying about the risk of inappropriate relationships springing up between staff and vulnerable patients. It would have been hard for him to have been more prescient.

II

The Walls Come Tumbling Down

Peggy Claude-Pierre considered hope and optimism her biggest stocks in trade. The parents and family members of every new patient were convinced that a full cure would be achieved at Montreux, and most of the patients thought so too. Claude-Pierre insisted that that factor alone helped them on the road to recovery. Parents who asked too many questions or expressed too many doubts just never made it to the top of the waiting list—not a problem for Montreux management, given that the waiting list was always described as years, if not centuries, long.

However, from the time of the first complaints to licensing, former staff members had been saying that the sense of hope created was a false one. They had realized that the cure rate in the residential program was nothing like 90 or 100 per cent, even by Montreux's unclear definition of "cure." It wasn't just those like Lena and Donna who said clearly they didn't think the program was working for them and removed themselves from it. It was also patients who had returned home apparently recovered, but turned up again after they'd relapsed. Some of the returnees became what staff at Montreux knew as "secret patients." From the beginning, they didn't stay in the main mansions, but rather in satellite sites with their own careworkers to look after them. Claude-Pierre sometimes instructed those workers that they weren't allowed to tell even other staff members who they were caring for. She explained that it would be harmful to the patients at the Rockland and St. Charles Houses if they knew that a patient who'd left apparently cured had, in fact, relapsed and had to return for more 24-hour care.

The promise of a potential 100 per cent cure rate had served Claude-

Pierre well in many ways. Nothing could have been a better marketing tool. From the first *20/20* program, the waiting list for Montreux had been hundreds of times longer than the number of patients who could possibly be admitted. Claude-Pierre could afford to pick and choose her patients from the hundreds of inquiries, selecting those for whom money would never be a problem, those with a connection to fame or celebrity status, those who had the potential to be the next media stars, or just those, like Dustin, who she found personally appealing or interesting.

It was the promised cure rate that had led to many of the high-profile media appearances and to a large advance from publishers for her book. No TV shows or magazines were going to be interested in a program that promised to cure half the eating disorder victims brought to it—even though that would have been an excellent outcome for a program dealing with patients with severe anorexia.

However, from the first time that concerns were voiced about aspects of the clinic's operations, the promised cure rate had also served another function for Claude-Pierre. It had been her last line of defence. She would admit that, as an "alternative" program, the clinic didn't necessarily follow the "bureaucratic rules" that authorities had set up to govern other facilities. Her self-proclaimed cure rate was the justification for that. She, David Harris, and their lawyers would all argue that they were doing what they had to do to save lives. She'd insist that those who wrote the rules didn't understand anorexia or the anorexic mindset, so couldn't comprehend why these patients had to be treated differently. They would accuse the authorities of permitting unnecessary deaths by insisting Montreux adhere to the rules—a serious condemnation for anyone in the health care system. Claude-Pierre argued that if they weren't allowed to continue running the program their way, some anorexics would die, and others would be condemned to a life of chronic suffering and torment.

This belief had been regularly proclaimed during the hearing before Dr. Stanwick. The parents who testified said repeatedly that they would far prefer a program that included imposed therapy to one that might let their children starve themselves to death. Many could not understand the differences between Montreux's approach and others that did impose therapy through, perhaps, nasal feeding tubes. Many were convinced that their child would not have survived without Montreux.

Staff members and managers echoed the same theme. Staff members said they'd persisted with feeding patients like Lena and Dustin to the point of physical violence because Claude-Pierre had convinced them that the only alternative for those patients was death. Few felt that they would be believed if they were to challenge someone who had been on *20/20* and *Oprah* and declared an "angel on earth." They still considered even the force-feeding compassionate compared to the alternatives for many of the clients. Noah Dobson argued that if the clinic wasn't allowed to persist in its efforts to feed residents, to continue its imposed therapy, "we might as well open a hospice." The man Montreux had hoped would succeed Dobson, Bob Enoch, said they needed to balance "theoretical risk" to some patients against "undreamed of amounts of therapeutic success." And Claude-Pierre said of her method, "It basically saves their lives in the end." In his closing remarks, Dennis Murray said that if all the rules had to be followed, "we don't have a clinic, and that part of the spectrum [of eating-disordered patients] is not dealt with.... They will be confined to the cycles from which they come," of improving briefly in hospital, but becoming worse again the minute they get out.

After Dr. Stanwick's judgment, Claude-Pierre still made the same argument. She told *Elle* reporter Stephanie Mansfield that she had done nothing wrong, that she should not be required to meet licensing standards. "Bureaucrats, who want every 't' crossed, don't understand that I'm dealing with a human life," she is quoted as saying. "My philosophy contradicts what health officials believe."[74]

But were her claims of an unprecedented success rate true?

From her first media appearances back in 1993, Claude-Pierre had implied, if had not said outright, that her clinic had a success rate of close to 100 per cent. "We do have the answer," she said in her first interview with *Focus on Women* magazine.[75]

"No evidence of failure whatsoever," said Lynn Sherr in the first *20/20* documentary—with no contradiction from Claude-Pierre.[76]

"Do you save most of the kids who come to you?" asked Oprah Winfrey in her first show about Montreux in 1996.

"There's no point in any recidivism," Claude-Pierre answered. "Of course we do." She did admit that some patients didn't reach the stage of being "cured" because the Mental Health Act allowed them to leave the program prematurely, but, asked Winfrey: "If the child, the person stays, you can save them?"

"Absolutely."[77]

In an interview with *Share International* magazine later in 1996, she reiterated: "Even if someone has only three or four days to live, we can turn them around completely within eight months to a year.... We have, and I say this with humility, found new ways of thinking, and have discovered how we can give to these children."[78]

The publication of her book in 1997 and the resulting media appearances prompted even stronger statements. "We have had wonderful success curing hundreds of the most seriously ill patients," she said in the *Cosmopolitan* article. "No patient who has completed our five-part program has relapsed, but a few have left without finishing."[79]

The Canadian magazine *Flare* went even further on Claude-Pierre's behalf: "With a new outpatient tracking system in place, Montreux can now substantiate claims of a near-zero per cent rate of recidivism for those who complete the program—the closest to a cure yet to be documented."[80]

In fact, there was not then, and still is not, any outcome study to prove or disprove Claude-Pierre's claims. Montreux consistently said it was on the verge of undertaking a proper scientific study of the results of their treatment—but one was never completed. When the provincial government first refused to fund the clinic in 1994, the health ministry committee urged Montreux to start the study so it could prove to officials that the results of its program were superior to others. Harris, the clinic manager at that time, agreed this was something that needed to be done, and said Montreux would pursue the resources needed for it to be undertaken. No study was ever begun, let alone completed. At another point, the clinic announced it would work with psychiatrist Dr. Elliott Goldner, a colleague of Dr. Birmingham's in Vancouver, on an outcome study. Again the proposal never came to fruition. During the hearing before Dr. Stanwick, Claude-Pierre testified that she had begun working with a University of Victoria psychology professor to develop the form of the study. However, the professor was later told that, given the difficulties with licensing, the research wouldn't be going ahead at that time.

That left Montreux with only testimonials to back up its claims. Certainly there was never a shortage of patients and parents willing to provide those testimonials. Some had been clients during the earliest days of Claude-Pierre's outpatient practice. Some were current residential patients prepared to say how much better, and more optimistic, they were feeling now compared to when they'd come. Some had moved from being acute-care patients to being careworkers themselves, but had never actually left the clinic.

Testimonials were invaluable for the media, putting a human face on the story to run alongside Claude-Pierre's theories and promises. That didn't mean they provided any valid, objective information to show that her treatment worked better than any other. They couldn't provide a comparison with the results of other programs. They couldn't show whether Montreux did better for all patients or only for some, and if so, which ones. Nor could they show what is of particular importance in anorexia studies: how long the "cure" or improvement would be maintained, or whether it would be sustained if a patient left the Montreux environment. They also couldn't show whether the Montreux system really did reduce the risk of relapse—a risk normally considered to affect at least one-third of those who have been seriously ill with anorexia, even after they appear to have recovered.

When the claims were made in the early magazine articles and TV programs, it wasn't even theoretically possible to offer a success rate. A patient is normally considered "recovered" only after a lengthy period of time has passed without a serious relapse (many eating-disorder professionals suggest five years as an appropriate period), and the clinic hadn't been open long enough to have those figures. However, neither Claude-Pierre nor the media ever explained this to those watching the TV shows.

Testimonials of the complete cure had to come from Claude-Pierre's first outpatients, for whom background data was sadly lacking. Even the number of patients Claude-Pierre had actually treated varied wildly depending on the interview. Some had never actually been diagnosed with anorexia by anyone other than Claude-Pierre. Some, like Sharon, looked back on their experience and remembered difficulties with eating but none of the key diagnostic criteria for anorexia—extreme and irrational fears of gaining weight and unrealistic view of their body shape. Many who gave testimonials were still linked to Claude-Pierre as long as a decade later, often having moved on to become part-time or full-time careworkers or counsellors at the clinic. The definition of "cured" remained vague. One "cured" patient, for instance, still took her own food with her everywhere, even to family Christmas and Thanksgiving dinners. She explained that, to her, "cured" meant she was no longer hostage to what society considered "normal" eating patterns; she was comfortable indulging in her own peculiar food preferences.

Even when the program had been in existence longer, no objective data of the outcomes for its patients was ever made public. Some experts from around the world became ever more vocal about their concerns that Montreux was continuing to claim its remarkably high success rate with no data to back that up. When they talked to each other at professional conferences they found that, more and more, they were seeing former Montreux clients who were relapsing, usually a few months after leaving the clinic.

They worried too that Claude-Pierre and her followers sometimes implied that those running mainstream programs would write patients off as incurable and allow them to die rather than treat them. That, they knew, was enough to make many patients and families afraid of becoming involved with the conventional medical system—and it was hardly ever true. During his testimony before Dr. Stanwick, Dr. Birmingham talked about his conviction that no doctor should ever accept that a patient should die of anorexia, and should always continue to provide care as they would for a chronic physical illness such as asthma.

At the same time, most mainstream doctors did believe that everyone providing treatment had to be realistic about the outcome—and the outcome for severe anorexia remained problematic. It still has one of the highest death rates of any mental illness, and a variety of careful, objective studies have shown that a small proportion of sufferers develop a severe and hard-to-treat form of the disease. No drugs appear to work for these patients, no treatment programs—residential, day hospitals, or outpatient counselling—appear to bring long-term, satisfactory results.

They are the ones who will most likely relapse, and in whom the disease often becomes chronic and unremitting in its course.

Still, the experts insisted, these cases should not be considered hopeless. "The point would seem to be that although some cases of anorexia nervosa may well be *incurable* in the sense that 'everything has been tried' ... no case can be thought of as *irrecoverable* in the sense that the disorder itself could not improve," wrote Dr. Bob Palmer from the University of Leicester.[81] Most clinicians know of individual cases where a sufferer has suddenly improved after many years of illness.

Claude-Pierre and Harris often insisted it was "professional jealousy" that pitted many doctors against them. They said the doctors were upset because Montreux was saving those who had been discarded as hopeless by the mainstream medical system. In fact, most of the doctors would have been happy if Claude-Pierre had proven she had found a treatment that would work for the group of sufferers for whom other programs did not work. Many (but far from all) of Montreux's residential patients fell into this group. They had gone through numerous programs, including some of the best in the world, but had responded to the treatment for only a short time, if at all. Many of their parents had been warned that their children were at high risk of death.

With still no evidence to back up her claims, however, the experts feared that Claude-Pierre was providing false hope to that group of anorexics and to their families and loved ones. Worse, they worried that at least a few patients suffering with anorexia would come to believe that Montreux was the only place that might possibly cure them; if they could not be one of the lucky ones admitted there, then there was no hope for them.

Postings on the Internet chatrooms after Dr. Stanwick's decision was made public showed they were not overreacting. "I kind of looked at the clinic as a place of hope, my own Mecca for my own ED [eating disorder] salvation," wrote one correspondent who had never come close to becoming a patient there.

"Knowing Peggy was in Canada working and helping us is what gave me the strength to go on and not give up," wrote another. "How dare anyone take away all I have left? Even if it is just an image, this is my life."

Some Montreux staff members and parent supporters reinforced that view by stressing their belief that closing Montreux would mean the death of anorexics—both those who were there and might have to return home, and those who would never get to come.

"Many people will die or suffer when they don't have to because of [Dr. Stanwick's ruling]," wrote Denise in one posting to a chatroom. And in the *Elle* article, Etta—who had at that point been at Montreux for more than a year and had not seen her family in that time—was asked what would happen if she had to go home at that point. "I would die," she answered.[82]

Still, the naysayers had no more data to work with than did Claude-Pierre. Their concerns about the clinic's success rate were also based on anecdotal evidence—mostly the stories they'd heard from patients who had sought treatment elsewhere after failing to achieve recovery at Montreux. Few experts had ever been allowed behind the doors of Montreux, and those who had had been there for a very short time and under carefully controlled conditions. They had no data to compare the success rates of their own programs with Claude-Pierre's. Even Montreux's own trusted doctors were not usually allowed to see patients alone; a member of management was almost always in the room during doctors' interviews or examinations.

When Dr. Allan Kaplan arrived, he was the first eating-disorder specialist with free access to the clinic and its patients. What he observed was a snapshot of the clinic at one moment in its history, far from the equivalent of a long-term outcome study. Still, it was enough to show him that the suspicions he and others had harboured were correct—Montreux showed no signs of "curing" every patient with severe anorexia who came through the doors. What it was doing, he found, in many cases was prolonging in-patient treatment and imposed therapy to a length seen in almost no other programs. Even in cases where patients didn't appear to be progressing after months or years, it was still holding out hope to them, and especially to their families: if the patient would just stay at Montreux long enough, that magical complete cure would eventually arrive. Some families had paid close to half a million dollars in fees, and still their children suffered from severe eating-disorder symptoms.

Claude-Pierre had repeatedly said publicly that the average length of stay at Montreux was about 12 to 18 months. From the time of the first complaints, staff members said the length of stay was much greater for a significant number of the patients. Even among those who provided testimonials, several had been in residence for three years and more. A few had even reached the four-year anniversary of their stay at the centre. As Dr. Kaplan interviewed the patients, he realized not just how long some had been living at Montreux, but that some of those long-term patients still suffered numerous symptoms of their eating disorders.

Like most other managers of conventional eating-disorder programs, Dr. Kaplan deplored the growing tendency in the U.S. for managed health-care providers to allow only the briefest of residential treatments for eating disorders. In many cases, plans now allowed only a week or two of hospitalization, which might not be enough even to stabilize a patient medically, let alone begin the necessary therapy to help them beat the disorder in the long term. Such unreasonably brief stays had frustrated the American parents of many of the Montreux clients.

However, Dr. Kaplan said in his reports, a program that maintained someone for years, even when they showed few signs of improvement, was little better for the patients. He tried to explain to Montreux staff that proper outcome studies have shown what length of stay is most likely to provide the best results. Data from his own program in Toronto had shown that a patient with bulimia who doesn't begin to respond to treatment within eight weeks of day-hospital admission is unlikely to respond to that program at all, even if kept on the ward for weeks or months more. For those with serious anorexia, he said, several studies have shown that in-patient treatment for about four months should be enough to stabilize the patient and begin treatment of psychological problems. After that, the patient will usually be able to continue making progress in a day-hospital program or with regular outpatient counselling. "There is no evidence to suggest that after years of treatment in a continuing symptomatic patient, that more of the same treatment is going to be effective," Dr. Kaplan wrote.

"It is simply not good enough to say 'we think this client should be treated for years and years because we know that this approach works.

Just trust us,'" he said—referring to the message Claude-Pierre had given to some parents for years. "This," wrote Dr. Kaplan, "is the same mantra that scores of self-proclaimed experts have used over the years to prey on vulnerable individuals and their families, to justify idiosyncratic unproven treatments for chronic, difficult-to-treat, potentially fatal illnesses." The treatments, he went on, "have no proven efficacy and ... serve only to feed the narcissism of the person making the claim or his/her financial coffers."

"At what point is more treatment at Montreux detrimental to the client?" Kaplan asked rhetorically in his report to Johnston. "Sometimes less is better. When is enough enough?"

The files Dr. Kaplan looked at were ones like those of Anna and Carrie. Both had gone through a difficult period when they'd first come to the clinic, but then had begun to show signs of improvement. They'd moved from "shakes" to solid food, begun to regain a healthier weight, and were less troubled by depression and obsessive-compulsive symptoms. However, neither had improved enough, by Montreux standards, to move off-care, where they would have had some responsibility for their own lives. Then, after between 18 months and two years in the program, they began to show signs of relapsing, even while still on 24-hour care. Anna had to go back on liquid food, and feeding her became just as much of a struggle as it had been when she'd first arrived. She again began begging to leave and go home almost daily. Carrie was actually able to lose several pounds while on 24-hour care, and she resumed her habit of pulling her hair out to the point that careworkers worried about her scalp bleeding.

One patient who was relapsing dangerously while living as an outpatient and taking counselling at Montreux was not even seen by Dr. Kaplan. Only a few days before he was scheduled to arrive, senior careworker Tricia told Marg Eastman and Pam Brambell that she was concerned about Esther. Esther had returned home just before the second licensing investigation started in the autumn of 1997 and had written a glowing letter in praise of the clinic then. She had later returned to Victoria, and was taking classes at the university and living in her own apartment, while still coming to the clinic for counselling. Brambell had worried about Esther when she'd assessed her health for the first time in February, because her blood pressure was so low. Now Tricia told Eastman and Brambell that it looked to her as if Esther was beginning to lose weight rapidly.

Later that same day, Eastman saw Esther having a counselling session with Claude-Pierre. The door was shut and she didn't want to interrupt, but afterwards, she asked Claude-Pierre about Esther's health.

"She's well," Claude-Pierre assured her, adding that Esther still weighed about 100 pounds. Eastman saw no need to put Esther on the list of patients to see Dr. Kaplan. A month after Dr. Kaplan had returned to Toronto, when Esther was to be formally discharged from the program, Eastman was told that, far from being 100 pounds, Esther's weight had actually dropped to the dangerously low level of 75 pounds. Her health was precarious enough to necessitate a trip to the hospital emergency ward.

Dr. Kaplan said in his reports that it wasn't fair to keep patients on-care forever at Montreux, assuming that at some point the "miracle cure" was going to happen for them. He suggested a variety of options that could be explored with that group of patients. Those patients who had never received treatment in a top-notch mainstream eating-disorder program should at least try such a program, he urged. He'd talked to several British clients who, like Samantha Kendall, had never been treated in a specialized eating-disorder program in their home country, even though several of the top programs in the world are located there.

For those patients who had not found success either in mainstream programs or at Montreux, he suggested two possibilities. One would be to set for them a date at which they would be discharged, along with goals for treatment to be accomplished during that time. The discharge date should be within two or three months, he said, and the clients should understand from the beginning that they would have to leave the program whether or not they met the goals. At that point they could be referred to programs in their home country with the understanding that they could return to Victoria at a later date—he recommended six months or more—if they then believed they could obtain more benefit from the Montreux program.

No suggestion, however, could have gone more against what

Claude-Pierre and her supporters believed. The part of Montreux that many parents and patients liked best was the clinic's "persistence," as they called it. The idea that a program would never give up on a patient, no matter how long treatment lasted, was extremely appealing to parents especially—at least to those who could afford to go on paying the fees. Many in the U.S. had been forced to worry from month to month about where their child might go next or how they could possibly care for them at home. Montreux's promise to provide treatment until a patient was cured eliminated that worry, even if the patients didn't appear to be making much progress at Montreux either.

For parents who did begin to have doubts after years of treatment, Claude-Pierre would insist that nothing could be worse than discharging a patient from her program because she wasn't making enough progress. It would, she argued, convince the patient that she or he was more worthless than ever, and the implication was that the parents would be conveying that negative and unloving message to their child if they sought to stop paying for her in the program.

Another alternative, Dr. Kaplan suggested then, would be to continue providing kind and compassionate care for those patients, but not to continue to insist that they would eventually recover completely. "There is a role for residential care of the type provided by a place like Montreux," he wrote. "What I object to is providing false hope to families, unsupported by data, that Montreux can cure these people when no one else has been able to.... If Montreux is to provide a safe haven for many years for chronically ill patients, it would be important that they be up front to families and clients about the fact that the expectation is not full recovery from the eating disorder, but rather the provision of support and a focus on quality of life and medical stabilization."

That proposal too went against Claude-Pierre's philosophy. She would never want to give the Negative Mind the satisfaction of hearing that it would always be part of a patient's life and could never be vanquished.

No matter the reason patients were staying years, Dr. Kaplan said, if this was to be a fact of Montreux life, the clinic urgently needed to develop some educational, rehabilitation, and vocational programs.

The clients needed programs that would allow them to be integrated with the real world outside the clinic's walls. He was particularly distressed to find that even clients who arrived at the age of 13 or 14 were not given the opportunity to keep up with their normal schoolwork. "The fact that adolescents are in Montreux for years without being involved in formal educational programs or vocational training is frankly shocking and difficult to justify," he wrote. The lack of school programs made it even more difficult for adolescents to return home, he said, because they became afraid of returning to school, where they would probably be years behind other students of their own age.

"A formal educational and vocational program has to be part of what Montreux provides if they expect to treat adolescents or young adults for years, removed from their families, peers, and homes," he said. He suggested the clinic could bring in a vocational counsellor who was experienced in treating patients of the same age with mental illnesses, and a teacher experienced in special-needs education. Without programs to help these clients move back into normal life in their home community, he said, "I am very concerned about their long-term capacity to function independently."

In any case, he recommended, Montreux should consider restricting its residential program to those aged 18 or over. For adolescents, recent research showed that family therapy was often one of the most essential parts of treatment. The families of Montreux clients lived too far away to participate in regular family therapy. All the patients he met were from outside Canada and even the youngest were not receiving any family therapy. Some, even those under the age of 18, hadn't seen their families for months, "or even years."

"The way Montreux is set up now, it appears to be functioning as a 'dumping ground' for families to abrogate their responsibility to their ill daughters, and to remove themselves for long periods of time from involvement with their child," he wrote. He predicted that those children, if they did return home, would be at high risk of future problems.

In fact, at least a few of the families of Montreux patients were openly attracted to it because of its very lack of family therapy programs. Some had been offended by the suggestions of doctors or social workers in other programs that the way the family functioned had been a factor in the development of their child's illness. They much preferred Claude-Pierre's theory, under which the only cause was the child's particularly sensitive and altruistic temperament. Some, such as Brenda's family, had withdrawn their children from facilities when doctors had insisted that family therapy was an essential part of the program.

Whichever route Montreux might choose to go, Dr. Kaplan said, one of the most important things Claude-Pierre could do would be to set criteria that would make it clear to everyone—clients, families, and staff—when a client would be considered to have completed the program and be ready for discharge. The criteria, he said, should be objective and specific: weight up to a certain level and maintained there for several weeks, the ability to eat normally, other symptoms reduced, depression and anxiety lessened. In Claude-Pierre's book, she writes of the Montreux Life Wellness Scale as the clinic's "way of clarifying a patient's progress."[83] The scale is divided into five stages, beginning with the acute and emergent stages and leading on to the Reality Stage, where a patient should be ready to move to partial care, and the Interactive Stage, where the patient can move to living independently while still taking counselling at the clinic. The final stage, at which a patient has completed the programs, ends, theoretically, when the Actual Mind, rather than the Negative Mind, is in control at least 86 per cent of the time. According to the book, this stage, known as the Environmental Integration Stage, and final completion of the program should occur when the patient has moved back home and lived there successfully for about a year. Despite the emphasis on the scale in the book, the licensing investigators who combed the patients' logbooks never found a single case in which it had been used to measure a patient's progress. Counsellors who prepared guidelines never noted where on the scale a patient might be, or how a treatment plan was designed to move her further along the scale.

Neither in the book nor elsewhere does Claude-Pierre explain just how "life wellness" is to be measured. Nowhere does she ever suggest the type of measures that Dr. Kaplan mentioned, nor could she specify to Dr. Stanwick just how the stages were reached. She and Margaret Dobson both said it was something that was easy for staff to determine subjectively, in the patient's visibly lessening anxiety and growing happiness.

However, Dr. Kaplan found that the process was, to the clients themselves, something "very mysterious." Even patients who'd been on-care for three years and more had no idea how it would be decided when they would leave. Virtually all the clients he interviewed told him "it was up to Peggy" to decide such things. That, he noted, leads to "an unhealthy dependence" on Claude-Pierre and the clinic, because the patients have no feeling of control over their lives. They don't know what the treatment plan is, they don't know what they should do to move towards discharge, and it often "leaves the clients feeling they will be staying in Montreux forever."

Although Claude-Pierre's book talked about "environmental integration" as involving the patient returning home successfully, that didn't seem to be the patients' view, as far as Dr. Kaplan could determine. Rather, almost all of them told him they planned on staying in Victoria when they finished treatment; most hoped to work at Montreux in some capacity. Many of those who had reached the "environmental integration" stage, in which they were expected to live independently, did not go home to complete it. Instead they stayed in Victoria and worked at the clinic in what was formally known as a "practicum." Some months after the licensing investigation began, the clinic had even written up a policy to govern those clients.

"As part of the 'environmental integration' stage of recovery," read the policy manual, "patients have the opportunity to apply for a practicum within Montreux." The policy stated that patients must meet the normal criteria of a clinic staff member: they had to be "of good character," have their immunizations and TB tests up to date, have a criminal record check, sign the regular clinic confidentiality agreement for staff, and have the agreement of their doctor that they were ready to undertake the job. Nowhere did it suggest that the patient actually had to be recovered from their eating disorder, or that the doctor had to agree that working with sicker patients would not jeopardize their recovery.

Dr. Kaplan's overriding concern was that the Montreux system overall led to the patients becoming ever more dependent on Claude-Pierre and on the clinic, just at the time when they should be looking forward to increasing independence and returning to their home communities and families. "The goal of the Centre should be clear," he wrote: "to help clients recover from their eating disorder so that they can return to their home and get on with their lives." To that end, he suggested that clinic staff should be encouraging patients in plans to return home, to go back to school or to go to work, not encouraging them to think about staying in Victoria "and working or continuing to have some kind of ongoing relationship with the Centre."

"Having an explicit rule that ex-clients cannot work at the Centre would certainly give a clear message to clients that there was an expectation that they work towards becoming independent of the Centre rather than becoming more enmeshed and dependent on it," he said.

The way the clinic appeared to work, with Claude-Pierre having all the decision-making power about how long anyone should stay or when they might work at the clinic as part of their treatment, amounted to "autocratic decision making [that] feeds into the 'cult-like' atmosphere that pervades Montreux," he wrote.

The cat—or the word—was out of the bag.

For years Montreux's opponents had whispered that there was something faintly cultish about the clinic, about the top-down decision making on every issue of importance, about the myriad of rules that dictated every aspect of patients' lives (and many aspects of staff's lives as well), about the slavish devotion of Claude-Pierre's most loyal supporters. Beginning with Andrew and Randi, several of those who complained to licensing had told the investigators that once they left the clinic, they realized how neither the veneration of Claude-Pierre nor the strict controls placed on every aspect of life were entirely normal. Gay remembered how shocked she was at staff meetings when Noah Dobson would, each time, introduce Claude-Pierre as "our angel" and the entire room would give her a standing ovation. Staff members who'd complained about being ordered to work huge amounts of unpaid overtime remembered being told, "This isn't a job, it's a way of life."

Some patients, such as Serena, had even worried before moving to Victoria that they might be coming into something vaguely cult-like. That awareness, she'd say later, didn't make it a bit easier to get out once you were caught up in the Montreux climate.

Even Claude-Pierre in the first *20/20* had described herself as "sort of the witch doctor in the world."[84]

National Post columnist Christie Blatchford picked up on the atmosphere at the news conference after Dr. Stanwick's decision when Claude-Pierre's supporters were strenuously attacking the judgment without even having read it. "It doesn't take an expert on cult-like behaviour to recognize that there is something really off about this bunch," she wrote.[85]

Even in the Internet chatrooms after the judgment, the vehemence of some of the Montreux defenders prompted others to note that they sounded more like advocates for a cult than individuals involved in a rational debate. Several of the clinic's supporters had posted very much the clinic's own version of events on a newsgroup, suggesting, for instance, that Dr. Stanwick's decision was "clearly being done on a technicality," and that the stories of force-feeding were "just rumours spread by disgruntled ex-employees." When others challenged them with actual quotes from the judgment or testimony, the challengers were attacked for everything from sarcasm to envy because they'd never been lucky enough to go to Montreux.

"The more you people post here to 'defend' yourselves and attack others, the more you sound like a cult," one correspondent finally wrote. The postings, she said, just didn't seem to reflect the compassion, kindness, and unconditional love that Montreux prided itself on, especially since most of the challengers involved in the chatroom were still eating-disorder sufferers themselves.

"Small mindedness would force you to write us off as a cult," snapped back "Tori," one of the Montreux defenders, whose specific role at the clinic was never disclosed. Denise, on the other hand, apologized if they'd sounded cult-like; they were, she insisted, just a group of people fighting for the survival of something in which they believed passionately.

However, until Dr. Kaplan wrote that sentence in his report, the suggestion had never been spelled out by any of the experts.

"Cult" is not a word currently in vogue among students of group behaviour. Over the past 20 or 30 years, it has come to conjure up too many negative images in the public mind to allow for objective study. Experts in the field now more often refer to "gurus and disciples," or "cultic relationships."

Margaret Thaler Singer, one of the renowned cult experts in North America, defines a cultic relationship as one "in which a person intentionally induces others to become totally or nearly totally dependent on him or her for almost all major life decisions, and inculcates in these followers a belief that he or she has some special talent, gift, or knowledge."[86] Even though Singer concludes that cultic relationships are harmful and destructive, there's little in that precise definition with which even Claude-Pierre could disagree. She explained in her book the need to have acute patients become entirely dependent on Montreux and its staff when they first arrive at the clinic. Her insistence that she had found a single cause of, and cure for, anorexia endowed her with special knowledge in the eyes of her followers.

Other experts put more emphasis on the way a group works when defining a cult-like group. Such groups are considered to be authoritarian in structure, to share deep-seated beliefs, to have close relationships among the members, and to believe the group leader has charismatic, or even divine, power.

Despite the negative connotations of the word "cult," research has shown that attaching oneself to a guru or a charismatic group is not always negative. It can provide psychological benefits to some people, especially in the short term. Research has shown that the simple act of joining a charismatic group is enough to substantially reduce a person's anxiety or "emotional distress." The closer the person feels to the newly joined group, the more their distress will be relieved.

"Surrender is one of the most powerful forces and emotional states that a human being can touch into," write experts Joel Kramer and Diana Alstad. The complete emotional surrender is as close as one can come in adult life to returning to the conflict-free innocence of infancy. As gurus encourage newcomers to surrender all control, they also try to show themselves as "the totally accepting parent—the parent one never had but always wanted."[87] Claude-Pierre again noted in her book that in the acute stage, a person with anorexia does in fact need to be "reparented" and considered as helpless as an infant.

The stories of numerous Montreux patients show this scenario being played out at the clinic. Many tell of having surrendered completely to Claude-Pierre's power the minute she greeted them on their arrival. Her hugs were felt as the hugs of an angel. Her voice, at that first moment calm, quiet, and compelling, brought them hope and reassurance that many had not experienced for years. For that moment, they felt totally cared for, totally understood, and totally accepted. And for that moment, they were utterly convinced that Montreux was the only place that could cure them.

The relief from anxiety experienced by Montreux patients had intrigued Dr. Paul Termansen, the suicide-prevention expert hired by Claude-Pierre and Harris in early 1999 to review the clinic's policies.

Dr. Termansen told Dr. Stanwick during the hearing that he'd interviewed three Montreux patients and found the same thing with all three. They all told him that their anxiety was much relieved since moving into the clinic, that they felt much better. However, none of them could tell him why. They had apparently not developed any understanding of their own anxieties, what caused them, how they reacted to them, or how they could cope better with them. Their description of their feelings matched well with the idea of surrender itself bringing relief from anxiety. With no deeper understanding or insight, however, Dr. Termansen feared it would be unlikely the patients would be able to maintain their reduced level of anxiety—and hence, of symptoms—once they no longer lived within the cloistered existence of the clinic.

Cult researcher Dr. Marc Galanter explains how guru-led groups use this "relief effect" to change behaviour—but only through growing dependence on the group or leader.[88] He terms it a "pincer effect" in which the group begins asking the new patient to do something that causes substantial distress—in the case of Montreux, to begin eating again. The only way for the newcomer to gain relief from that distress is to surrender ever more completely to the clinic and its philosophy. Groups like Montreux, in which new arrivals are competely isolated from family, friends, and all old contacts, strengthen the effect even further, since the person has nowhere else to turn for friendship, warmth, companionship, or relief. If they say or do anything that alienates them from the Montreux staff, they are completely psychologically alone.

For those who surrendered themselves to the program, the relief of anxiety and distress could seem like a miracle. For a while at least, a virtuous circle was set up—they were mostly easy to care for because of their reduced anxiety, so careworkers found it easy to treat them with kindness and gentleness. That reduced their anxiety even further, and they found it easier yet to make progress in the program. Staff would encourage them and promise them that they too could soon join the Montreux staff, stay on at the clinic, and help others suffering from the mental torment of anorexia.

"I was going to be the next Peggy. We were going to change the world," remembers Natalie,* who'd gone to Claude-Pierre for outpatient counselling for bulimia and stayed on to become one of the first careworkers when the residential program opened. "I was just unbelievably idealistic."

The greatest promise, though, she says, was the promise of becoming part of Claude-Pierre's most trusted, innermost circle. "The promise was that that way [if you moved up the Montreux ladder], you'd have Peggy forever."

Clients like this often became the ones who would be the stars of the next media appearance. A high proportion of those interviewed for TV, newspapers, and magazines were either the complete newcomers, awed by their arrival, or those who had been there a few months, whose anxiety had been relieved and whose physical and mental state would show major improvement from their time of arrival. The relief from anxiety was so great that not only did those who surrendered say they felt better, but they also appeared healthier and happier to those who knew them before.

It didn't work for everyone who came to Montreux, not even in the short term. For some, it was because they had too many other physical or psychiatric problems to be treated in any non-hospital setting. Others who never did well in the program appeared to be those who never could or would surrender entirely to Claude-Pierre's charisma or the Montreux group. Donna Brooks said even before she came that she doubted she could turn control of her whole life over to others.

Lena Zavaroni told investigators that older patients at least needed to have some autonomy and independence. Sylvia, one of the few patients ever discharged because Montreux couldn't handle her behaviour, insisted, sometimes violently, that she would remain in control of her own life. Their anxieties did not appear appreciably lessened by coming to Montreux, and therapy had to be "imposed" more and more often.

Even for those who did experience the immediate reduction of anxiety, however, improvement most often came at the cost of their autonomy, independence, and self-determination. At the clinic all information was tightly controlled, for patients and family members. As long as they were on 24-hour care, patients were essentially cut off from the outside world. Their reading materials were censored, as were any movies they might want to watch, TV shows they might like to see, or CDs or radio stations they might want to listen to.

"The sensitive and impressionable disposition of acutely-ill patients require [*sic*] the close monitoring and censoring of televised programming that could prove emotionally harmful," read Montreux's policy and procedures manual. Among the items patients were not normally allowed to watch were any advertisements that might feed into their eating disorder, such as ads for diet programs or low-fat products; "negative talk shows"; or any material, factual or fictional, involving violence or sex. Bold-face type is used to emphasize the policy that "It is suggested that no patient is to watch news programming." The rules banning watching or reading the news, or discussing it, were so effective that most acute-care patients were not aware of the death of Princess Diana or of the world's massive outpouring of grief for her, even weeks later.

Similar guidelines applied to books and magazines, CDs, tapes, the radio, and movies. Videos, the manual suggests, should be "uplifting in theme and content." One staff member was the designated "movie reviewer" who'd have to watch any new movie or video that came out before staff could decide whether it was suitable for any or all patients.

Senior staff members had to approve any activity the patient wanted to take up, from music lessons to exercise programs. Something as simple as a 20-minute walk or a trip downtown for coffee had to be approved by Claude-Pierre or a counsellor, even if the patient was going to be within arm's length of a staff member at all times. Nothing could be done spontaneously.

Even when patients advanced to the status of "partial care" or "off care" so they didn't have a careworker with them at all times, Montreux still exercised considerable supervision over them—ensuring they engaged only in approved activities and ate only food on approved meal plans. Because of liability issues, no one under the age of 19 was ever allowed to live independently.

Many of the patients didn't know a single person in Victoria other than those they'd met at the clinic. Their communication with their former friends, schoolmates, or workmates had been broken off for months or years. Because they were from outside Canada, immigration rules didn't allow them to work, and younger adolescents were still not involved in any school program. Although some did eventually volunteer outside the clinic or take a course or two, in most cases their lives remained dominated by their involvement at the clinic.

It was not surprising that, on any given day at Montreux, large numbers of the partial-care and off-care patients could be found spending the day at the mansion—working in the garden out back, joining in art projects or the informal educational program, or just hanging out and talking to the other patients and staff members who were the only friends they had in the city. Others began their "practicum" at that point, spending 40 hours and more a week as careworkers with the newer patients. One patient on "practicum" was assigned by Claude-Pierre to work regular 16-hour days because Claude-Pierre didn't want her to have much time to go back to thinking about her problems.

However, as Dr. Termansen pointed out, these patients still did not know how to cope with any increasing stress or anxieties in their life themselves. They had not come to understand the emotional conflicts that led to anxiety or to find ways of handling it other than through disordered eating, harming themselves, or perhaps obsessive-compulsive symptoms. For some, the ability to cope with anxiety was so fragile that even moving to partial or off care would be enough to start them backsliding. Montreux records are rife with examples of patients who had to be returned to 24-hour care when their progress couldn't be maintained with any less structure from the clinic in their lives.

For a few, like Anna and Carrie, even 24-hour care ceased to provide the anxiety relief it once had. They lost any belief that the Montreux program would lead to a complete cure, at least for them. They again began to demand repeatedly to go home; they began to demand a choice. For them, more than for any other clients, the "illusion of no choice" stopped being an illusion and became the reality of their lives.

Most patients coped with the move to partial care and again to off care, perhaps with a few ups and downs, perhaps with a little extra support from clinic staff on occasion. However, as Dr. Kaplan pointed out, what they were not prepared for was the move back home—a move in which they would have to manage their anxieties and stresses on their own. Some simply never left at all. Denise, for instance, moved seamlessly from being a patient to being a careworker before her seventeenth birthday and remained living in Montreux housing until she got married—to another Montreux staff member. Caroline is another who, in more than six years, had never spent more than a few days completely away from the clinic. Some of the earliest outpatients shifted immediately to jobs as counsellors and stayed connected to Claude-Pierre for 12 years or more.

Many others did move home for a period of weeks or months, and then returned to Montreux. Some relapsed and returned to 24-hour care. Others recognized the increase in anxiety and stress in their lives and came back before they reached that point. "I can't be well at home," said Emily,* who returned to Victoria after a few months back in the U.S. "I can only be well here." Still others convinced themselves that they could cope perfectly at home, but just preferred to stay connected with the clinic that, in their minds, brought them such relief from torment. Many of this latter group joined the Montreux staff, but few had proved they could actually do well living independently without ongoing support from the clinic.

As for those patients who did leave Montreux permanently, it still remains unclear what their long-term outcomes have been. As Drs. Strober, Yager, and Kaplan have noted, some have turned up at other clinics, relapsing and in need of more treatment. Others, according to their families at least, are now doing well.

Dr. Kaplan again urged Montreux to start work on a long-term outcome study, assessing clients when they arrive at the clinic, when they leave, and for several years thereafter, "in order to be able to establish what approach at Montreux works for which type of patient and for how long."

He concluded: "Montreux's credibility has been severely tarnished by claims made in the national media by its founder that she has found the cure for anorexia nervosa. Anyone who knows anything about this disorder cringes at hearing such a thing from someone who has no training (not even a B.A.) and presents not one shred of hard evidence to support such a claim, when clinicians who are trained at the highest levels have been struggling to treat this disorder for the past 400 years."

12

The End

Marg Eastman knew she had a lot of learning to do, fast. When she arrived to take over as manager of Montreux, she threw herself into learning as much as she could about two things. One was eating disorders; the other was the responsibilities of a manager under the Community Care Facilities Act. Unlike Bob Enoch, she was not prepared to learn only Peggy Claude-Pierre's theories of eating disorders. She wanted to learn how other treatment centres operated, how they minimized risks to their patients, how they dealt with medical and psychiatric problems that arose. She wanted to know the medical complications of eating disorders and what symptoms she and Pam Brambell should be watching out for.

She didn't see herself acting as therapist for any of the clinic patients. Rather, she saw her job as bringing together the resources that would not only bring the clinic into compliance with the rules, but also improve the service to its patients. She came to Montreux convinced that if the best parts of its care—the idea of uniformly kind and compassionate treatment, the caring and devotion of so many staff members—could be enhanced with upgraded medical and nursing professionalism, Montreux could be a world-class centre second to none. If there was one thing she'd become convinced of through all her reading, it was that eating disorders, as much as any medical problem, needed a team approach. The caring and devotion of the staff needed to be backed up with nursing and medical expertise, with a psychiatrist on hand for consultation, with the skills of a dietitian, with strong links to the patients' families.

When she'd been interviewed for the job by licensing, she'd agreed to spend time observing the program run by Dr. Birmingham and his colleagues in Vancouver. She spent a week learning as much as she could, with Brambell joining her for a day as well. Along with Dr. Clinton-Baker, they registered for an international conference to be held just a few hundred miles away in Edmonton. They tried to get local help from Victoria's eating-disorder centre as well, but found the staff there unhelpful and hostile as soon as they mentioned where they came from. Montreux had obviously long since burned its bridges with the local eating-disorder community.

At the same time, Eastman was reading through every section of the licensing act and regulations. She came to understand that the person appointed as manager of any licensed facility was expected to be responsible for the day-to-day management of the centre—budget, hiring and firing staff, ensuring that care plans were in place and being followed for each resident. Although Steven Eng and Kim Macdonald had approved her as facility manager, they had suggested she not take on the position of "co-ordinator of care," another post required under the legislation. That, they said, should go to someone with greater background in eating disorders.

Eastman met several times with administrator John Noble to ensure everything was in place for meeting the new conditions on the license. Noble told her he saw his role as being the link between the clinic, the regional licensing investigators, and the provincial licensing branch that had granted the stay. He didn't expect to be a day-to-day administrator, but he did spend time at the clinic, helping management draft even more policies and procedures which they hoped would satisfy licensing's requirements.

The plan had been that the new conditions would be in place for only three or four months until the full appeal could be heard. However, Montreux's new lawyer, Chris Considine, quickly realized he was never going to be able to meet his commitments to his other clients, plus digest the entire Montreux file and be ready for the appeal by May. Since the clinic was still open, the pressure to complete the full appeal was reduced. Considine said the earliest he could possibly be ready was the end of November, a full 10 months away. With the time he had bought the clinic, he hoped that Montreux would be able to show that it could operate a successful program within the parameters of the licensing regulations as well as the strict conditions placed upon it.

Eastman became aware almost from the day she joined that Claude-Pierre was less than 100 per cent enthusiastic about her new role. Claude-Pierre worried aloud that the presence of so many nurses was going to "turn the clinic into a hospital," and she wouldn't be soothed by Eastman's assurances that she approved of the non-institutional atmosphere and saw her role mainly as a co-ordinator of resources.

The same day that the staff were told that Eastman would be coming on board as manager, they were also told that Emma* would become the co-ordinator of care. Eastman found one of her first uncomfortable jobs was putting the brakes on that idea.

Emma had certainly been a qualified nurse before her eating disorder grew so bad she ended up coming to Montreux. However, she had arrived as an acute-care patient only about 18 months earlier, and was still listed as a client taking counselling at the clinic. Eastman thought it was unfair to put so much pressure on Emma, not to mention the fact that she doubted licensing would accept in that job someone who was still officially a Montreux client.

Emma was not the only patient being promoted rapidly through the ranks at Montreux. As far as Eastman could tell, Serena was running the clinic practically singlehandedly. It still was less than two years since she had arrived as a 24-hour care patient, and she too was still listed as receiving counselling on an outpatient basis. Serena's background was in business and marketing, but—in the absence of any other decision-makers—she'd ended up doing everything from chairing staff meetings to deciding on readmissions of patients who weren't doing well. Several staff members told Eastman how pleased they were to have a proper management structure in place. Eastman was surprised at how little time Claude-Pierre and Harris were spending at the clinic. They often wouldn't turn up to planned meetings and, when problems arose, would simply phone Serena and tell her to "handle it." They spent several weeks that spring in the home they'd bought in Maui, letting their wishes be known by phone calls, again usually to Serena.

When Eastman first arrived, most of the patients remained scattered in the satellite sites throughout Victoria. She found she could keep in touch with them—and with their careworkers—only by spending hours each day reading the detailed patient logs compiled by every worker on each eight-hour shift they spent with a patient. She soon realized that the workers were painstakingly conscientious in describing every detail of a patient's health and behaviour. However, most of them didn't have the training or experience to spot the signs of problems that should be passed on to one of the nurses. As well, she soon discovered, careworkers were still following the same rules as before: the people to be paged in the case of any problem were a patient's counsellor or Claude-Pierre herself, not the manager or nurse. As she read the reports, she came across several instances where patients, some with a history of suicide attempts, had talked about wanting to hurt or kill themselves. In each case, they'd been referred only to Claude-Pierre, not to a nurse or doctor. Other patients had shown signs of physical problems, including an episode in which a patient with a serious heart condition had a blackout spell, but no one had thought it serious enough to let either of the nurses know. This, Eastman realized, wasn't good enough. If the nurses had been placed on staff to improve patient safety, it was essential they know when safety might be jeopardized.

The other person Eastman badly wanted to bring more into the loop was the centre's dietitian, Susan Trefz. Officially, Trefz had been on contract with the centre for almost a year, ever since it was pointed out to management that licensing regulations demanded a nutritionist as part of the team of any residential facility. She had 20 years' experience as a dietitian, including work at almost a dozen licensed care facilities. She had worked with young people and with sufferers of eating disorders. However, until Eastman came, her role with the patients at Montreux had been minimal. She had neither written food plans for the residents, nor provided counselling about nutrition and healthy eating. She had not even been allowed to read the patients' files, except for the occasional one that she was asked to provide a recommendation on. Claude-Pierre had made it clear to her that she was on the staff list solely because of the licensing requirement, and she was not invited to play any meaningful role.

Eastman, however, had quite a different idea of how Trefz might fit into the program. From her studies, she knew that nutritional counselling was considered a valuable part of therapy for almost all eating-disordered patients, many of whom harboured positively weird ideas about the relationship between eating and weight. Eastman also thought Trefz's background might provide better nutrition and food plans for the residents than the ones drawn up by either the counsellors or Claude-Pierre, none of whom had any background in nutrition. From the beginning, Eastman had found it unusual and concerning that the counsellors had so much power over every aspect of patients' health, including what they were to eat and how much activity they were allowed. Many of the counsellors were actually the least trained members of the Montreux staff. They were Claude-Pierre's early patients, some of whom had never even completed high school.

And in the original health assessments, Brambell and Trefz had worried that some of the patients didn't seem to be taking in enough fibre or even enough liquid to keep their digestive systems functioning properly.

Eastman asked Trefz to review the patients' histories and undertake proper nutritional assessments, something that she'd found was required by the regulations.

That was the first surprise for Trefz. As Eastman and Brambell began discussing the various patients with her, she realized that the satellite sites were teeming with patients she'd never even heard of, let alone properly assessed. She figured there were at least three times as many patients "on care" at the clinic as had been discussed with her. She first heard of Carrie in March 2000, although Carrie had come to the clinic in April 1997, and had been on 24-hour care ever since.

Trefz began spending as much as 15 hours a week at the clinic, trying to meet with each patient individually and catch up on the long-overdue assessments. It wasn't easy. The counsellors made it clear they weren't happy with her meeting with patients alone, let alone providing them with counselling about food issues. Just as a Montreux staff member was normally always present when a patient was seeing a doctor, the counsellors expected the same system to prevail when the patient was seeing the nutritionist. The patients wouldn't feel comfortable being alone with Trefz, they insisted.

Trefz was adamant. In all her years of experience, she'd never run into a circumstance where she wasn't allowed to meet with her clients privately. And no matter what the counsellors said, several of the patients, as they grew accustomed to seeing her around the mansion, began to ask her questions about nutrition and to ask Eastman how they could talk to her.

In March, with Eastman's help, Trefz set up a meeting with the counsellors. She wanted to address the counsellors' concerns and explain the value of nutritional counselling for eating-disordered patients. The meeting was not a great success. Since, in Claude-Pierre's theories, eating disorders had absolutely nothing to do with eating, the counsellors couldn't see why nutritional counselling would be of any benefit to the patients. And, they explained, they didn't like the patients seeing anyone untrained in the Montreux system without a counsellor there, because Trefz might be "tricked" or "manipulated" by the patients' Negative Minds.

Trefz wasn't sure what curve balls the patients might throw at her that she hadn't seen before, but she realized she was going to have to proceed more slowly to obtain the co-operation she needed. She agreed that she would, for the time being, allow the counsellors to be present when she met with the patients. Most of the counsellors were comfortable with that, but some still didn't like the idea of a nutritionist being involved with their patients at all. That minority included Claude-Pierre's two daughters, Nicole and Kirsten, as well as the senior counsellor, the former bank teller, Tessa.

Even though she was progressing slowly and attempting to work co-operatively with the counsellors, Trefz still found roadblocks being put in her way. Patients told her they weren't allowed to meet with her unless the counsellor was present. She'd be told a patient was unavoidably busy with another appointment so couldn't see her, and then spot the patient talking casually with a careworker only minutes later. When she talked to Claude-Pierre about the problem, Claude-Pierre blamed the patients and said they were all lying.

Eastman, meanwhile, found it wasn't just the systems related to licensing inspections that were in need of improvement. She quickly grew distressed at how poorly the careworking staff, most of whom were young and untrained, were treated. They were, she found, expected to work an eight-hour shift without a single break for lunch or coffee. Meals were all expected to be taken at the same time, and at the same table, as the patient, usually eating the same food as well. Even finding a minute to use the washroom could be a problem if you were working with a patient who could not be let out of a staff person's sight for the briefest moment. One of the first things Eastman did was find a way for every staff member to have at least a short break during their shift.

She found that many careworkers were actually ending up out-of-pocket paying for Montreux expenses. The way the system was supposed to work was that the careworkers would pay for meals out, special activities, movies and the like, and then be reimbursed by the clinic. But the system was always slow and inefficient, and careworkers ended up waiting weeks to get their money back. Sometimes they just gave up altogether.

She and Brambell also wanted to improve living conditions for the patients, especially those living in the satellite sites. Brambell had been unhappy about the sites since the first visit she'd made to Carrie's apartment the day after she was hired. She found the 15-year-old girl living in a dark, dingy, and damp basement suite. It was poorly furnished, but Carrie had no choice but to spend most of her waking hours in it, with no company except her caregiver. Brambell wasn't surprised that Carrie was complaining she felt like she was in prison. The basement suite didn't seem much of an improvement on a jail cell for a teenager. The clients at the third facility, Richmond House, weren't much better off. Weeds grew tall in the front yard, and paint was peeling off the door. The inside of the house never seemed clean.

Yet it didn't seem to Eastman and Brambell that they ever got a full day to work on the system changes they knew needed to occur; every day, a crisis of some kind seemed to happen with one patient or another.

One Friday evening, when Eastman had been there only a couple of weeks, a taxi driver drove up to the front door with Anna in tow. Anna, who was then supposed to be living independently, had wanted a ride home, but then had refused to pay the bill. In her four years at Montreux, Anna had taken so many taxi rides that she was well known to most of the cab drivers in town, and he'd brought her home anyway. But in his opinion, she was behaving so bizarrely this time that he figured he'd better put her into the charge of some adult who knew what they were doing.

Eastman went to talk to Anna but found her irrational and belligerent, screaming in the basement of the mansion. She seemed so unreasonable that Eastman at first wondered if she had taken some recreational drugs on her outing, but eventually Anna told her that she had abruptly stopped taking the antidepressant she was on because she was having unpleasant side effects and didn't think she needed it any more. Eastman checked and found out the drug was one that should never be stopped abruptly because of the risk of producing worse psychiatric symptoms. Eastman talked to Dr. Clinton-Baker about the need to deal with Anna's medications.

Less than two weeks later, she was told that Anna had found herself a part-time job, babysitting a 14-month-old child. She was appalled. It must, she thought, have been obvious to anyone that Anna wasn't emotionally stable enough to be put in charge of a toddler for hours on end. When she went to investigate, she was even more appalled to discover that Anna had been apparently hired, at least in part, on the basis of a reference letter written by a Montreux manager. Judy* had worked for the clinic in various capacities for more than four years and was now designated the family liaison officer.

"I have known Anna for the past three years and find her a helpful and capable young woman," Judy had written. "I feel she will succeed in any field she wishes to pursue and would feel comfortable having her care for my granddaughter." Eastman couldn't believe it. It was as if Judy was writing about some person altogether different from the one whose logs at Montreux showed she had spent the past three years on 24-hour care, scarcely ever able to swallow solid food, frequently self-harming and suicidal.

The End

But Judy agreed cheerfully that she'd written the letter a few weeks earlier, thinking it might be good for Anna to get a job and have something to focus on other than her problems. Eastman managed to put a stop to the idea.

The arrival of Dr. Kaplan the next week proved a welcome relief to Eastman and Brambell. Eastman picked him up at the airport, and as they drove to the clinic, she explained to him what she was trying to accomplish in her new job.

"We could make this a double-ended week," he told her. As well as undertaking the assessments he'd promised Johnston, he'd spend as much time as he could teaching Eastman and Brambell and showing them places they could go to learn more. He met with the clinic doctors, discussing the use of psychiatric medications and other medical problems. As well, he agreed to conduct a seminar with any staff members who wanted to attend, answering as many of their questions as possible. He found the staff desperately hungry for information and for hints on handling some of the more difficult problems that arose with their patients. But as well, he noted how lacking they were in even the most basic information about eating disorders, outside the Montreux framework. They did not even know that other agencies had developed guidelines to help keep people with anorexia safe and healthy, let alone what those guidelines were. They had no links to any others working with sufferers in Victoria or elsewhere in B.C. They didn't even have anyone to call for backup in cases where something went wrong.

As he examined the Montreux patients, Dr. Kaplan insisted he would see them alone. He was aided in this by Carrie, one of the first on the list, who firmly told Kelly,* the clinic's medical liaison officer, to "get out ... what the hell are you doing in here?" before Dr. Kaplan had even asked her her name. As well as the officially "on-care" patients, Dr. Kaplan examined two others—Anna and Sharleen. Dr. Bertoia asked him if he would examine Sharleen, whose progress seemed shaky, and Eastman persuaded Anna to talk to him because she remained worried about Anna's mental state. Sharleen had long been beset by serious obsessive-compulsive symptoms, and Dr. Kaplan talked to her about prescription medications that might help her with those.

She agreed to try that but, a few days later, Sharleen was again full of doubts. The full report from Dr. Kaplan, laying out exactly what medications she should be prescribed, had not yet arrived, and in the meantime, Claude-Pierre, now returned from Hawaii, had told her, "You can try the medication, but it probably won't work." A frustrated and discouraged Sharleen began once again talking about harming herself. Eastman, Brambell, and several of Sharleen's favourite staff members spent more than an hour convincing Sharleen that she had trusted Dr. Kaplan at the time and that he'd explained carefully to her why it would work.

Claude-Pierre grew increasingly unhappy with Dr. Kaplan as his week at the clinic continued. She didn't like the questions he was asking the patients, especially the ones about sexual harassment or sexual activity at the clinic, or other instances in which the boundaries of a professional relationship might have been crossed. She again asked Considine if he couldn't find a way to get Dr. Kaplan fired from the consultant's job, but Considine explained she had no legal grounds for that. Eventually Claude-Pierre took to meeting with each patient alone before they went for their assessment with Dr. Kaplan, letting them know they were free not to answer any questions that made them "uncomfortable." Some staff members suspected that Claude-Pierre was hoping the patients wouldn't provide Dr. Kaplan with any useful information at all. But Dr. Kaplan developed a good rapport with most of the patients, and nearly all ended up feeling comfortable talking to him and answering his questions.

The clinic held a reception for Dr. Kaplan one night at the mansion. Many of the staff members enjoyed having a chance to ask him questions informally about issues that had arisen with their patients. Claude-Pierre's hostility increased when she and Harris spotted Dr. Kaplan having dinner one evening with Kersteen Johnston, John Noble, and Marg Eastman. She and Harris became more convinced than ever that the doctor's visit was all part of what they still saw as a government conspiracy to put the clinic out of business. Now they were sure Eastman, and by association Brambell and Trefz, were part of that conspiracy too.

Eastman and Brambell, on the other hand, felt vastly reassured by the week with Dr. Kaplan that they were on the right track in what they were trying to do. A week or so later, when he was back in Toronto, Eastman phoned him to talk about steps she might take, based on the general findings he would be putting in his report. Dr. Kaplan told her his two largest areas of concern: the dependency on the clinic and lack of school or rehabilitation programs, and the repeated crossing of therapeutic and professional boundaries. It would, he noted, take longer to deal with the need for rehabilitation programs. Staff would have to be hired and programs developed; some plan would need to be created to try to bring a level of expertise to the existing staff members. On the other hand, most of the boundary issues could, and should, be dealt with immediately. The scheduler could ensure that male staff were not alone with female patients on overnight shifts. Clear rules could be set up governing the circumstances in which patients could be physically touched or hugged. Therapy sessions with the counsellors could be restricted to the counselling offices. Any outside counsellors used could be told to follow the same rules (and certainly not to take the clients to any more AA meetings).

Eastman agreed with all the suggestions and began trying to put them into place. Claude-Pierre did agree to chair a "special" training session for staff to deal with the issue of touching and hugging clients. Claude-Pierre continued to insist that an encouraging hug could be therapeutic and effective for eating-disorder sufferers; human touch should continue to be an important component of the Montreux strategy. She did, though, concede that touch must remain within "appropriate boundaries." A series of guidelines were put forward in which it was made clear that staff members must not initiate hugs with residents without the clear permission of the resident, and not when a worker was alone with a resident. A brief touch on the hand or arm could then be used instead when a staff member wanted to show emotional support and encouragement. Claude-Pierre agreed with the new boundaries, but shortly afterwards photocopied cartoons of two friendly-looking bears engaged in a full frontal hug, which were then stuck up on walls all over the clinic.

Eastman also began trying to establish a system under which staff members could take additional training, and have it paid for by the clinic. When she was told the clinic itself didn't have any money for such training, she approached the non-profit society, now headed by Dee,* a school principal and mother of an early Montreux patient. Dee agreed with the idea and promised that the society would provide $10,000 for the year, to be divided among any staff members who wanted to take courses on anything from medication administration to first aid. Pleased, Eastman posted a notice signed by Dee on the clinic bulletin board inviting applications from staff members.

A few days later she was approached by Claude-Pierre and Harris, asking where the memo had come from. Eastman explained, but Harris made it clear that donations raised by the society were not to be used for that purpose. The purpose of that money, he said, was to help pay the fees of those residential patients at the clinic who couldn't afford the full cost of care themselves. Eastman said that, as a member of the reconstituted society, she'd thought it was clear the society's emphasis now was, and legally had to be, training and education, not direct support of the profit-making corporation.

But later that day the notice disappeared from the bulletin board. Serena told Eastman that Claude-Pierre and Harris had ordered her to take it down. Eastman had to manoeuvre behind the scenes to get staff trained in such basics as medication administration and safe food handling.

It was Easter week when Eastman heard that Johnston and her lawyer, Brian Young, wanted to visit Montreux. She and other staff members scurried around, tidying and decorating the mansion to look as if celebrating Easter would be a major event at the clinic. John Noble had explained that the two wanted to meet with Eastman and himself. They drove up at precisely 10:00 a.m. Eastman had also invited Brambell and the centre's business manager, Drew Firth, to join the conversation. Firth and Harris had been complaining about the number of hours Brambell was working, and Eastman hoped Johnston would help explain the need for the extra hours, especially until all care plans and health assessments had been brought up to date. Firth, though, wanted to extend the conversation further. As well as managing the books, his job involved dealing with parents and sponsors in arranging payments; he ended up doing much of the marketing of the clinic to prospective families. He began his sales pitch with Johnston and Young, stressing that he told parents of the large and comprehensive health team that was available to clients. "If they need a chiropractor, we'll get them one," he said. "The same with any other health professional." But patients and families didn't want to see nurses prominent around the clinic, he said. Most of them had had more than their fill of anything that looked like a traditional medical model. Eastman and Brambell were stunned. One thing they'd already learned was that it was next to impossible to persuade Montreux management to bring in outside health professionals. But Johnston and Young seemed to be taking it all in.

Firth talked about how difficult it had been for the clinic financially since Johnston had ordered them to admit no new patients, even as outpatients. He did hope, he said, that the clinic would soon be able to show it had made enough improvements that Johnston would change that condition. Johnston and Young seemed understanding and sympathetic.

They turned to Eastman. "How long do you think you'll need before you would be able to admit new patients?" Young asked.

Eastman was flustered. She was having such difficulty getting changes accepted that she was beginning to doubt if it would ever be safe for Montreux to admit new patients, except with extremely well-defined admission criteria. "Well," she said, "we still have quite a bit of work to do. Maybe eight to 12 weeks."

A few minutes later, Melanie,* the patient admitted just two weeks before the stay hearing, walked by the doorway of the office where the meeting was taking place. Claude-Pierre and Harris were there too.

"Ah," said Harris, "you must meet our doctor." Eastman knew Melanie hated being introduced as a doctor, even though she held her MD in her native Switzerland. While she was at Montreux, she'd told staff, she wanted to be just plain Melanie, a patient like any of the other patients, working to overcome her eating disorder. But Eastman realized Harris was sending a subtle message—Montreux must be a safe place, or why would a doctor stay here?

After a few minutes of polite chat, Noble realized he had to leave. Johnston and Young still wanted a tour of the facility. Before Eastman could say anything, Claude-Pierre and Harris took over, inviting the visitors to come over to see St. Charles House, and especially some of the patients' art. Eastman watched as the four of them headed through the back garden over to the other building. They didn't return for close to an hour. Only later did she realize how inappropriate it was for the person who would have to sit as judge on any complaints of breaches of the stay order to spend time alone with the facility owners. Neither McDannold nor the licensing investigation team had even known Johnston and Young were planning to visit the clinic.

More and more, Eastman was beginning to feel that her efforts to make any major changes at the clinic were being undermined. Claude-Pierre and Harris wouldn't allow her to put a want ad in the newspaper to search for a suitable candidate for the co-ordinator of care. Instead, when she'd insisted Emma wasn't acceptable, they put forward another name they'd heard about privately. Eastman, Brambell, and Trefz all interviewed the woman and concluded that her knowledge of eating disorders was far too limited for her to ever be accepted by licensing for the job. Still she could not get permission to run the want ad.

Eastman also pointed out that the regulations required a staff person to be appointed as co-ordinator of social and leisure activities, and Judy was appointed to that position. She called a meeting of managers and counsellors to establish a better system for co-ordinating the residents' activities. Eastman was pleased, thinking this could be the first step towards a proper rehabilitation program as had been suggested by Dr. Kaplan. But the minutes of the first meeting showed clearly that if any patient wanted to start a new activity, Judy "would speak with Peggy to ensure that there are no safety or financial concerns that would inhibit the residents from pursuing that activity." Eastman couldn't figure out why it wouldn't be one of the nurses or doctors who should be deciding about health and safety concerns, rather than Claude-Pierre.

Despite repeated requests, neither Harris nor Firth would ever give her a copy of the budget so she could see what money might be available to hire the outside professionals she thought were needed. Instead, she found she had to fight for every cent she wanted to spend on the patients, even on simple things like a new mattress for a patient with back problems.

Eastman was also finding difficulties in having roles and responsibilities clearly delineated around patient care. Becca, one of the patients who'd been trying to live independently since the stay order was granted, was brought back onto 24-hour care, not on the advice of her doctor or any of the nurses, but rather of Serena. Becca had been relapsing, but the decision appeared to be based as much on the fact that Montreux now had spare staff available for another patient as it was on an evaluation of her symptoms.

Of all the patients, the one showing the most problems was Anna. Claude-Pierre had also moved Anna to "off-care status," with her last regularly scheduled careworkers having worked with her the day after the stay was granted. But along with the episodes with the taxi driver and the babysitting, virtually all the staff members who saw or spoke to Anna knew things were not going well for her. For various parts of the spring she and her dog had stayed in a basement suite at the Richmond Avenue house and then moved to the basement of the St. Charles mansion.

At one point a staff member complained about the filthy condition of the suite where Anna was staying. Another time the dog's persistent barking brought the police on a noise complaint; they too let Montreux management know they thought the suite was so dirty as to be a health concern. On another occasion, a staff member who was working with Naomi in her suite in Richmond House complained that Anna wasn't ordering groceries or buying food, but just taking Naomi's on the rare occasions when she did want to eat anything.

In early April, a team meeting was held with Anna to talk about her future. She had moved back to St. Charles by that point and planned to live there independently. She told staff she planned to move away from the Montreux facilities altogether soon and begin taking college courses in Victoria in the fall. She was volunteering at a deli to gain work experience, and she said she wanted to begin taking driving lessons to increase her independence. The team agreed those were reasonable goals if she was going to remain living independently—

even though her weight had been dropping ever since she'd been assigned to live off-care. It wasn't mentioned that Dr. Kaplan had recommended that Anna—who had by then been at Montreux for four years with little improvement—be discharged and returned to her home in England. Dr. Kaplan had even recommended physicians and facilities in England that might be able to provide help and support to Anna and her family.

The weekend after Easter, Brambell, Eastman, and Dr. Clinton-Baker went to Edmonton for four days for the eating-disorder conference. They went to seminars on treatment options, talked to experts from around the world, and returned fired up with enthusiasm to do even more to make Montreux a world-class centre.

Their optimism was short-lived. They returned to find that in their absence problems had developed with patients, as well as, apparently, with the clinic's finances. As Eastman checked the workers' logs on the patients for the weekend, she found reports that Jessica,* one of the newer patients, had been talking about harming herself. Jessica had a lengthy history of suicide attempts; staff had become so worried she was going to hurt herself that they'd removed the glass from the picture frames in her room and the paper clips that held her sheet music together. Although Eastman and Brambell had made sure that substitute medical personnel were on call while they were away, no one had bothered to tell the on-call nurse or doctor of their concerns. When Eastman checked the guidelines written for Jessica's care, she found that the risk of her harming herself was emphasized—but staff were still told to seek help from her counsellor or from Denise, her team leader, rather than discuss it with medical personnel.

Carmen, who for most of the spring had been living with her mother in an apartment but still receiving help from careworkers as much as 24 hours a day, was officially discharged from the Montreux program while the others were away. However, a few days later, the logbooks still contained notes for staff to check Carmen's room for sharp objects or toxins that she might use to harm herself.

Problems with finances were growing increasingly acute as well. At the end of April, Brambell had found her paycheque reduced unilaterally by about $1,500 from the bill she'd submitted for the hours she'd worked. When she asked about it, she was told that Harris and Firth had concluded that, despite what Dr. Kaplan said was required, she hadn't needed to put in as many hours as she had, so they'd "adjusted" the bill accordingly. Firth had suggested that a private nursing company could provide any services they really needed. Brambell almost quit on the spot, but was persuaded to stay on an extra month once Eastman convinced Firth to pay her the money for the time she had already worked.

At the beginning of May, other paycheques were bouncing. On May 3, Trefz announced she was quitting, in part because of the difficulty in getting paid. She'd change her mind, she said, only if Montreux would pay her in advance for any work done. Two days later, Harris called Brambell and told her that Montreux was prepared to pay her for a maximum of two hours "on call" work a day, now that most of the health assessments had been completed. That was less than half the hours she'd actually been working. Other staff members came to Eastman and complained that their paycheques had bounced too—although that was remedied in less than 24 hours by Harris and Firth.

For Eastman, it seemed as if the place was falling apart around her. She could not see how she could even keep things up to minimal standards with no dietitian and only about one-third the number of nursing hours available to her. She still had no authority to hire the health professional staff she needed to live up to the licensing regulations and the terms of the stay order.

Angry and discouraged, she wrote a letter specifically to Claude-Pierre on May 5. "With the withdrawal of the services of Susan Trefz and reduction of Pam Brambell's services, I am unable to be responsible for the health and safety of the residents as required by the Act." She made sure John Noble had a copy as well as Considine, Claude-Pierre, and Harris. Eastman and Brambell did, though, both agree to continue working to the end of the month to ensure care was provided to the residents.

In fact, neither of them made it. From that day on, everything just seemed to get worse and worse, faster and faster. Patients weren't doing well, families were unhappy with what was going on, careworkers seemed overwhelmed. Staff members told her the story of Jacob and Marcie's love affair. More than ever, Eastman felt she couldn't obtain the authority to make the decisions or bring in the resources needed to get things back on an even keel.

Kelly, the medical liaison officer, was trying to take over more and more of the nurses' role, although she had no nursing training. Her only experience was having a job as an assistant in a pharmacy for three years. Eastman and Brambell found her trying to do nutritional counselling with the patients, making reports to the doctors, and even bypassing the nurses to take orders from the doctors on medical issues like changes to patients' medications. Eastman spoke to her about it, but to no avail.

Eventually she told Claude-Pierre that she was worried that Kelly could get the clinic into legal difficulty if she continued making medical decisions without consulting with the nurses, even when they were sitting only a few feet away. Kelly, she pointed out, was not a registered nurse and shouldn't be doing jobs which, in health care facilities, were restricted to those who had proper nursing training.

Claude-Pierre replied that it shouldn't be a problem because, "I trained her."

Openly exasperated, Eastman pointed out to Claude-Pierre that she didn't have any nursing training either.

Jessica was having a bad month, and so were Etta and Carrie. Jessica didn't want to move back in to the Rockland mansion, especially not the attic suite, which she found was kept at far too warm a temperature for her liking. At a case conference it was agreed that she wouldn't have to move until returning from her first visit home at the end of May—but less than a week later, Eastman and Brambell found her, tense and anxious, unpacking her bags in the attic suite. When Eastman complained about the decisions of a case conference being overturned unilaterally, she was told that Jessica's counsellors had persuaded her that the move would be fine and then had convinced Dr. Clinton-Baker of the same thing.

Etta alternated between self-destructive urges and grandiose plans, like wanting to go bungee jumping and wanting to go on holiday to

The End

Hawaii, taking her team leader with her. Her careworkers and counsellors said that all of this was just Etta's Negative Mind speaking. But they said the same thing when Etta asked permission to go to spend time with her sister, who was visiting Victoria all the way from Sweden and was staying at a downtown hotel. Eastman couldn't see anything unreasonable about that request and allowed Etta to go, thereby incurring the disapproval of several other staff members.

Carrie was managing to lose weight, even while on 24-hour care. Her anxieties around gaining weight and eating were becoming extreme again. She complained constantly of how bored she was, said she felt like she was in prison, and that she didn't want to lose any more school time. Her family, which had been passionately supportive of Montreux during the hearing a year earlier, were changing their tune. When they visited Victoria that month, they complained bitterly that they had not been allowed to talk to Claude-Pierre, that their phone calls weren't being returned, and that they couldn't get any useful information out of any staff members they did talk to. Carrie was refusing to talk to them because she was so angry about having to stay at the clinic. At an emotional case conference, it was decided that plans should be made for Carrie's discharge by the end of the summer.

Also visiting in town towards the end of May was Anna's father. Even Claude-Pierre recognized that the experiment of allowing Anna to live independently was not going well. While her father was in town, Claude-Pierre suggested a meeting with herself, Anna, Eastman, and Dr. Clinton-Baker to try to persuade Anna that she was not yet ready to live independently.

This time everyone realized that Anna was indeed looking thinner. Anna, however, was adamant that she would not return to 24-hour care. She wanted to be independent, she said. She pointed out that she'd gone through every part of the Montreux program, including all the suggestions her counsellors could make for her and years of round-the-clock care. "I have self discipline," she said. "It's up to me now."

She was persuaded to return to an antidepressant medication that Dr. Clinton-Baker would prescribe. She would allow the Montreux counsellors to monitor her weight, and she and her father would meet jointly with Dr. Clinton-Baker to discuss her longer-term future within a week or two. She would be formally discharged from the Montreux program when her weight had stabilized again.

On the morning of May 25, Eng and Macdonald turned up at Montreux to do an unannounced inspection. Trefz had talked to them after quitting, to warn them of the problems she saw developing. They'd also heard from others still in contact with the clinic that, far from improving, things there appeared to be becoming more chaotic than ever. Dr. Clinton-Baker also chose that morning to visit the clinic, in part to talk about Anna, whom he'd seen in his office the day before. Thus it was with the licensing investigators present that the whole thing appeared to unravel.

Even Dr. Clinton-Baker, accustomed to seeing anorexics in their most acute stage of illness, had been shocked at Anna's appearance. The girl had obviously deteriorated drastically in the six days since he'd seen her last. When he persuaded her to step on the scale, he found she weighed only 90 pounds, a loss of eight pounds in the previous nine days. Since moving towards independent living at the end of January, she'd lost 25 pounds, more than one-fifth of her body weight. It would have been a drastic weight loss for anyone, but for someone whose body was already compromised by years of malnutrition, it was clearly a medical emergency. She eventually admitted to the doctor that she hadn't eaten a bite of solid food for the previous five days—presumably since the last planning meeting about her future—and that she'd been suffering from diarrhea.

Dr. Clinton-Baker ordered her returned to 24-hour care immediately. When Brambell came to assess her a couple of hours later, she found her temperature to be below normal, her heart rate to be slow, and her blood pressure to be low. After a discussion with Dr. Clinton-Baker, Eastman took Anna to the emergency room of the local hospital to see if she needed to be admitted to hospital to be medically stabilized. However, after talking to Dr. Clinton-Baker, the emergency doctors thought she could be cared for at Montreux. Less than four hours later, Anna was back at the mansion.

Eastman and Brambell knew that, as far as they personally were concerned, this was the end. Both had always prided themselves on maintaining the highest standards of practice, according to the codes of the nurses' professional organization. They knew there was no way they could maintain those standards at Montreux. The clinic refused to provide either the resources or the expertise needed to deal with the crisis. Although Anna's blood pressure and temperature needed regular monitoring, the clinic didn't even have a blood-pressure cuff that would fit her or a thermometer on site. That night, with Trefz gone, there was no one with any expertise in nutrition to tell them what Anna should start eating. She'd eaten nothing at all for a long time and was adamantly refusing any "shakes." Eastman tried to phone the experts she'd met at the St. Paul's Hospital program, but by then it was too late in the day to contact them. Eventually Claude-Pierre and Dr. Clinton-Baker consulted by phone and decided that Anna's meal plan for that night should be a cup of yogurt, a banana, and a glass of grape juice.

The next morning Eastman and Brambell both resigned, reiterating that it was impossible to be responsible for the patients' health and safety in the circumstances that prevailed at Montreux. Brambell left at 6:00 p.m.; Eastman agreed to stay until 10:00 p.m. that night to allow Montreux to find someone else to take over the on-call nursing duties.

Both Eastman and Brambell expected that their departure would lead Johnston to order the facility closed under the terms of the stay order. Not only did they no longer have an approved manager or approved nursing services, but the three health professionals who'd been hired had all quit on the grounds that they felt that the health and safety of the patients was being put at risk. They had explained all the circumstances of their abrupt departure to Noble.

It didn't happen. Don Caverley, whose background was in social work, had already been hired to take over when Eastman went back to her old job, and he hastily assumed the manager's position. Nursing services had been cobbled together too, using at first a nurse who volunteered her time, and then a psychiatric nurse who was quickly promoted to become the supervisor of care as well. It made Eastman and Brambell uncomfortable, but, they concluded, they had done the best they could; it wasn't really any of their business what Johnston chose to do next. However, Eastman continued to receive phone calls from staff members who had come to trust her during her time at

Montreux. It was clear that life was not improving, for either the patients or the staff.

Eastman and Brambell had been reluctant to make further official complaints to licensing. For one thing, both had signed confidentiality agreements before starting at Montreux—something the clinic demanded of all its staff members—and they weren't sure what they could disclose without risking legal trouble. For another, Eastman had kept Noble up to date on problems as they'd developed at the clinic. That, they thought, should have been sufficient to make clear to Johnston the extent of the difficulties. As more and more bits of information leaked out to them, however, they grew increasingly worried about what was happening since they had left. Eventually they talked to a lawyer from the nurses' professional association, who told them they were well within their rights to disclose exactly what they'd observed at the clinic to the licensing investigators. They phoned Kim Macdonald, and on June 30, Eastman sat down in a conference room with Macdonald, the nurses' association lawyer, and a shorthand reporter to begin to detail her experiences. The interview lasted for three hours—and didn't cover half the questions that Macdonald had. The long weekend would begin the next day, so they arranged to meet again at 9:30 Tuesday morning.

But on the Saturday, Canada Day, Eastman got a phone call at home from one of the clinic staff members with whom she'd developed a good relationship. The staff member was terrified of being identified publicly, but desperately wanted advice from Eastman. The problem, she said, was Anna. Things had gone from bad to worse in Anna's case since Eastman and Brambell had departed. Although Anna had originally agreed to return to 24-hour care, she was now bitterly opposed to it again and insisting on returning home to England. Plans had been made in mid-June to allow her to leave, but they continued to be delayed, the latest delay occurring the previous Wednesday. Meanwhile, Anna was emotionally distraught and she was losing more weight. The staff member was convinced that, with the latest delay in Anna's departure, not only was she being kept against her will, but her physical and mental health and safety were in serious jeopardy.

Eastman concluded that the information was so critical it couldn't be

The End

ignored until Tuesday. She phoned Noble to pass on the staff member's concerns. On Monday evening she repeated her concerns in an e-mail to Johnston so it would be there first thing when Johnston came in to work in the morning. As well, she explained to Kim Macdonald what had happened as soon as they met on the Tuesday morning. That week, she and Brambell spent two more days completing their interviews with licensing. When Eastman checked her e-mail after finishing her interview on Tuesday, she found a reply from Johnston, saying she'd asked Noble to investigate as quickly as possible and report back to her. On Thursday she received an e-mail from Noble, repeating that Johnston had asked him to investigate, "and I have." He said he would be sending a confidential report to Eng as soon as possible.

Eastman and Brambell were satisfied. People in authority appeared to be taking their concerns seriously at last. However, their peace of mind was short-lived. Eng never received a report of any kind from Noble. Instead, the next news they heard from their Montreux sources was that on July 28, Anna had been put on the plane for England, accompanied by several clinic staff members who would stay with her at her home for the first few weeks of the transition.

Macdonald and Eng, meanwhile, were frustrated and distressed by the information they'd received from Brambell, Eastman, and Trefz. It seemed that everything McDannold had predicted, both at the hearing before Dr. Stanwick and at the stay hearing, was coming true. Claude-Pierre and Harris couldn't be trusted to make the changes needed for the residential clinic to operate within the law. They weren't even prepared to make changes sufficient to allow the health professionals that they themselves had hired to stay on the job. It sounded as if patients might be at even more risk now than they had been at the time Dr. Stanwick gave his decision.

Macdonald had asked a few direct questions at the end of each interview, and had learned that the clinic was still practising the "illusion of no choice" and that boundaries were still sometimes being crossed with unwanted hugging and holding. As well, they realized that moving Anna, Becca, and Carmen back onto 24-hour care could well be considered "new admissions," against the terms of the stay order, since all three had previously been declared by Montreux to have moved to outpatient status, not to be counted in the list of "on-care" patients. It was, they decided, time to talk to lawyer Guy McDannold again and see what options were legally available.

McDannold agreed. He concluded that the best route would be to go back to Johnston and ask for a reopening of the stay application. Licensing would, he said, urge Johnston to follow through on her plan to have the clinic close if it was found not to be living up to the licensing rules and the terms of the order. He told the licensing team to bring together as much evidence as possible, just as they had done when first preparing the case for Dr. Stanwick. Less than a week after the interviews with Brambell and Eastman, McDannold sent a letter to Considine, advising him of what licensing was planning to do, backed up by the interviews with the nurses and Trefz and all the evidence that the investigative team had found up to that date.

Montreux fought back with vigour. Less than a week later, the centre filed a 13-page report from its new "acting manager," Caverley, disputing nearly everything Brambell and Eastman had said. Caverley's report implied that if anything had gone wrong during the three months while Eastman was manager, the blame must be laid on her. He cited "communications breakdowns" between the care staff, Eastman, and Brambell as the reason the nurses had not known key information. If Brambell wasn't told what she needed to know, that was Eastman's fault. If Trefz didn't know what was going on with the patients nutritionally, that was Eastman's fault too. He blamed the abrupt resignations of both Trefz and Brambell for putting residents at risk. He included a letter from Firth, in which Firth said that Brambell had told him she could not stay because Anna was "beyond her professional ability to provide nursing."

When Brambell read the letter later, she couldn't believe her eyes. It wasn't that Firth had misinterpreted what she'd said about her resignation, it was that she hadn't even been at the clinic at the times he mentioned, had not talked to him at all on the day she resigned, or ever, about her reasons for resigning. As far as she could tell, the entire story had been made up out of thin air.

Caverley admitted that Eastman might have had some trouble gaining enough control over finances and policy but promised that "this has been rectified" since he took over the job. "To date, after aprox [*sic*] two months of being associated with Montreux, I have not had my decisions undermined by Peggy Claude-Pierre nor David Harris."

Caverley then spent several pages detailing the improvements Montreux had made, yet again, to its policies and procedures, and promising that even more would be forthcoming. He insisted that Montreux "does not teach an 'illusion of no choice' at this time" and that this had been stressed to all staff members. Psychiatric nurse Maureen Harrison had come on board as supervisor of care, he noted, and a new dietitian had been hired as well. "Montreux has had, and will continue to have, staff with adequate experience, competence, and training to ensure the health and safety of the residents," he wrote.

Considine attached the report when he wrote to Johnston, urging her to dismiss licensing's application out of hand. He noted that Claude-Pierre and Harris had moved their offices out of the mansion and were "not involved in daily operations" of the residential program, and that Montreux was being operated by Caverley and his team.

"It is my submission that Montreux residential facility has made tremendous strides in the last six months," he argued. "No patient has died or nearly died at the facility. Concerns which have been raised by Licensing have been addressed and will continue to be addressed to ensure the best possible care for the patients."

He wanted Johnston not only to continue the stay order, but also to insist that licensing approve Caverley and Harrison as the centre's management team and to allow Montreux to admit new clients once again.

Johnston had no appetite for another formal hearing on whether the stay should be continued. She didn't ask for a response from Eastman, Brambell, or Trefz, or even send them a copy of Caverley's report. Eastman and Brambell were concerned for their reputations when they heard Caverley had written a report. Eastman went to the trouble of personally phoning Young to ask about the report, but he told her there was nothing in it about which she needed to be concerned personally.

Instead of holding a hearing, Johnston wanted the two sides to meet informally with her, Young, and Noble. At such a meeting, she was apparently convinced, a compromise could be worked out that would meet licensing's concerns while allowing Montreux to stay open.

Eng and Macdonald couldn't believe it. As far as they were concerned, they had more than enough evidence to show that Montreux had again broken the licensing rules, breached the conditions of the order, and weren't showing any more signs of co-operation than they'd done before Dr. Stanwick's ruling.

McDannold was equally outraged. He didn't think it proper for someone sitting essentially as a judge to decline to hold a proper hearing and instead insist on trying to broker a compromise herself. After much discussion, they decided that licensing would not attend the "informal meeting" proposed by Johnston.

That, however, didn't deter Johnston. The meeting went ahead with only Noble, Considine, and Caverley attending. When they realized that the licensing team wouldn't be coming, Montreux seized upon the chance to convince Johnston of the amount of progress they'd made and the value of allowing the program to remain open. Caverley, Harrison, and dietitian Marg Yendel were introduced as the new management team, who, they argued, had much more understanding of eating disorders than the former team headed by Eastman. As in Considine's letter, they emphasized the progress the clinic was making and described it as the only alternative to death for desperately ill anorexics.

This time McDannold, Eng, and Macdonald were not surprised at Johnston's decision to allow the clinic to remain open. She was, she wrote, satisfied that the clinic was doing all it could to minimize health and safety risks to its residents. Given the sort of patients they dealt with, it was not possible for them to eliminate all risks, she said, but they were as small as reasonably possible. It wasn't reasonable, she said, for them to be expected to implement Dr. Kaplan's recommendations immediately and, she noted, he hadn't found any of the patients he examined to be at serious immediate medical risk. The clinic could stay open without the necessity of another formal hearing being held. Noble would continue to monitor Montreux's operations for her.

It would have been easy for the licensing team to leave it at that. They had done all they could; it would be on Johnston's head if anything went badly wrong in the months before the appeal was decided. But they just couldn't do that. They had become fierce advocates for the health and safety of the Montreux patients, and if they had given up at that point, they would have felt as if they were abandoning them. They were genuinely afraid someone would die at the clinic before the full appeal could be heard and decided. Yet another Montreux staff member, one with health care experience, had come to them with confidential information, and they realized the situation was not improving. For some patients, it even appeared to be getting worse. Montreux laid off several staff members, including the only careworker who could speak Japanese to Naomi, and Steven,* one of the most popular counsellors. Several patients were distraught that their favourite staff members were no longer there for them.

If they wanted to fight on, McDannold told Dr. Stanwick and the licensing team, one option remained. They could take the entire case to the B.C. Supreme Court and ask a judge to overrule Johnston's decision.

McDannold wrote a 20-page brief, stressing the continuing pattern he'd seen in the clinic's operations. They were always promising to change but they didn't, he said, and even genuine professionals like Brambell, Eastman, and Trefz couldn't get them to. The stories they were hearing now were no different from the stories they'd heard during the first investigation, during the second investigation, and during the hearing.

Eng and Macdonald put together as many documents as they could find to back up their argument. They included full transcripts of the interviews with Eastman, Brambell, and Trefz, the full text of both Dr. Kaplan's reports, and, yet again, dozens of pages of patient logs describing the occasions when things were going wrong. When McDannold went to the courthouse to file his application, he took with him a cardboard grocery carton filled with more than 1,200 pages of documents.

The hearing was scheduled for the last week of August. At 6:00 p.m. on August 25, 2000, just days before it would begin, reporters around Victoria began receiving calls from Considine's office. They were told to stand by for an important fax that would be coming in to their newsrooms. When the reporters read the fax, they were shocked.

It was Montreux who had thrown in the towel. Peggy Claude-Pierre and David Harris had, that afternoon, handed back their operating licence to Kersteen Johnston. They would not try to operate a residential program in Victoria.

"Montreux has been emotionally exhausted and financially depleted by its struggle with the local licensing authority," said the official statement. "It deeply regrets that it is not able to continue with this important humanitarian work in Victoria in a residential setting.

"Montreux surrendered the license due to its extreme frustration with the local ... licensing authority who have refused to participate in constructive dialogue with respect to the facility over the last three months and with the general activities of Licensing over the last 3½ years."

It quoted the parts of Johnston's decision in which she said the clinic was minimizing risk, and also those in which she criticized licensing for not attending the "informal meeting."

This time there was no large news conference, no cast of parent and patient supporters surrounding Claude-Pierre and Harris, no appearances on *20/20*. Considine was the clinic spokesman. Serena had joined the ranks of the many former staff persons who no longer cared to be associated with Montreux. It was, Considine said, too early to say what Montreux might do instead. They might run a program strictly for outpatients, which wouldn't need a licence. The non-profit society might apply again for a licence to run a residential program, independent of Claude-Pierre and Harris.

The news had been kept so quiet that not even Eng or Dr. Stanwick knew of Montreux's decision until other reporters and I phoned them that evening.

This time Montreux staff members did not send postings to the Internet chatrooms. Their public support level had slowed to a trickle. Etta was the one patient who went public, bemoaning the closure and suggesting it was the result of a "witch hunt" by government authorities.

Christie Blatchford wrote one last column in which she described Claude-Pierre as "a helpful amateur" rather than a professional, and as "a wingnut who broke provincial safety regulations with abandon and ignored the several second chances to clean up her act that were given her by the province's fair-minded health officials."[89]

The End

Licensing knew it was the best they could expect. But they knew too that they had not succeeded in shutting down Montreux entirely. It would emerge in another incarnation, or in another place. Claude-Pierre was too determined to ever give up her work, and the world too full of desperate sufferers and families. They needed an angel, even a fallen one, too much to turn their backs on the person who professed to work miracles, no matter what the evidence. They needed an angel more than they needed the truth that was spread before them.

Epilogue

In the days immediately after it had turned in its licence, there was much conjecture about Montreux's ultimate fate. One option raised by lawyer Chris Considine was that the non-profit society might consider applying for a new residential licence as a completely separate entity from any company that Claude-Pierre and Harris might be running. Alternatively the program could relocate somewhere outside British Columbia. Claude-Pierre and Harris had talked previously about establishing what they then called "a teaching clinic" in Hawaii; she'd also talked about offers to relocate in places as far away as Great Britain or Norway.

However, no new application for a licence was ever received by health authorities, and the clinic didn't move anywhere. Instead, Claude-Pierre and Harris adapted their program with the requirements of B.C. legislation in mind. The law requires an operating licence only for establishments providing their services on a residential basis.

Those who want to run a day program or outpatient counselling program require no licence from the government, no matter how ill—physically or mentally—their clients may be. Unlike residential facilities, such programs have no requirements for the qualifications of either the operators or the staff they hire.

As a result, Montreux changed its programming to provide "intensive outpatient counselling, multiple daily sessions and therapy," (as it wrote on the Internet) but with no residential component run by the clinic. Clients who are so ill upon arrival that they need 24-hour care may bring a family member to provide it or hire their own careworkers. Although the clinic may help families find such careworkers, none of these workers are clinic employees. The clinic may also help families to find a place for a client to live, even in the same facilities previously used by Montreux, but the families pay rent like any other tenant. Under this system, Montreux is not subject to any government oversight.

Because the clinic is no longer required to submit reports to provide accountability through any official body, it is not possible to say how many clients it is serving in its new set-up, the sort of information that must be provided to licensing authorities by residential facilities. Neither need it submit to the authorities "incident reports" in which any particular problems with a client are expected to be noted.

As of February 1, 2002, Montreux Counselling Centres had not filed the legally required annual reports under the B.C. Companies Act for either 2000 or 2001. The non-profit Montreux Society for Eating Disorders had not filed its required reports for 2001 either.

Peggy Claude-Pierre has not been featured on any major radio or television shows or in magazine articles in Canada or the U.S. since relinquishing the clinic's residential licence.

As for some of the other key characters in this book:

Noah and Margaret Dobson returned to Victoria but are no longer associated with Montreux. Margaret has returned to a career in retail sales, while Noah is developing a successful new career as a realtor.

Nicole and Kirsten Claude-Pierre have both moved to Vancouver where Nicole is pursuing a career in photography.

Chloe underwent several years of effective outpatient therapy in Victoria, remarried, and is living happily in Victoria with her family.

Jeannie chose to stay in Canada, married a young man she met in Victoria, and is working in the community social services sector.

Anna returned to her home in England where she is receiving psychiatric treatment and managing to live semi-independently.

Louise also returned to her home in England where she is pursuing her interest in a career working with pre-school aged children.

Dustin is getting good marks in fourth grade at the private school he attends in New York. He lives with his parents and spends much of his spare time indulging in his hobby of working with computers.

Serena broke away completely from the clinic but stayed in Victoria.

Epilogue

She found a ready-made family, including stepchildren, and is involved in a successful business development project.

Emma, the nurse from Australia, also stayed in Victoria after breaking away from the clinic. She is now practising her profession and on staff at the Vancouver Island Health Authority.

Gay Pankhurst is now working as assistant manager for a chain of thrift shops whose profits go to help community projects in Greater Victoria.

The other staff members who provided information to licensing, including Marg Eastman, Randi, Andrew, and Gavin, have all returned or moved on to careers in the health or social services field.

Steven Eng moved to Vancouver to take on a similar job with a health authority; Kim Macdonald is now responsible for licensing of residential facilities in Greater Victoria.

Dr. Richard Stanwick has assumed the role of medical health officer for all of Vancouver Island with the reorganization of health services delivery in B.C.

Dr. Allan Kaplan is serving his term as president of the international Academy for Eating Disorders as well as managing the eating disorders program in Toronto.

Funds are being raised for a memorial statue dedicated to Lena Zavaroni to be erected in her home town of Rothesay in Scotland.

Other former Montreux patients, including Stacey and Sheila, continue to struggle to cope with their eating disorders.

One who lost her battle was Becca Heitling. She left Montreux on July 1, 2000, two months before the clinic gave up its licence. She had been a residential patient for more than three years. Back home in the southern U.S., her family was unable to find her any further long-term, residential treatment. She died of complications from her eating disorder on May 12, 2001.

Chronology of Montreux Counselling Centre

1988	Peggy Claude-Pierre founds Montreux as an out-patient practice.
May 1993	Residential program opens in SafeHouse in Victoria.
August 1993	Residential program moves to mansion at 1560 Rockland Ave.
January 1994	Caroline* becomes first high-profile patient.
January 1994	Non-profit society incorporated to acquire donations.
May 1994	Samantha Kendall arrives from England to begin program.
June 1994	Provincial government declines to provide funding to Montreux.
September 1994	Donna Brooks arrives from England to begin program.
December 1994	Hour-long documentary on Montreux airs on ABC's *20/20*.
May 1995	A second positive report on Montreux airs on *20/20*.
June 1995	Montreux receives its first licence from regional health authorities.
August 1995	Lena Zavaroni arrives to begin program.
August 1995	Samantha Kendall goes home to Britain and refuses to return to Montreux.
October 1995	Three-year-old Dustin* arrives from New York to begin program.
January 1996	Claude-Pierre makes first appearance on *Oprah*.
March 1996	Dustin becomes a residential patient.

January 1997   First complaints made by staff member to health licensing authorities.
January 1997   Claude-Pierre, patients, and staff make second appearance on *Oprah*.
January 1997   Lena Zavaroni is allowed to return home to Britain.
May 1997   On the day of a licensing inspection, Dustin is returned to his mother's care.
July 1997   Medical health officer Dr. Richard Stanwick allows Montreux to keep its operating licence after it promises to improve its practices.
October 1997   Samantha Kendall dies at her home in Britain.
November 1997   On the basis of new complaints, a new licensing investigation begins.
February 1998   Police conclude there is no evidence to pursue criminal charges.
November 1998   Licensing investigators submit report to Dr. Stanwick, urging that the licence be cancelled.
December 1998   Dr. Stanwick orders that Montreux not accept any new patients, pending a hearing on the future of its licence.
May 1999   Public hearing into the future of the clinic's licence begins.
July 1999   Hearing concludes after 26 days of evidence and arguments.
October 1999   Lena Zavaroni dies after a brain operation in Britain.
November 1999   Donna Brooks dies only days after returning to England from Victoria.
December 1999   Dr. Stanwick rules that Montreux has put the health and safety of some of its patients at risk and must surrender its residential licence by January 31, 2000.
January 2000   B.C. Director of Licensing Kersteen Johnston allows Montreux to remain opening pending a hearing of its appeal of Dr. Stanwick's decision.
February 2000   Nurses Pam Brambell and Marg Eastman begin work at Montreux to meet the licensing conditions.
March 2000   Eating-disorder expert Dr. Allan Kaplan visits

	Montreux to evaluate the patients as a condition of Johnston's order.
May 2000	The two nurses and dietitian hired as a condition of Johnston's order all resign.
July 2000	Licensing applies to Johnston to review her order allowing the clinic to stay open, but Johnston declines to hold a new hearing.
August 2000	Licensing applies to B.C. Supreme Court to force Johnston to review the situation.
August 2000	On the eve of the court hearing, Claude-Pierre turns in her residential licence to Johnston, effectively promising not to run a residential program in Victoria any longer.

Notes

1. Peggy Claude-Pierre. *The Secret Language of Eating Disorders* (Random House, 1997), page 9.
2. *Ibid.*, page 10.
3. *The Maury Povich Show*, May 24, 1994.
4. Claude-Pierre, page 30.
5. *Victoria Times-Colonist*, April 3, 1993.
6. *Victoria Times-Colonist*, April 4, 1993.
7. *The Province*, April 25, 1993.
8. *The Maury Povich Show*, November 16, 1993.
9. *The Maury Povich Show*, February 22, 1994.
10. *The Daily Mail*, May 9, 1994.
11. *The Guardian*, May 10, 1994.
12. *The Independent*, May 10, 1994.
13. *Ibid.*
14. *The Maury Povich Show*, May 24, 1994.
15. *Vancouver Sun*, May 19, 1994.
16. *Victoria Times-Colonist*, June 28, 1994.
17. *Victoria Times-Colonist*, July 11, 1994.
18. *The Daily Mirror*, August 26, 1994.
19. *The Telegraph*, October 23, 1994.
20. *Victoria Times-Colonist*, June 8, 1994.
21. *20/20*, December 2, 1994.
22. *USA Today*, December 2, 1994.
23. *Victoria Times-Colonist*, December 2, 1994.
24. *20/20*, December 9, 1994.
25. *Columbus Dispatch*, January 22, 1995.

26 *Columbus Dispatch,* August 30, 1995.
27 *Columbus Dispatch,* August 19, 1996.
28 *20/20,* May 19, 1995.
29 *The Oprah Winfrey Show,* January 17, 1996.
30 *The Telegraph,* October 3, 1999.
31 *Ibid.*
32 *The Oprah Winfrey Show,* January 13, 1997.
33 Deborah Wilson, "Starved for Love?" *Chatelaine,* February 1997.
34 *20/20,* September 18, 1997.
35 *Scottish Sunday Mail,* October 5, 1997.
36 Claude-Pierre, page 65.
37 *Ibid.,* page 71.
38 Vivian Smith, "The Martyr of Montreux," *Elm Street,* Holiday edition, 1999.
39 Claude-Pierre, page 87.
40 *Newsletter of the Academy for Eating Disorders,* Fall 1997.
41 *Canadian Medical Association Journal,* August 11, 1998.
42 *Eating Disorders Review,* November/December 1997.
43 "Anorexia: Eating Disorders Investigation," *Cosmopolitan,* October 1997.
44 *Cosmopolitan,* February 1998.
45 *The Montel Williams Show,* December 1, 1997.
46 Keith Stanovich. *How to Think Straight About Psychology,* Third Edition (HarperCollins, 1992), page 59.
47 *The Daily Mail,* October 19, 1995.
48 Stephanie Mansfield, "All You Need is Love," *Elle,* June 2000.
49 Column by Elizabeth Nickson, *Globe and Mail,* September 1, 1999.
50 *The Brenda* Story,* Channel 9 TV, Melbourne, Australia.
51 *People,* August 23, 1999.
52 ABC's *Good Morning, America,* August 23, 1999.
53 Smith, *Elm Street.*
54 Mansfield, *Elle.*
55 Stephanie Nolan, "The Secret Language of Force-Feeding," *The Independent,* June 4, 1999.
56 Column by Christie Blatchford, *National Post,* July 22, 1999.
57 Column by Christie Blatchford, *National Post,* July 23, 1999.
58 Column by Christie Blatchford, *National Post,* July 24, 1999.
59 *The Sunday Mirror,* October 10, 1999.

Notes

60 *20/20*, December 2, 1994.
61 Column by Christie Blatchford, *National Post*, December 2, 1999.
62 *Ibid.*
63 Column by Margaret Wente, *Globe and Mail*, December 2, 1994.
64 Kim Lunman, "The Case of David Bruce," *Globe and Mail*, December 2, 1994.
65 *20/20*, December 6, 1999.
66 Letter from Dr. David Clinton-Baker, *Victoria Times-Colonist*, December 24, 1999.
67 *Globe and Mail*, December 9, 1999.
68 Decision by Dr. Stanwick, December 1, 1999, page 27.
69 *U.S. News online*, September 29, 1997.
70 *20/20*, December 2, 1994.
71 *20/20*, May 19, 1995.
72 *20/20*, September 28, 1997.
73 Nolan, *The Independent*.
74 Mansfield, *Elle*.
75 *Focus on Women*, February 1993.
76 *20/20*, December 2, 1994.
77 *The Oprah Winfrey Show*, January 17, 1996.
78 *Share International* magazine, December 1996.
79 "Anorexia: Eating Disorders Investigation," *Cosmopolitan*.
80 "Where Angels Tread," *Flare*, October 1997.
81 Bob Palmer. *Helping People with Eating Disorders* (John Wiley & Sons Ltd.), page 228.
82 Mansfield, *Elle*.
83 Claude-Pierre, page 144.
84 *20/20*, December 2, 1994.
85 Column by Christie Blatchford, *National Post*, December 2, 1999.
86 Margaret Thaler Singer. *Cults in Our Midst* (Jossey-Bass Publishers), page 7.
87 Joel Kramer and Diana Alstad, *The Guru Papers* (Frog, Ltd.), page 49.
88 Marc Galanter. *Cults: Faith, Healing and Coercion*, Second Edition (Oxford University Press), page 82.
89 Column by Christie Blatchford, *National Post*, August 28, 2000.

Bibliography

BOOKS ON EATING DISORDERS

Abraham, Suzanne, and Derek Llewellyn-Jones. *Eating Disorders: The Facts.* Oxford University Press, 1997.

Agras, W. Stewart, and Robin F. Apple. *Overcoming Eating Disorders: A Cognitive-Behavioral Treatment for Bulimia Nervosa and Binge-Eating Disorder.* TherapyWorks, 1997.

Apostolides, Marianne. *Inner Hunger: A Young Woman's Struggle through Anorexia and Bulimia.* W.W. Norton & Co., 1998.

Bode, Janet. *Food Fight: A Guide to Eating Disorders for Preteens and Their Parents.* Simon & Schuster, 1997.

Boskind-White, Marlene, and William C. White. *Bulimarexia: The Binge/Purge Cycle.* W.W. Norton & Co., 1987.

Brownell, Kelly D., and John P. Foreyt, eds. *Handbook of Eating Disorders.* Basic Books, 1996.

Bruch, Hilde. *The Golden Cage: The Enigma of Anorexia Nervosa.* Harvard University Press, 1978.

Bryant-White, Rachel, and Bryan Lask. *Eating Disorders: A Parent's Guide.* Penguin Books, 1999.

Claude-Pierre, Peggy. *The Secret Language of Eating Disorders.* Random House, 1997.

Duker, Marilyn, and Roger Slade. *Anorexia Nervosa and Builimia: How to Help.* Open University Press, 1988.

Garner, David M., and Paul E. Garfinkel, eds. *Handbook of Treatment for Eating Disorders*, Second Edition. Guilford Press, 1997.

Gilbert, Sara. *Counselling for Eating Disorders.* Sage Publications, 2000.

Goodman, Laura J., and Mona Villapiano. *Eating Disorders: A Time for Change.* Brunner/Mazel, 2001.

Gordon, Richard A. *Eating Disorders: Anatomy of a Social Epidemic*, Second Edition. Blackwell Publishers, 2000.

Gottlieb, Lori. *Stick Figure: A Diary of My Former Self.* Simon & Schuster, 2000.

Kedesky, Jurgen H., and Karen S. Budd. *Childhood Feeding Disorders.* Paul H. Brookes Publishing, 1998.

Kinoy, Barbara P., ed. *Eating Disorders: New Directions in Treatment and Recovery.* Columbia University Press, 1994.

Kirkpatrick, Jim, M.D., and Paul M.C. Caldwell. *Eating Disorders: Anorexia Nervosa, Bulimia, Binge Eating and Others.* Key Porter Books, 2001.

Lask, Bryan, and Rachel Bryant-Waugh, eds. *Childhood Onset Anorexia Nervosa and Related Eating Disorders.* Psychology Press, 1993.

Lawrence, Marilyn. *The Anorexic Experience*, Third Edition. The Women's Press, 1995.

Levenkron, Steven. *Anatomy of Anorexia.* Lion's Crown Ltd., 2000.

Marx, Russell, M.D. *It's Not Your Fault: Overcoming Anorexia and Bulimia Through Biopsychiatry.* Penguin Books, 1991.

Mehler, Philip S., M.D., and Arnold E. Andersen, M.D. *Eating Disorders: A Guide to Medical Care and Complications.* Johns Hopkins University Press, 1999.

Natenshon, Abigail H. *When Your Child Has an Eating Disorder.* Jossey-Bass Publishers, 1999.

O'Neill, Cherry Boone. *Starving for Attention.* Continuum Press, 1982.

Palmer, Bob. *Helping People with Eating Disorders: A Clinical Guide to Assessment and Treatment.* John Wiley & Sons Ltd., 2000.

Ronen, Tammie and Ayelet. *In and Out of Anorexia: The Story of the Client, the Therapist, and the Process of Recovery.* Jessica Kingsley Publishers, 2001.

Sandbek, Terence J. *The Deadly Diet: Recovering from Anorexia and Bulimia*, Second Edition. New Harbinger Publications Inc., 1993.

Schwartz, Mark F., and Leigh Cohn, eds. *Sexual Abuse and Eating Disorders: A Clinical Overview.* Brunner/Mazel, 1996.

Siegel, Michelle, *et al. Surviving an Eating Disorder.* HarperCollins, 1997.

Vandereycken, Walter, and Pierre J.V. Beumont, eds. *Treating Eating Disorders: Ethical, Legal and Personal Issues.* New York University Press, 1998.

Wilkinson, Helena. *Beyond Chaotic Eating: A Way Out of Anorexia, Bulimia and Compulsive Eating.* Marshall Pickering Press, 1993.

Woodside, D. Blake, M.D., and Lorie Shekter-Wolfson, eds. *Family Approaches in Treatment of Eating Disorders.* American Psychiatric Press Inc., 1991.

Yager, Joel, M.D., Harry E. Gwirtsman, M.D., and Carole K. Edelstein, M.D., eds. *Special Problems in Managing Eating Disorders.* American Psychiatric Press, 1992.

Zerbe, Kathryn J. *The Body Betrayed.* Gurze Books, 1995.

BOOKS ON PSYCHOLOGY

Armstrong, Louise. *And They Call It Help: The Psychiatric Policing of America's Children.* Addison-Wesley Publishing, 1993.

Barnes, Fiona Palmer. *Complaints and Grievances in Psychotherapy: A Handbook of Ethical Practice.* Routledge, 1998.

Bongar, Bruce, *et al.*, eds. *Risk Management with Suicidal Patients.* The Guilford Press, 1998.

Cameron, Paul, Jon Ennis, and John Deadman, eds. *Standards and Guidelines for the Psychotherapies.* University of Toronto Press, 1998.

Cytryn, Leon, M.D., and Donald McKnew, M.D. *Growing Up Sad: Childhood Depression and Its Treatment.* W.W. Norton & Co., 1996.

Frances, Allen, M.D., and Michael B. First, M.D. *Your Mental Health: A Layman's Guide to the Psychiatrist's Bible.* Scribner, 1998.

Kennard, David. *An Introduction to Therapeutic Communities.* Jessica Kingsley Publishers, 1983.

Levenkron, Steven. *Obsessive-Compulsive Disorders: Treating and Understanding Crippling Habits.* Warner Books Inc., 1991.

Marcus, Eric. *Why Suicide.* HarperCollins Publishers, 1996.

Osborn, Ian, M.D. *Tormenting Thoughts & Secret Rituals: The Hidden Epidemic of Obsessive-Compulsive Disorder.* Pantheon Books, 1998.

Plous, Scott. *The Psychology of Judgment and Decision Making.* McGraw Hill, Inc., 1993.

Pope, Kenneth S., and Melba J.T. Vasquez. *Ethics in Psychotherapy and Counseling: A Practical Guide*, Second Edition. Jossey-Bass Publishers, 1998.

Shermer, Michael. *Why People Believe Weird Things: Pseudoscience, Superstition and Other Confusions of Our Time.* Freeman Press, 1997.

Stanovich, Keith E. *How to Think Straight About Psychology*, Third Edition. HarperCollins Publishers, 1992.

Strong, Marilee. *A Bright Red Scream: Self-Mutilation and the Language of Pain.* Penguin Books, 1998.

Welfel, Elizabeth Reynolds. *Ethics in Counseling and Psychotherapy: Standards, Research, and Emerging Issues.* Brooks/Cole Publishing Co., 1998.

BOOKS ABOUT GURUS AND CULTIC RELATIONSHIPS

Cialdini, Robert B. *Influence: The New Psychology of Modern Persuasion.* Quill Press, 1984.

Galanter, Marc. *Cults: Faith, Healing and Coercion*, Second Edition. Oxford University Press, 1999.

Hassan, Steven. *Combatting Cult Mind Control.* Park Street Press, 1990.

Kramer, Joel, and Diana Alstad. *The Guru Papers: Masks of Authoritarian Power.* Frog, Ltd., 1993.

Langone, Michael D., ed. *Recovery from Cults: Help for Victims of Psychological and Spiritual Abuse.* W.W. Norton & Co., 1993.

Mithers, Carol Lynn. *Therapy Gone Mad.* Addison-Wesley, 1994.

Shaw, William. *Spying in Guru Land: Inside Britain's Cults.* Fourth Estate, 1994.

Singer, Margaret Thaler. *Cults in Our Midst: The Hidden Menace in Our Everyday Lives.* Jossey-Bass Publishers, 1995.

Tobias, Madeleine Landau, and Janja Lalich. *Captive Hearts, Captive Minds: Freedom and Recovery from Cults and Abusive Relationships.* Hunter House, 1994.

Acknowledgments

A book such as this requires so much help and co-operation from so many people that oftentimes I felt more like a team captain than an individual author as the many pieces came together. I cannot adequately express my thanks to:

My collaborator, Michelle Stack, who is completing her PhD thesis, using Montreux as a case study. Her research, organizational, and editing skills were invaluable. Even more invaluable was her insistence that the book meet the highest ethical standards in dealing with such a vulnerable population.

Editor Karen Hanson and all the folk at HarperCollins Canada who have exercised so much patience and given so much help in bringing this story to life.

My friend and fellow-author Rebecca Godfrey, who blazed the path for me by having her first book published six months before mine.

My team of volunteer editors and advisers at home in Victoria—Alan, Ann, Chris, Charley, Kim, and Shirley. No one could have better friends.

Lorne Smith, Fabian Dawson, Malcolm Kirk, Andy Ross and the rest of my colleagues at *The Province* newspaper. They gave me the opportunity to work on the story of Montreux in the first place, and were tolerant, flexible, and helpful when it metamorphosed into a book.

My lawyer, John Orr, who not only read contracts and organized paperwork, but cheered me on all the way.

Acknowledgments

The many eating-disorder experts who so willingly shared their knowledge with me and Michelle: Dr. Gillian Wellbourne, Dr. Kelly Vitousek, and the doctors and staff at the Menninger Clinic in Topeka, Kansas; the Laureate in Tulsa, Oklahoma; Rader Programs in Tulsa; Renfrew Centres in Pennsylvania; and Rhodes Farm Clinic in London, England.

The many participants in this story, who were always prepared to answer questions, ensure accuracy, and tell me just one more anecdote.

And, most of all, the patients, families, and staff from Montreux who so generously shared their time, their insights, and their stories. Without them, this book could never have been written. It is really their book.